Commercial Property Law

Commercial Property Law

ALAN MORAN

LawMatters
PUBLISHING

Published by Law Matters Publishing
Law Matters Limited
33 Southernhay East
Exeter EX1 1NX
Tel: 01392 215577
www.lawmatterspublishing.co.uk

British Library Cataloguing-in-Publication Data

A catalogue record for this book is available from the British Library.

ISBN 13: 978 1 84641 024 6

Typeset by Pantek Arts Ltd, Maidstone, Kent

Preface

This book aims to provide an introduction to commercial property which is accessible to the reader who has not studied the subject before. After some years doing commercial property work in practice, I have taught commercial property for many years but there has never been a suitable course book available. Inevitably, the plan of the book closely mirrors the course I teach which is an undergraduate option for LLB students. I hope, however, that those taking LPC and BVC courses may find the book helpful, as well as those non-lawyers taking such courses as land management and surveying. It may also be of use to the younger (perhaps) lawyer in practice who finds himself or herself required to get involved in commercial property work – which is how I got into this field.

Much legal work involves dealing with matters of business, and so all solicitors in practice should have some knowledge of business tenancies. The market for commercial property plays such an important role in the nation's economy that to have no awareness of this subject is to be at a disadvantage in serving the interests of clients. The book tries to strike the right balance between laying out the legal background and seeing the subject in its practical context.

There have been many developments in commercial property law and practice in recent years and in the last two years especially. Changes of the utmost importance have been wrought by, for instance, the Land Registration Act 2002 and the reforms to the Landlord and Tenant Act 1954 Part II. Case law likewise has made some significant strides in very recent years: the number of cases cited in this book from 2005 and 2006 bears this out.

It is usual in a Preface to extend thanks to those who have helped in the production of the book. My first thanks must go to Peter Luxton and Margaret Wilkie; without their generous and unstinting help as colleagues and friends over the years, I would never have been equipped to teach this subject or to think of writing this book. My debt to them cannot be repaid. My thanks go also to the publishers who have given prompt and unstinting help throughout the writing of the book. I would also like to thank those of my students who have read some draft chapters and given me feedback as to how it seemed from the consumer's point of view: I mention in particular Mark Reading, Caitlin Stickler and Asad Arif whose comments in particular were very useful. I have not managed to include all their suggestions – perhaps next time.

I have tried to state the law as at 24 June 2006 (a quarter day, and so a day on which many rent payments must have been made!).

Alan Moran.

Contents

Table of cases

Table of statutes

Table of statutory instruments

Table of abbreviations

ADR	alternative dispute resolution
AGA	authorised guarantee agreement
CVA	company voluntary arrangement
FRI	full repairing and insuring (lease)
JCT	Joint Contracts Tribunal
L&T(C)A 1995	Landlord and Tenant (Covenants) Act 1995
LLP	limited liability partnership
LPA	Law of Property Act
LRA 2002	Land Registration Act 2002
LTV	loan-to-value ratio
DCLG	Department for Communities and Local Government
OMR	open market rent
RICS	Royal Institution of Chartered Surveyors
SDLT	stamp duty land tax
SSSI	site of special scientific interest
UORR	upwards only rent review

1 Introduction

1.1 Meaning of commercial property

Commercial property is generally understood to mean business leases because a large majority of businesses rent their premises rather than own the freehold. Business tenancies typically have terms of five or seven years and so there is constant legal activity in advising on the granting and renewing of leases. The trend recently has been towards shorter leases but longer terms are not unusual: business leases of 50 years may be encountered. Retail tenants tend to require leases which are rather longer than average – say, 12 years. Commercial property also includes business premises which are not rented; the practitioner will sometimes come across, say, a long-standing family firm which owns the freehold of its premises; institutions such as universities (which are charities) and hospitals normally own the freehold of their property, and the estate management departments of such premises generate a variety of work for property professionals. Also counted as commercial property work is development work which means the acquisition of a site and its development for a certain use such as a business park or industrial estate. This is specialist work requiring expertise in the wider area of conveyancing: see **Chapter 2**. Many businesses, however, occupy part only of some building or site – one floor of an office block, or a warehouse on an industrial estate – and the lease is the appropriate way of managing multiple occupation. This book focuses on business tenancies.

All rented property has a foundation of general landlord and tenant law made up of both common law and statute. Specific statutory regulation is then superimposed on top of the general law. There are three areas of statutory regulation: residential, agricultural and business, such regulation having to do largely with security of tenure for the tenant – that is, being able to stay on when the lease ends. Residential tenancies are the most regulated because of the basic importance for people of having a roof over their head. They are regulated by the Rent Act 1977 and the Housing Acts of 1985, 1988 and 1996. Agricultural tenancies by their nature require a particular form of regulation which is found in the Agricultural Tenancies Act 1995 for farm leases created on or after 1 January 1995 and in the Agricultural Tenancies Act 1986 for those created before that date. Business tenancies are regulated mainly by the Landlord and Tenant Act 1954, Part II (as amended); this is dealt with in **Chapter 15**. Most aspects of business tenancies are still governed by the common law of landlord and tenant but in recent years there has been an increase in statute law affecting business tenancies.

Commercial property, then, consists of property which is not residential or agricultural. It may be categorised as retail, office and industrial. It ranges from a lock-up corner shop to a city centre complex of shops and hotel, from a local insurance broker's office in a suburban shopping parade to a bank's premises at Canary Wharf, London, and from a small unit on an industrial estate to a steel works. The type and size of rented premises varies enormously. This variety is one of the things which makes the work so interesting for the practitioner.

1.2 Commercial property in context

Despite the huge range of types of business premises, renting is the norm across the board. Landlords of commercial property range from a local investor who owns a few shops to internationally-known financial institutions with billions of pounds invested in property. For all landlords, the commercial property market is a source of income, called 'income stream'. Tenants range from multinational corporations to the local sole trader. For tenants, leasing premises keeps capital free for other uses, and a lease is more flexible for businesses: it is easier to walk away from a lease when it ends than to market freehold premises, perhaps at a time when the market is unfavourable. Where occupation is of part, the lease will be the only available means of occupation.

For the citizen, it is impossible to avoid commercial property: in a day one might go to work in the factory, shop, office or university, call at the bank, visit the garage, buy some flowers at the florist, book a holiday at the travel agent, and shop at the supermarket – a day full of entering commercial property. Almost every business (and 'business' includes charities for the purposes of commercial property) needs to operate from some premises, and commercial businesses have customers who visit: after all, if you do not have customers, you do not have a business! Of course, not all premises which fall to be dealt with by the commercial property professional are places of business: patients in hospitals and the congregations of churches are not customers. It is worth noting that in certain parts of the retail sector, there is some challenge to the traditional shop from the use of online shopping.

Financially, the commercial property market is a vital part of the national economy. For the landlord, investment in commercial property provides rental income and capital growth and, in recent years, commercial property has performed better than some other investment media. At times of inflation, a portfolio of properties let on leases with upwards only rent reviews (UORRs) is very valuable. The property market can, however, suffer from occasional troughs; in the recession of 1988 to 1992, rental growth fell by at least 50%. Many landlords of the more substantial properties such as shopping centres and City office buildings are financial institutions; an insurance company or pension fund will undoubtedly have a portfolio of commercial property as part of its investment strategy. Policy holders' premiums are partly ploughed into property and the strength of the rental income helps to generate the return on the investment. So, the rental levels in the commercial property market play a part in determining the value of an endowment policy or pension fund and thus how much a pensioner may have to live on in retirement. Notice in the cases how often insurance companies and pension funds are parties. Owners of property also have the choice of entering into sale and leaseback arrangements; here, an owner sells the property to an investor and then takes a lease of that property from the investor. This way of releasing capital has become popular in recent years. The vast majority of tenants are small to medium businesses but in the retail sector, the much-criticised trend of homogenous high streets has resulted in many more large, national companies being the tenants of local shops.

Professionally, the commercial property market generates jobs for a range of professionals and their support staff. Consider how many staff are employed by firms of lawyers, surveyors and agents who work in this field. For the lawyer and the surveyor, there are career opportunities ranging from working in a small local firm in a provincial town and acting for local shopkeepers and other businesses to working in a large City firm advising major corporations in multi-million-pound deals.

1.3 Commercial property in practice

Commercial property work in legal practice may be general or very specialised. In smaller firms, the practitioner may have to handle both the granting of the lease and the procedures for renewal and termination. In larger firms, this latter work is considered to be 'court work' and so will be handled in the litigation department or, in very large firms, the property litigation department.

The complexity and changes which now characterise commercial property work make specialisation desirable. Commercial property work for lawyers involves commercial property conveyancing, property litigation, and property finance. Even in smaller firms, the conveyancing practitioner will not presume to be able to advise clients on matters such as development funding which requires the expertise of the property finance specialist or at least of the banking lawyer.

1.3.1 Obtaining instructions

Commercial property work in practice involves lawyers and surveyors using their respective skills and co-operating to achieve their mutual client's aims. Suppose the client landlord is some local company which has land and buildings to spare at its factory premises. It decides to turn this spare capacity to account. The chartered surveyor advises that workshop units to be let out can be made from the buildings. The surveyor recommends basic lease terms, draws up plans for proposed leases and markets the units. When prospective tenants are found, the surveyor sends instructions to the solicitor indicating the parties' names and addresses, the name of the prospective tenants' solicitors, a plan of the premises and the basic lease terms. These terms may be brief indeed, even as little as 'FRI', ie 'full repairing and insuring', meaning that the burden of these matters is to be borne by the tenant. The solicitor will ask the client to confirm these instructions and then prepare a draft of the proposed lease which is always done by the landlord's solicitor.

It may happen, of course, that the client instructs the solicitor directly. The solicitor may act for some large corporation and deal regularly with a property services manager, who may be a solicitor or chartered surveyor (and be more experienced in the property industry than the solicitor acting!).

The prospective tenant's solicitor must also obtain the client's instructions and ensure that these match the terms of the draft lease.

As the conveyancing process continues, the client's instructions must always be obtained on any variation of the original terms.

There is a Code of Practice for Commercial Leases which was published in 2002. This Code was an attempt by the Government to get the commercial property industry to regulate itself following concern about tenants' complaints of a lack of flexibility in lease terms generally, and about upwards only rent reviews in particular (see **7.2.2**). Research from the University of Reading commissioned by the Government and published in 2005 showed that the industry had taken very limited notice of the Code of Practice. The problem of upwards only rent reviews remains but is diminished in importance by the trend towards shorter leases. The Government is concerned about inflexibility in alienation clauses and the operation of break clauses (see **13.3.4**). This is so, notwithstanding that, as far as alienation clauses are concerned, British Property Federation members have said that they will allow subletting at market rent even if that is below passing rent (see Glossary), thus mitigating the decision in *Allied Dunbar Assurance plc v Homebase Ltd* [2002] 23 EGLR 23 (see **11.8.4.3**).

1.3.2 Commercial awareness

The property professional must cultivate commercial awareness to the extent necessary to advise the client properly. For example, a client may have several adjoining properties, all but one let on various leases which all have the same termination date. If instructed to prepare a lease of the remaining part of the site, the solicitor should realise the potential development value of the whole site if vacant possession could be offered at the time when the leases end. Instructions should be taken from the client on whether it wished to have the option of taking this development opportunity, in which case care must be taken to ensure that the lease of the remaining part of the site will end on the same date as the existing leases.

It is natural to want to be as helpful to the client as possible but care must be taken only to advise within the scope of one's competence. In the example given in the previous paragraph, the solicitor, though having awareness of the development potential of the site, should not give commercial advice but refer the client to a chartered surveyor. It is for the client to make its own commercial decisions.

1.3.3 Drafting

It is unlikely that a solicitor working in a firm will have to draft a commercial lease from scratch, and even so, a precedent book would be used. No client wants to pay at an hourly rate for original and creative drafting!

Most firms of solicitors have a bank of precedents for all occasions, and these will have been tried and tested over time. Medium and large firms may well have drafted their own documents. There is also the *Encyclopaedia of Forms and Precedents*, and a range of model leases and clauses (see Ross, *Commercial Leases*, the British Property Federation model clauses at www.bfp.org.uk/publications/documents, and law stationers such as

Oyez). Precedents are model forms of documents and obviously save a great deal of time, but they must be used with care. Precedents must always be adapted to the particular job in hand, and will require more or less amendment according to how closely the precedent fits the instructions received.

If any drafting has to be done, then it should be according to what is currently considered best practice which is to avoid archaic language, 'legalese' and Latin words and phrases. No modern attestation clause should read, 'In witness whereof the parties hereto have set their hands and seals . . . '! Language is the tool of the lawyer's job, and that job cannot be done effectively if language is not used with clarity, accuracy and precision.

The aim of a legal document is to set out in straightforward, unambiguous language the bargain struck by the parties. This means, as far as possible, that drafting should be the process of providing the legal machinery which will make the commercial agreement work, and not be the forum for negotiating items which should already have been agreed.

The document should be comprehensible to anyone who needs to read it, and that may include surveyors and others as well as lawyers. It should certainly not end up being read by a judge in a case caused by bad drafting. Judges cannot rewrite the document for the parties; as Lord Simon made clear, 'the question to be answered always is, "What is the meaning of what the parties have said?" not, "What did the parties mean to say?"' : *L Schuler AG v Wickman Machine Tool Sales Ltd* [1973] 2 All ER 39 (quoting from *Norton on Deeds*). The language used should be as simple as possible – that means plain English save where well-recognised legal terminology is necessary to achieve accuracy and avoid doubt. Sentences should not be so long that the reader loses the thread of the meaning. Short sentences are better than complex compound sentences. Double negatives should be avoided.

Paragraphs – and a commercial lease has a lot of them – are best numbered (1.1, 1.2, 1.3 with subdivisions 1.1.1, 1.1.2 and so on, as in this book). For an excellent guide to drafting, see *Ross on Commercial Leases*.

Unfortunately, not only legal documents but also statutes are sometimes badly drafted: see, for example, the Courts Act 2003 and the comment on it by Burnton J in *R (on the application of the Lord Chancellor) v Chief Land Registrar* [2005] EWHC 1706 (Admin). The Act contains – incredibly – a provision that reads, '[w]here the transfer takes place by way of the creation of a lease . . .'. As his lordship points out, '[t]he creation of a lease does not transfer any rights and obligations'.

It can, though, be dangerous to oversimplify language; the law is a specialist discipline like medicine and it has its own terminology for good reasons which are precision and clarity. Some words and phrases may have no popular meaning or they may have a meaning different from their popular meaning. In *Welsh v Greenwich London Borough Council* [2000] EGLR 41 (on which see **10.7**), an attempt by a local authority landlord to use tenant-friendly, simple language led to its being found to owe a degree of liability to repair it did not suspect (see Sandi Murdoch, 'Not so limited liability', (2000) Estates Gazette, 21 October, 172).

There are many cases in which the judge has commented on the poor standard of drafting (and not only commercial property cases). Bad drafting can itself have been the cause of the litigation as in *Westminster City Council v HSBC plc* [2003] 1 EGLR 62 (see below).

When reading another solicitor's draft document, it is essential to do so with the utmost care. Making amendments to that draft obviously involves using writing and drafting skills. The two solicitors involved in the process of producing a draft lease should aim at producing a document which reflects the intentions of their respective clients; it should not be a contest to see who can force the most concessions from the other side just for the sake of it. Nor should solicitors try to take advantage of another's drafting errors: see *Littman v Aspen Oil (Broking) Ltd* [2005] EWCA Civ 1579 (see below, and comment in (2006) Estates Gazette, 3 June, 172).

Inevitably, mistakes do occur. If the parties and their advisors cannot agree to deal with these themselves, the court may be asked to determine the position. The court will construe the lease according to the usual rules of interpretation and construction and determine the issue. The law in this respect was set out in *Holding & Barnes plc v Hill House Hammond Ltd (No 1)* [2002] 2 P & CR 11 by Clarke LJ. In the same case, Peter Gibson LJ commented that the problem in the case illustrated the dangers of the unthinking use of word processors. In *Westminster City Council v HSBC Bank plc*, Mr Recorder Michael Black QC followed the guidance of Lord Hoffmann in *Investors Compensation Scheme Ltd v West Bromwich Building Society (No 1)* [1998] 1 WLR 896 where his lordship said (at 913):

> . . . if detailed semantic and syntactical analysis of words in a commercial contract is going to lead to a conclusion that flouts business common sense, it must be made to yield to business common sense.

Mr Recorder Black was faced with a provision which did not make sense; he imposed sense by deciding that the wrong word had been used and construed the clause in such a way as to give commercial purpose to the agreement. See further on this case **9.4**. In *Littman v Aspen Oil (Broking) Ltd* [2005], a clause which was intended to provide that a tenant's notice to break was conditional on the tenant not being in breach of covenant mistakenly had the word 'landlord' instead of 'tenant' in the condition. This was manifestly wrong and the judge corrected the mistake (which worked in favour of the landlord).

If appropriate, rectification may be ordered. The law on rectification was set out in *Swainland Builders Ltd v Freehold Properties Ltd* [2002] EWCA Civ 560 by Peter Gibson LJ. In *Tilfen Land Ltd v London Logistics Ltd* [2005] EWHC 1456, the scant evidence persuaded the court that there had been a common mistake in not including a break clause, and rectification was ordered so as to include a break clause. The case, incidentally, illustrates the difficulties which can arise from poor office procedures, especially failure to keep attendance notes.

Since 19 June 2006, there is a requirement for most leases granted on or after that date to contain 'prescribed clauses' under Part 2 of the Land Registration (Amendment)(No 2) Rules 2005 (SI 2005/1982). In practice, firms will doubtless include the prescribed clauses rather than maintain separate precedents for those leases which require them and those which do not. There are 14 prescribed clauses set out in Schedule 1 to the Rules. Their purpose is to make registration of leases easier by providing ready reference to details such as the date, title details, parties, property, term, options and break clauses, and rights granted and reserved (see below at **1.4.6**).

1.3.4 Dates in documents

It is worth making a point separately about the putting of dates in documents. In some circumstances, time may be said to be, or found by the court to be, 'of the essence'. This expression is not unknown outside the law, but it has special importance in the law, particularly in connection with deadlines for serving notices but also in calculating the length of the term granted by a lease.

Take a common way of describing the term of a lease in the lease document. The wording is often something like this: 'to hold the premises for a term of 10 years from 29 September 2006'. What does this mean? Is 29 September included or not? And when, then, does the lease end? On 28 September 2016, or 29 September 2016? When notices which are date sensitive have to be served by a certain date which may have to be calculated by reference to the term of the lease, clearly getting the date right matters. There is a convention that 'from' excludes the date mentioned so that, in the example given, 29 September is not included and the term starts at the very first moment of 30 September. Thus, it would end at the very last moment of 29 September 2016. This convention is seen in legislation such as 'r 10, computation of time', Family Procedure (Adoption) Rules 2005 (SI 2005/2795).

As far as some matters are concerned, such as ending the lease, the court may not allow a mistake of one day to render the procedure invalid: see *Whelton Sinclair v Hyland* [1992] 41 EG 112, CA. But time may be of the essence in the service of some notices, and then a mistake of one day will cause the mistaken party to lose its rights; this could be the case in the operation of a break clause (see **13.4**).

Dates should be given in a way which avoids any ambiguity. For the calculation of time periods and of the dates on which notices must be served, it is essential that expressions, however well known, which may cause doubt must be avoided. 'From' such and such a date is arguably unclear: it is better to put, 'from and including'.

See also **Chapter 5**.

1.3.5 Dealing with others

Obviously, property professionals, whether solicitors or chartered surveyors, must act at all times in accordance with their respective professions' ethical requirements, not only in relation to the client but in relation to other professionals with whom they deal, including financial institutions. Apart from professional requirements, a professional person should act at all times with honesty, integrity and courtesy whilst at the same time keeping paramount the interests of the client. In the professional and business community, people generally recognise the value of being courteous and helpful to their fellow professionals which can mean not taking advantage of another's slips or errors provided the client's interests are preserved. You might one day be grateful for a similar good turn. In *Littman v Aspen Oil (Broking) Ltd* [2005] (see **1.3.3**) a solicitor tried to be clever in her drafting of a clause in a lease by introducing an advantage for her landlord client which had not been negotiated and made a mistake in so doing. Because of the 'blunder', the matter ended up in the Court of Appeal where Jacob LJ agreed with the judge at first instance that the clause as it stood was 'an absurdity' which the landlord needed 'in the same way that a fish needs a bicycle'. Her opposite number in the matter tried to be even more clever by keeping silent in the hope – vain as it turned out – that the clause would be found to be meaningless. As Jacob LJ pointed out (at para 23), trying to take advantage of the other side's drafting error imprudently exposes the client to an argument for a meaningful construction of the clause (successful in the case) and is inequitable.

Take a case from practice: A and B are solicitors. L is a corporate landlord with an in-house lawyer. A is acting for T1, an assignor of a lease, and B is acting for the assignee, T2. The assignment is almost complete and L, whose consent is needed, has so far not indicated to A any reservations about T2 but has approved the licence to assign. At the last minute, L demands a large rent deposit from T2 (a sum of money that goes on deposit as a guarantee against T2 not paying the rent). T2 thinks that this last-minute obstacle must be B's fault. To help B, A should be prepared to write a 'sympathy letter' to B which B can use to persuade the client, T2, that the problem arose only from L's inefficiency or bad behaviour.

On the other hand, if a solicitor X has written something in open correspondence (not 'subject to contract') and this tends to serve the interest of solicitor Y's client, Y cannot turn a blind eye to the advantage given, provided the client instructs Y accordingly, since it is not the solicitor's job to provoke acrimony between parties who have good relations.

Professional conduct should be governed by the injunction, 'do to others what you would want them to do to you'. One should never lose sight of the ethical dimension in professional life however business-focused it may be.

1.4 Conveyancing

This section deals with the essential points of leasehold conveyancing. It is not possible here to go into any detail about conveyancing, and readers should refer to one of the many conveyancing text books available, such as R Abbey and M Richards, *A Practical Approach to Conveyancing* 7th edn. (Oxford: Oxford University Press, 2005). Such books have sections on commercial as well as general conveyancing. One very basic distinction needs to be made clear at this stage, namely that between the 'grant' of a lease and the 'assignment' of a lease. The grant of a lease is when a new lease is created and the parties to it are the first – original – landlord and tenant. An assignment is the transfer of an already-existing lease from the outgoing tenant to the incoming tenant. The assignor is the person getting rid of the lease: the assignee is the person taking it over. Books and judges sometimes talk about an assignment 'of the term': it is the same thing, namely, the assignment of the term (or what is left of it, ie the residue) created by the lease when it was first granted.

The formalities for creating and assigning leases are dealt with at **3.7**. Although the trend has been towards leases for terms of less than seven years, a significant number of leases will be of more than seven years, and these, and assignments of them, will require registration at the Land Registry.

1.4.1 Contract

It is usual on the grant of a lease not have a contract but to go directly to the completion of the lease. A contract is only used where, for example, the premises are not yet built and the grantor wants to tie future tenants to the development. The lease to be entered into must be agreed and annexed to the contract.

Any contract for a sale or other disposition of land must comply with s 2 of the Law of Property (Miscellaneous Provisions) Act 1989 (except a lease within the Law of Property Act, 1925, s 54(2) and a contract made in the course of a public auction: 1989 Act, s 2(5)(a) and (b)). Of especial note is the requirement in s 2(1) of the 1989 Act that the contract must incorporate 'all the terms which the parties have expressly agreed'. This can mean that it is difficult to know whether correspondence must be made 'subject to contract' or 'subject to lease'. Solicitors are cautious people and will think that it is better so to qualify correspondence to avoid the possibility of creating an express term. For a long time, solicitors have used 'side letters': these are letters evidencing some understanding personal to the parties and so not appropriate for inclusion in the lease. The questions is, are these terms of the contract, non-inclusion of which makes the contract invalid under s 2(1), or are they collateral contracts (that is, related contracts side by side with the main contract) which are purely personal to the parties? Side letters need careful drafting so as to avoid any argument in this respect.

A contract is more usual for an assignment of a lease, and is likely to be conditional on certain matters such as getting the landlord's consent to the assignment (and, perhaps, to other matters such as a change of use or an alteration), or obtaining planning permission (which is also likely to need the landlord's consent). The assignor will prefer an unconditional contract, and such matters as mentioned may be resolved beforehand to enable this to happen.

The assignor's solicitor will draft the contract which may make use of standard forms such as *Standard Commercial Property Conditions* (published by the British Property Federation). The contract will deal with, among other things, the deposit payable on exchange, VAT, and payment of the landlord's costs for giving consent. This is a matter for negotiation but often the assignor pays the landlord's costs.

A contract to grant a lease which is not then granted will be effective to create an equitable lease under the doctrine in *Walsh v Lonsdale* (see further K Gray and S F Gray, *Elements of Land Law* (4th edn, Oxford: Oxford University Press, 2004), 9.61–9.76).

1.4.2 Grant

On the grant of a lease without any contract, the draft lease is prepared by the landlord's solicitor and sent to the tenant's solicitor who will have to spend some hours checking it. It is certainly tedious going through a long lease but it has to be done. One should not assume that others always do their job perfectly, nor should the young and less-experienced assistant solicitor take it for granted that the 'admitted-for-decades' partner on the other side must be right. Simple matters should not be overlooked; for example, it is necessary to check whether there are pages or clauses missing, and whether the names of the parties and the premises are properly described. Where applicable, the dates for rent review must be correct and clear, and any dates for the service of notices also clear. It is not uncommon for companies in a group to have similar though not quite identical names and one must be sure then that the correct company name is given: in *3M United Kingdom plc v Linklaters & Paines* [2006] EWCA Civ 530, getting the name of the company wrong caused the loss of a valuable break option for the claimant (see further, **13.4**). As a matter of good practice, reference should be made to the unique company number. If in doubt, get instructions.

Much trouble is often caused by inadequate plans and these must be checked. The plan and the verbal description of the premises must agree. The Land Registry is now strict about what it requires from plans: see below at **1.4.6**.

The tenant's solicitor must ensure that his client understands the obligations it is taking on. Major commitments include the amount of rent (check when it is reviewable); the amount of service charge (if any); the cost of insurance (if that is the tenant's responsibility); and the cost of repairs. The tenant client must understand what alterations it can and cannot make, what signs it can put up, and so forth. These and others matters are dealt with in this book.

For all but the very shortest of leases – and some solicitors would say in every case – the landlord should deduce title (ie provide proof of this title) to the tenant's solicitor. This is necessary for the grant of a term of more than seven years if the tenant is to obtain absolute leasehold title at the Land Registry: see below at **1.4.6**. On the grant of an underlease, 'title' includes the head lease. Where the landlord's title is registered, there should be no difficulty since the Register is open to public inspection: s 66 of the Land Registration Act 2002; but it would be a perverse landlord who refused to deduce title since registered title details are now available at a nominal charge from the Land Registry.

When the lease is agreed, completion may take place. The lease is prepared in duplicate, one copy being the lease and the other the counterpart. The landlord executes the lease and the tenant the counterpart. The two are then exchanged and dated. It is essential that both parts are identical but in the event of discrepancy, the lease prevails over the counterpart. It is dangerous to leave blanks, for dates perhaps, for filling in at the last minute since it is possible to overlook filling in the blanks. Also on completion, any apportioned rent which is due must be paid. For apportionment of rent, see **7.1.6**.

Where the lease is registrable at the Land Registry, the tenant then applies for registration in the prescribed way: see below at **1.4.6**.

If registration is not applied for and then there are further dealings with the land, problems may arise. In *Sainsbury Supermarkets Ltd v Olympia Homes Ltd* [2005] EWHC 1235, failure by an individual who bought land to register and to respond to requisitions from the Land Registry caused the title to revert to the seller of the land. The individual had entered into an option agreement with Sainsbury's to enable Sainsbury's to build a roundabout on part of the land. The individual's lender sold the land to the defendant which believed the option was binding. But the Land Registry registered the defendant's title without the option. However, the defendant had bought an equitable title from the lender, and since Sainsbury's option was first in time, the option prevailed. The Land Registry had been wrong to register the defendant's tile without mention of the option.

Rectification was ordered to note the option on the register. (In fact, the Land Registry had been wrong to register the defendant's title at all, but the judge thought it served no purpose to take that point.)

1.4.3 Assignment

Both the landlord's freehold interest, the reversion as it is known, and the tenant's interest, the lease, may be assigned. Both transactions typically proceed by way of contract and completion. The landlord may assign the reversion to rearrange its portfolio or merely to raise capital; the tenant may assign, subject to the terms of the lease (see **Chapter 11**), because the premises are now too small or, indeed, too big. A deed is necessary to assign any lease, whether the lease is in writing or not. Failure to use any writing will mean that the purported assignment has no effect whatever. Any writing which is not a deed will take effect only in equity (see further, **3.7**).

An assignment by a tenant of its lease will invariably need the consent of the landlord. The deed of consent is drafted by the tenant's solicitor and approved by the solicitors for both the assignee and the landlord, and all three parties will execute it. Usually, the alienation clause in the lease has a condition that the assignee will give the landlord a direct covenant to observe and perform the tenant's covenants in the lease, and this covenant will be included in the deed of consent. For assignments, see further at **11.5**.

1.4.4 Searches and enquiries

In the case of an assignment of a freehold reversion, the usual conveyancing procedure for a transfer of a freehold estate must be followed though obviously this will be done subject to the lease granted out of that freehold. Thus, the full range of pre-contract and pre-completion searches will be made.

Whether on the grant or the assignment of a lease, it will be necessary to decide what searches and enquiries to do. It will be a question of judgment for the solicitor as to which searches to make. The combined cost of local authority and environment searches is now significant, and clients taking grants of leases may want to keep such costs down. The landlord's solicitor may provide a copy of a local authority search, though it could be some months old. The prospective tenant's solicitor must advise on the pros and cons of taking a lease without such searches or accepting the landlord's searches. If the lease is longer than three years, the advice must be to carry out all usual searches. In any event, junior practitioners must follow the policy of their firm. The longer the lease and the more high value the transaction, the more important is this decision. The solicitor must consider the length of the lease to be taken, or, in the case of an assignment, the amount of the term that is left, and the location and character of the premises being acquired, and form a view of just what searches and enquiries ought to be done. At a minimum, local authority searches and enquiries and a water and drainage search should be done, and a company search where the landlord is a company. It must be ascertained, in particular, that planning permission exists for the use authorised in the lease. Standard Commercial Property Enquiries may be used and any further enquiries raised as the transaction requires. Before completion, a Land Registry search should be done, assuming the landlord's title is registered. For details of further searches and enquiries, see a conveyancing text book such as Abbey and Richards, *A Practical Approach to Conveyancing,* 7th ed (OUP).

Where the tenant is responsible for repairs – and this will be often – it is essential that the premises are inspected by a surveyor whose report must be carefully considered before the transaction becomes binding. For more about this very important matter, see **10.3**.

1.4.5 Sublettings

The formalities and procedures on the grant of a sublease are essentially the same as those in the grant of a head lease. However, the head lease and any assignments of it forms part of the title, and should be investigated. Also, any consents under the head lease must be obtained – normally, this will be the superior landlord's consent under the alienation clause. Though s 44(4) of the Law of Property Act 1925 prohibits the proposed sublessee from calling for the leasehold out of which the sublease is to be granted, s 44(4A) provides that subsection (4) does not apply where the grant triggers first registration under s 4(1) of the Land Registration Act 2002. Since leases of more than seven years trigger first registration, only shorter leases are caught by s 44(4) of the Law of Property Act 1925. In any case, the subtenant's solicitor should insist on a full deduction of title, save for the very shortest of leases, though, again, readers in a solicitor's firm should follow that firm's practice.

The subtenant's solicitor must check that the draft sublease sent for approval corresponds with the head lease, especially with regard to user and repairs. The planning situation must be looked into, and correspondence with the superior lease must be checked. In *Hill v Harris* [1965] 2 QB 601, a subtenant was unable to use the premises for the use authorised by the sublease since the head landlord objected to the fact that this was different from the authorised use in the head lease. The Court of Appeal held that there had been no warranty as to use by the sublandlord, though, of course, the subtenant's solicitor was negligent.

The grant of a sublease must reserve a reversion for the sublandlord, even if of only one day. If the head lease is due to expire on a certain date, and a sublease is granted which will end on the same date as the head lease will end, that operates as an assignment. In *Keydon Estates Ltd v Eversheds LLP* [2005] EWHC 972; [2005] 21 EGCS 139, the defendant solicitors were negligent in advising that a sublease which ended at the same date as the head lease did not operate as an assignment. When the subtenant failed financially, the head tenant denied any liability to pay rent to the claimant which therefore lost its income stream, which had been the very reason it had bought the property.

1.4.6 Registration at the Land Registry

Estates in or granted out of land title to which is unregistered may be subject to compulsory first registration either on creation (such as the grant of a lease of the kind which triggers first registration) or when there is a transaction which triggers first registration (such as the assignment of a lease whose term is such that the transfer triggers first registration). A transaction with an estate title to which is already registered is called a dealing: see **1.4.6.2**.

1.4.6.1 Compulsory first registration

Section 4 of the Land Registration Act 2002 (the 2002 Act) provides that the following trigger first registration if they are a qualifying estate:

(a) a transfer for value or other consideration (whether moving in either direction);

(b) a transfer by way of gift;

(c) a transfer pursuant to a court order;

(d) a vesting assent.

A lease granted for a term of more than seven years from the date of the grant is a qualifying estate, so such a grant triggers first registration: s 4(1)(c) of the 2002 Act. The grant will only be effective to create a legal estate if the lease is registered at the Land Registry: s 4(1)(c)(i). The grantee should register the lease within two months: s 6(4) of the LRA 2002. The consequences of failure to register are that no legal estate will be granted, and the transaction will have effect only as a contract which is vulnerable unless protected by priority protection under s 72 of the 2002 Act. In reality, the Land Registry will accept late applications for registration but late registration is not good practice.

An unregistered lease which has more than seven years to run when it is assigned is a qualifying estate, so such an assignment triggers first registration: s 4(1)(a) of the 2002 Act.

Leases which are not subject to compulsory first registration – leases for seven years or less – will be overriding interests: Sch 1, para 1 to the 2002 Act.

Full details are set out in the pages at:

www.landregistry.gov.uk/education/leases/when_to_reg/.

Plans

Land Registry Practice Guide 40 and the Land Registry's requirements for lease plans to be found at www.landregistry.gov.uk/education/leases_plans1a/ make clear how strict now are the Registry's requirements regarding plans. Clients in the past were sometimes reluctant to spend money on plans, and the Registry's requirements are to be welcomed after many years of poor plans which sometimes led to litigation and judges being critical of poor plans.

Where there is a lease of part, one must check that no part of the entire premises is left out of account, otherwise there will be doubt and so perhaps argument about who is responsible for repair.

The Registry's requirements are summarised as follows:

(a) the plan must be drawn true to an approximate scale in metric measurements only, show the scale, and have a North point to show orientation;

(b) dimensions must be in metric units to two decimal places only;

(c) sufficient detail must be shown to enable the land to be identified on the Ordnance Survey map and, where necessary, the landlord's title plan;

(d) the property the subject of the transaction must be clearly identified by suitable colouring, edging, or hatching;

(e) edging must not be so thick as to obscure detail on the plan [this had been a very common problem];

(f) different floor levels must be identified both on the plan and in the verbal description in the lease;

(g) disclaimers of the plan, eg that it is not to scale, or it is for identification purposes only, are unacceptable;

(h) references to colours in the lease deed must be matched by the colours on the plan.

The Land Registry website (cited above) has examples of how not to do plans, and examples of how they must be done for registration to proceed. See also K Fenn and A Colby, (2006) Estates Gazette, 27 May, 122.

Consents

The consent of the relevant third party may be required in the following cases:

(a) where there is a caution against first registration;

(b) where there is a restriction on the grantor's title;

(c) where there is a charge on the grantor's title;

(d) where the application concerns the grant of an underlease and consent under the alienation clause of the head lease is required.

Full details are set out at www.landregistry.gov.uk/education/leases/consents/.

Prescribed clauses

These are described in detail in Land Registry Guide 64. The Land Registration (Amendment) (No 2) Rules 2005 introduced a new set of standard lease clauses which must be used as required or else registration of a lease will not be done. With very limited exceptions, leases granted on or after 19 June 2006 must contain the prescribed clauses. Precedents of leases will include prescribed clauses, and so the actual work to be done is not great and prescribed clauses do not present problems; what is required is that they are done accurately.

The prescribed clauses must appear at the front of the lease. 'Front' means immediately after any cover sheet (usually like a title page) or after the contents page if there is no cover sheet. Both parts – lease and counterpart – must contain the prescribed clauses and they must be an integral part of the deed.

There is no room for mistakes in setting out the prescribed clauses: the Land Registry will not enquire beyond what is presented. Registration will proceed on the basis of the information given. The Registry's advice on uncertainty as to what to include is, 'if in doubt, include it'. The prescribed clauses are of such importance that they are briefly described here.

There are 14 prescribed clauses as follows:

LR1 Date of lease

This must be done according to UK convention which is date, month as a word, year. So, it must appear thus: 25 June 2006. The American convention, which puts the month first, is well known since '9/11', ie September 11, 2001. However, this format is likely to cause confusion since, in UK usage, it means 9 November.

LR2 Title number(s)

Most commonly, this will be the landlord's title number where the landlord's title is registered.

LR3 Parties to the lease

Full names and addresses of the landlord, tenant and any other party (such as a guarantor) must be given. Where any party is a company, its company number must be given. Foreign companies must have their territory of incorporation given.

LR4 Property

Here must be set out either a full description of the land being leased or reference to the description in the lease. It must be noted that if what is put here at LR4 differs from the rest of the lease, then what is put here prevails. The consequences of such a mistake are likely to be serious. Practice Guide 64 specifically draws attention to the requirements regarding plans in Practice Guide 40.

LR5 Prescribed statements etc

Certain statements are required in the case of leases granted to a charity, or under the Leasehold Reform Act 1967 and the Housing Acts. The commercial property lawyer is likely to have to act for a charity at some time, and reference must be made to Practice Guide 14.

LR6 Term for which the property is leased

What is said above at **1.3.4** about dates is clearly vital here. The Land Registry's preferred method for stating the term is 'From and including' and 'To and including'. Two alternatives are offered.

LR7 Premium

Any premium inclusive of VAT must be given here.

LR8 Prohibitions or restrictions on disposing of the lease

This is discussed at **11.4**.

LR9 Rights of acquisition etc

This requires details of:

(i) Tenant's contractual right to renew (as opposed to statutory right);

(ii) Tenant's covenant to (or offer to) surrender the lease;

(iii) Landlord's contractual right to acquire the lease.

LR10 Restrictive covenants given in the lease by the landlord in respect of land other than the property

This requires details of any restrictive covenants in the lease which bind land owned by the landlord, other than the reversionary interest described in clause LR4.

LR11 Easements

In a lease of part, it is likely that easements will be granted for the benefit of the property being let, and easements granted or reserved by the lease over the property being let for the benefit of other property. These must all be set out here or the relevant part of the lease referred to.

LR12 Estate rent charge burdening the Property

Rent charges are described in s 1(2)(b) of the Law of Property Act 1925.

LR13 Application for standard form of restriction

There are standard forms set out in Sch 4 to the Land Registration Rules 2003 (SI 2003/1417). Details of restrictions are found in Practice Guide 19. Restrictions are commonly used where the consent of a third party (such as a superior title owner or a chargee) is required before any dealing is to be registered, and where there is a tenancy in common.

LR14 Declaration of trust where there is more than one person comprising the tenant

This clause deals with the tenant which comprises co-owners, whether joint tenants (which would be unusual in business) or tenants in common (as is usual in business).

NB: Practice Guide 49 sets out the criteria under which the Land Registry will reject applications. These criteria apply to the prescribed clauses. Furthermore, if the prescribed clauses are not drawn up in the correct manner, or if any of clauses LR2.1, LR3, LR4, or LR6 have not been completed, the application will be rejected. It is the landlord's solicitor who drafts the lease and that includes the prescribed clauses. Given that a grant of a lease requiring registration or an assignment requiring registration will not, respectively, grant or transfer a legal estate, the interests of tenants must be served by their solicitors getting the registration requirements right.

1.4.6.2 Dealings

Dealings with registered title are provided for in s 27 of the Land Registration Act 2002. If a lease is registered, an assignment of it will be a transfer requiring to be completed by registration (s 27(2)(a)). Section 27(2) sets out which dispositions are required to be completed by registration. For present purposes, they include a transfer of a registered lease and the grant out of a registered estate in land of a lease for a term of more than seven years. It is likely that by statutory instrument under s 118, this period will be reduced to three years. A disposition which fails to comply with the registration requirements does not operate at law, though it will in equity.

2 Development and leases

2.1 Introduction

This book focuses on the law of landlord and tenant as it applies to business tenancies, and on the statutory regulation of such tenancies by the Landlord and Tenant Act 1954, Part II. Many leases are granted following development of a new site, and this chapter looks at some of the matters to be considered in such development. Examples are out-of-town retail centres, business parks, industrial estates, and large shopping centres such as Bluewater in Kent, Meadowhall in Sheffield, and the Metro Centre in Gateshead. Also, existing sites may be redeveloped such as has happened in the centre of Birmingham. Such development has been rapid in the last 20 years and is not always without controversy. Retail centres and shopping centres are blamed for the decline of traditional town centres and the demise of local shops. They also require significant infrastructure in terms of transport, especially highways, since the vast majority of the public visit such places by car. These developments are often carried out in association with the local authority which, in some cases, is the freeholder owner of the site. Recently, there has been a trend away from out-of-town development towards mixed development in urban areas and as part of the regeneration of town centres. The cost of such retail development is very considerable, and regeneration and development agencies are often involved in these schemes.

Many sites are offered as redevelopment or conversion opportunities. Disused and redundant buildings, 1950s and 1960s office blocks, old hospital buildings, dated shopping centres, and the like are the kinds of sites which investors and developers will buy. An example is the current £110m project to demolish and redevelop Edgbaston Shopping Centre in Birmingham. One of the best-known retail blocks in England, Cavendish Square in London's Oxford Street, is to be redeveloped to reconfigure and improve the retail space on the site. A consortium bought the site in November 2005 for £425m from the BP Pension Fund.

Development is a highly specialised area of property legal practice, and only an outline can be presented here so as to draw attention to those areas which are likely to need consideration. The role of the lawyer is to ensure that the developer client acquires the chosen site on the agreed terms and without legal obstacles to the client's aims. Practitioners wishing to gain expertise in this field will learn from experienced colleagues and will attend special courses such as those offered by the College of Law. Practitioners need to be able to manage and co-ordinate a range of functions including site acquisition and assembly, planning issues, construction and professional contracts, funding the development, and preparing leases for the letting of units on the development.

2.2 **Development leases**

A development lease is simply a lease which incorporates the agreement between the developer and the landowner for the development of a site. The agreement will have regard to the interests of others such as prospective tenants (or subtenants). The developer will covenant in the lease to develop the site in accordance with the agreement. An example of a development lease can be found in *Ashworth Frazer Ltd v Gloucester City Council* [2001] UKHL 59.

2.3 **Site acquisition**

This is commonly called 'site assembly'. When acting in the disposal or acquisition of a development site, the basic conveyancing procedure is similar to that for any sale and purchase of land. All the usual searches and enquiries must be made. For details of conveyancing procedure, the reader should refer to the standard conveyancing texts. Almost certainly, the title to the site will be registered. The file plan and any plans accompanying the title will be of vital importance; plans must be studied scrupulously. Title must be checked in the usual way but, in commercial deals, a certificate of title may be negotiated. This involves the seller producing a report on title effectively holding out the title to be good. The buyer accepts the certificate of title if its terms are satisfactory. The title must be free of anything which could compromise the buyer's ability to develop the site as intended; restrictive covenants and easements must be checked, and all appropriate searches carried out.

In some areas, special searches must be done, for example mining subsidence searches in areas such as South Yorkshire, and enquiries about radon in parts of Derbyshire, Northamptonshire, Devon and Cornwall. Whether a site may be in a flood plain is clearly something to be investigated, especially given concerns about global climate change. In the ordinary course of residential conveyancing, the buyer's solicitor will not see the house which is transferred. With site acquisition, the solicitor may well go to the site, put on a hard hat and walk the site with the client's surveyor or property services manager in order to check that what is visible on site accords with plans and documents. Points to be checked include access and rights of way, the means of connection to services (water, electricity and gas), rights of air and light, building up to boundaries, party walls and boundaries features.

Sites are generally classified as 'brownfield' or 'greenfield'. The former are sites that have previously been built on, such as derelict industrial sites. Development of brownfield sites is encouraged. In these cases, a crucial matter to be investigated is whether the site is contaminated land. A former industrial site may well be contaminated, and the cost of clean-up can be considerable, sometimes running into seven figures. There are higher standards for clean-up where the land is to be developed for housing. The local authority has a duty under the Environment Act 1995 to identify contaminated land. If there has been previous use of the land which suggests possible contamination, an environmental survey is advisable. There are civil and criminal liabilities for escaping pollution, and statutory liability for the cost of clean-up: see the Environment Protection Act 1990. The basic aim of the legislation is that the polluter should pay for clean-up costs. At common law, liability may be strict: see *Cambridge Water Co v Eastern Counties Leather Ltd* [1994] 2 AC 264. Liability may be transferred from one owner to another. The person responsible for clean-up, which the legislation calls 'remediation', is called the 'appropriate person'. In *R (on the application of National Grid Gas plc) v Environment Agency* [2006] EWHC 1083 the claimant sought judicial review of the defendant's decision that the claimant was the 'appropriate person' under the Environment Protection Act 1990. The site had been a gas works and had later, in 1966, been developed for housing. Contamination was discovered in 2003. The developer of the housing would have been liable but no longer existed. The claimant was not the polluter, but it was the successor to its statutory predecessors, making liability retrospective. Therefore, the claimant was the 'appropriate person' and so liable (for remediation estimated to cost £700,000). For comment, see M Edwards and J Thornton, (2006) Estates Gazette, 17 June, 168. Clients involved in development are aware that contamination is a key issue and time may be spent negotiating terms to deal with remediation. Lawyers acting for mortgagees need to take account of their interests in this respect.

Greenfield sites are sites that have not been developed before, and a key question then is whether such land is or forms part of common land. If it does, a commons search will be necessary. Wider environmental concerns may arise. For example, parts of the Thames Gateway project and plans for housing in parts of the south-east of England will have to take account of advice from English Nature regarding the protection of the habitat of rare birds such as the woodlark, nightjar, and Dartford warbler: see (2006) Estates Gazette, 6 May, 38. Enquiries may be made of English Nature. Where a sensitive site is involved, particularly a site designated as a Site of Special Scientific Interest (SSSI), a developer may face delay caused by protesters. Less obvious problems may arise from watercourses which can damage foundations. Insurance companies are well acquainted with such risks and enquiry of them can be useful.

There may be problems, from a developer's point of view, if the site is of archaeological interest or turns out to be so. If the site is located in an area where there are known archaeological remains, then this will be taken into account in planning the development. The developer's surveyor will have local knowledge of this factor. A current example is the St Botolph's Master Plan in Colchester (the town promoted by the local authority as 'Britain's Oldest Recorded Town'). The development of this area includes plans to preserve and enhance access to the Roman walls and the remains of the medieval St Botolph's Priory. Where archaeological finds are unexpected, the situation is more difficult. Then, the local authority's archaeological service will inspect the site and there may be some delay whilst 'rescue archaeology' takes place. The local archaeological service will work with the developer to resolve matters. In rare cases, the archaeological finds may make the site of such importance that development cannot proceed. Special measures must be taken if human remains are found. Developers should always commission an archaeological survey before contracts are entered into. There are specialist firms of surveyors which do this work: further information is available from the Institute of Field Archaeologists. It must be borne in mind that the developer is responsible for the costs incurred for field work, analysis of finds, conservation of finds, and museum archiving. Finds are, however, the property of the landowner unless they are treasure within the meaning of the Treasure Act 1996.

Site acquisition will proceed by way of contract and then completion. If all pre-contract matters are found to be satisfactory, the matter can proceed by way of an unconditional contract. Often, however, a conditional contract will be entered into.

2.4 **Planning**

The principal statute governing planning is the Town and Country Planning Act 1990 (the 1990 Act). Section 57(1) says that any 'development' needs planning permission. Section 55 says what 'development' is: it includes any building, engineering, mining or other operations in, over or under land. It also includes making any material changes in the use of buildings and land. Building operations include demolition, rebuilding and structural alterations. Engineering operations include laying out roads. Accordingly, development involves both building operations and changes of use (which may involve no structural change at all). Practitioners should be aware of the planning legislation which deals with use. The relevant secondary legislation is:

(a) Town and Country Planning (Use Classes) Order 1972 (SI 1972/1385);

(b) Town and Country Planning (Use Classes) Order 1987 (SI 1987 764) (amended with effect from 21 April 2005 – see H Williamson QC, (2005) Estates Gazette, 2 July)

The 1972 Use Classes Order may be found mentioned in leases created when that Order was current, so it is necessary to know about it. The 1987 Use Classes Order was significantly revised in 2005 by SI 2005/84. The website of the Department for Communities and Local Government (DCLG) has details of the revision in its Circular 03/2005 which can be downloaded from the site. The 1987 Use Classes Order has been further amended to cover regulation of casinos: see SI 221/06 and Circular 02/2006.

Some development may be impliedly permitted under the General Development Order 1995 (SI 1995/418); boundary walls and fences up to a certain height and extensions up to a certain size are permitted under this Order. Development of shopping centres, business parks and the like will need express planning permission from the local planning authority. Permission may be outline or full.

It is likely that an architect or chartered surveyor, rather than a solicitor, will deal with the application for planning permission. Once obtained, planning permission benefits the land rather than the applicant personally and so a transferee from the applicant can take the benefit of it. Permission does not require the development to be carried out but the permission does have a 'shelf life'. If permission has expired, there must be a fresh application. Planning permissions are registrable as local land charges and those given will appear on the local authority search.

If planning permission is refused, or problematic conditions are imposed, the applicant can appeal to the Secretary of State. This is usually done by written representations, but in the case of large developments there could be a public enquiry led, usually, by a planning inspector. Beyond that, there may be an appeal to the High Court or a judicial review.

Breaches of planning law, ie carrying out development without permission or in breach of conditions, may be dealt with by the local planning authority by way of enforcement. Enforcement action must be taken within four years of the carrying out of operations without permission or in breach of conditions. An enforcement notice is served on the landowner and may require remedial steps to be taken such as alterations to or removal of buildings.

A significant aspect of planning law is the s 106 agreement. Section 106 of the 1990 Act provides for agreements between local authorities and developers designed to deal with the negative aspects of a development which cannot be covered by conditions attached to planning permission. Such agreements aim to strike a balance between the impact of development and the existing infrastructure of the affected area. The planning authority assesses this impact and then negotiates terms with the developer for the mitigation of that impact. This involves placing obligations on the developer to make a positive contribution to the amenities of the area. A cash settlement may be negotiated instead. Local authorities have dedicated s 106 case officers who negotiate with the developer. Section 106 agreements are especially common in affordable housing developments.

The need for a s 106 agreement will be considered before the planning application is approved, and heads of terms agreed with the developer. This process is done in the light of government guidelines contained in Circular 05/2005. The obligations placed on the developer must be fair and reasonable and relate to the proposed development. The benefits to be delivered by the developer to the affected area may include: affordable housing, employment opportunities, improvements to highways and pedestrian areas, provision for recreation spaces and improvements to public facilities such as schools. The local planning authority has power to enforce a s 106 agreement: s 106(5) and (6).

2.5 Construction

The developer may be a company, or may have a company in its group, which undertakes the design and construction of the buildings on the site. Otherwise, a team of contractors and professionals will have to be put together. The team will include (depending on the scale of the project) a main building contractor, subcontractors, the architect, and a quantity surveyor. Most building contracts are those issued by the Joint Contracts Tribunal, and so are called JCT contracts. There are different forms of contracts depending on whether the traditional type of contract is used, ie where the developer employs the contractor and then separately engages professionals such as architects, or whether there is a design and build arrangement. In 2005, Sweet & Maxwell were appointed to manage and publish JCT contracts which are, as a result, currently being revised. It is said that about 90% of UK construction projects use JCT contracts. Consulting engineers will advise on such matters as electrical systems and heating and ventilation. There must be a project manager or supervisor who may be the architect or surveyor. Design and build arrangements are very common: in these contracts one company assumes responsibility for both design and construction. Whatever approach is taken, suitable contracts need to be made between the developer as employer and the contractors. Such contracts are not the province of the property lawyer.

On physical completion of the project, the developer's architect will issue a certificate of practical completion. The terms of practical completion are not defined and are not dealt with in JCT contracts; the certificate is the product of the architect's professional expertise. There is likely to be a defects liability period, usually 12 months, in which the contractor undertakes to make good any defects. A schedule of outstanding minor matters to be attended to is commonly called a 'snagging list'.

Of course, there may be defects in construction. If there are, the question as to who is liable will arise. The law of contract and tort may help the party which is in sufficient legal proximity to the negligent party, though success in tort is more difficult to achieve and will not cover pure economic loss (see *D & F Estates Ltd v Church Commissioners for England* [1989] AC 177). It is necessary, however, to consider the position of a buyer from the developer, of tenants of units (especially where, as may be the case in independent premises, the lease puts all responsibility for repairs on the tenant) and – it should not be forgotten – any future mortgagee. The Contracts (Rights of Third Parties) Act 1999 may help though it is common to contract out of the Act. In commercial construction, there is no equivalent of the National House Building Council (NHBC) cover which is available for new houses; therefore, no well-advised buyer of a development or an original tenant of premises on the development (including an assignee from the original tenant) will proceed without collateral warranties. These are standard guarantee documents issued by the British Property Federation. Collateral warranties set up a contractual relationship between those giving the warranties (contractors and professionals) and those third parties for whose benefit they are given. Warranties may be either under hand or by deed; since the limitation periods for these are respectively 6 and 12 years, it follows that those acting for third parties should look for warranties by deed and, in fact, the use of a deed is the norm.

2.6 Funding and investment

The price to be paid for a site is a matter for the developer and the solicitor should not seek to give advice to clients on commercial decisions. Development funding is likewise the sphere of the specialist. In some law firms, staff in the company and commercial department will advise on funding, not staff in the real estate department. In large firms, there will be lawyers who specialise in banking and property finance. This area of expertise has its own terminology (eg 'senior loans', 'junior loans', 'mezzanine lending', 'equity lending', 'debt finance') which has meaning only to those who work in the field.

Sources of funding and funding products vary enormously. For very large projects, institutional investors may be involved. Reading commercial property cases will show how many developments are funded and owned by insurance companies and pension funds. Shopping centres are often funded and owned by financial institutions, partly because tenants – usually well-known retailers – are considered to offer good covenant strength, lease terms are longer, and because yields are consistent, usually at about 7%. The amount that can be borrowed by a developer will depend on the investor's assessment of the value of the site, but what is known as the 'loan-to-value ratio' (LTV) may be 80% to 90%. Institutional investors look for long-term growth, bearing in mind that the asset will generate both rental income and capital growth, like any property that is rented out. Insurance companies and pension funds have to meet future liabilities such as policy payouts and pensions to scheme members, and so require a great level of certainty.

Some specialist investors look only for income and may be private investors or a group of private investors. It was such 'income stream' to fund retirement that the private investor in *Keydon Estates Ltd v Eversheds* (see **1.4.5**) was seeking. Other investors may be specialist property companies which actively engage in management with a view to constantly enhancing the performance of a development. Some developments may offer less certainty, such as smaller industrial estates where traders, holding under shorter leases, may be here today and gone tomorrow. These represent higher risk and so attract the more courageous investor.

Funding may be very short-term simply to cover the cost of development. Specialist lenders may advance, say, 60% of site valuation and 100% of build cost but over only two years or even one year. In such cases, the project must show a significant profit on cost, say, 25%.

Regeneration projects especially may attract public sector finance, in whole or in part. Funds may come from local authorities, central government or the European Community. An example of mixed funding is the Oxford Castle regeneration project whose £40m funding came from the Royal Bank of Scotland, the South East England Development Agency and English Heritage.

In funding arrangements, lenders are usually advised by their own lawyers separately from those advising the developer.

In 2005, banks lent £156bn on commercial property, and there is concern at the level of debt in the commercial property market with some lenders requiring no equity even for long-term loans.

2.7 Letting

On completion of the project, the developer has the choice of selling the developed site or granting leases of the units. To speed up occupancy and to help with funding the development, the developer will seek to secure tenants by way of pre-let agreements which are essentially agreements for lease or forward funding agreements. Pre-let agreements are a way of getting tenants committed to premises in the development before it is finished. Such agreements are essentially agreements for lease in which the developer contracts to carry out the development and to grant the lease in the form which is attached to the agreement. Forward funding agreements are complex but basically involve the sale of an agreement for lease to a fund which meets monthly invoices from the developer up to an agreed limit. The surplus on completion of the development is the developer's profit. Such agreements help directly with the costs of development.

Forward funding agreements must not be confused with forward purchase agreements. These involve the developer contracting to sell pre-lets to an investor.

Where the developer chooses to keep the freehold (or head lease), it will engage commercial property agents to market the various premises in the development (in the absence of pre-lets). The developer's solicitor will have drawn up draft leases (or underleases) in readiness, perhaps also with standard documentation including a local authority search, any special searches, copies of collateral warranties, and replies to standard commercial property enquiries. This document pack will be sent to the solicitors of prospective tenants and the granting of the leases will proceed in the usual way.

3 Leases

3.1 Introduction

Interests in land are often described and defined by reference to the remedies available for their protection. Leases have their origin in the Middle Ages when the common law regarded them as personal contracts outside the system of tenures and estates, and protected them as such. This meant that a dispossessed tenant had only an action in trespass for damages. From 1235, a dispossessed tenant could take action for recovery of the land against his landlord and, from the end of the fifteenth century, against anyone. Thus, having complete protection, a lease became an estate in land, and so the Law of Property Act 1925 declares that a lease – a 'term of years absolute' as it is there called – is one of the two legal estates in land: s 1(1)(b).

This historical background to leases has results which are still relevant. Leases are still classed as personal, not real property. Also, after their long metamorphosis into an estate in land, their early contractual character is again to the fore. This has led to leases being described as 'hybrid', ie having characteristics of real property and of contracts. Gray and Gray describe the 'conceptual ambivalence' of leases and consider their proprietary and contractual perspectives (7.75 et seq). Judges have focused on the 'contractual perspective' of leases in many cases. So, contractual rules and remedies have been applied to leases, for example frustration (*National Carriers Ltd v Panalpina (Northern) Ltd* [1981] AC 675), and repudiatory breach (*Hussein v Mehlman* [1992] 2 EGLR 87).

Furthermore, the simple fact remains that leases necessarily serve a dual function. They operate not only as an executed demise of land, conferring an estate, but also as executory contracts with many of the terms waiting to be fulfilled throughout the term, either at fixed intervals (such as a covenant to decorate every five years) or at an unknown time in the future (as with a covenant to repair).

3.2 Relationship of landlord and tenant

Essential to the relationship of landlord and tenant is land, the tenure of which may be freehold or leasehold. No one calls the parties to an agreement for the renting of a car 'landlord and tenant': such an agreement is a contract for the hire of personal property, a chattel. Also essential is a demise, a letting from one party to the other for a certain period of time – in other words, the creation of an estate. Accordingly, the relationship of landlord and tenant must involve the two land law doctrines of tenure and estate. C Harpum, *Megarry & Wade: The Law of Real Property* (6th edn, 2000), 2–006, describes these doctrines thus:

> In short, the tenure answers the question 'upon what terms is it held?'; the estate answers the question 'for how long?'.

A tenant thus 'holds' land from the landlord on terms ('tenure' comes from the Latin *tenere*, 'to hold'). The LPA 1925 confirms this by defining 'land' as including 'land of any tenure': s 205(ix). Relevant legislation calls what the tenant has a 'holding' (for example, Landlord and Tenant Act 1954 Pt II, s 23(3)). It is the doctrine of tenure which underlies the very practical fact that a landlord is able, in the event of failure by the tenant to pay rent, to turn to the tenurial remedy of distress.

A further practical result of the doctrine of tenure is that when a tenant assigns its lease, it ceases to hold anything from the landlord: the assignee acquires the estate and *it* then holds that estate from the landlord. This lay behind the decision of the House of Lords in *City of London Corporation v Fell* [1994] 1 AC 458, which made it clear that, provided there was no contractual obligation to the contrary, a tenant is not obligated to the landlord after it has parted with the estate at the end of the term.

What the tenant holds is an estate, but that estate must be for a period of time – a 'term of years' – which is less than that held by the landlord. In the case of a lease granted out of a freehold estate, any determinate term is bound to be less than the freehold which is indeterminate, even if that determinate term is as long as 999 years. (The word 'determinate' has its root in the Latin word *terminus*, meaning 'boundary'.) If a lease, usually called a sublease, is granted out of a lease, it must be for a lesser period of time, even if by only one day, otherwise there is an assignment (see **1.4.5**).

3.3 Definition

The foregoing section (ie **3.2**) allows us now to consider the definition of a lease. *Woodfall: Landlord and Tenant* (hereafter *'Woodfall'*) (at 1.003) asks the question, 'what is a lease?', and answers that a '"demise" or "lease" is the grant of a right to the exclusive possession of land for a determinate term less than that which the grantor has himself in the land'. Similarly, in *Prudential Assurance Co Ltd v London Residuary Body* [1992] 3 All ER 504, Lord Templeman said (at 506) a 'demise for years is a contract for the exclusive possession and profit of land for some determinate period'. These definitions contain two features which are essential for the existence of a lease: exclusive possession and a determinate – or certain – term.

3.4 Essential elements of a lease

3.4.1 Exclusive possession

Exclusive possession is considered at **4.3.2**. For the time being, it is enough to note that it means the right to exclude everybody from the premises let, including the landlord, save where the landlord has reserved rights of re-entry (for instance, to inspect the state of repair). So, for the time that the tenant has the premises, it can treat them in much the same way as a freeholder: the tenant has physical and legal control of the premises. Note, as is mentioned in **4.3.2**, that exclusive possession and exclusive occupation are not the same: exclusive occupation is something much less.

3.4.2 Certain term

Statute uses the expression 'term of years' in referring to a leasehold estate: s1(1) of the LPA 1925. The word 'term' comes from Greek and from Latin and means 'end' or 'limit'. The Roman god Terminus was the god of boundaries. Applied to leases, it means that a lease must have a certain beginning and a certain end in time. The definition in *Woodfall* indicates the requirement for a 'reversion'. This means that a lease must be for a certain period of time which is less than the time enjoyed by the grantor (see **3.2**). A 'term of years' or certain term can be for a period of years, and also for less than a year. Even a periodic tenancy – a monthly or weekly tenancy – is a term of years and therefore a certain term: (LPA 1925, s 205(xxvii)). Equally, discontinuous periods of time may, taken together, still be a term of years, as in the case of timeshares.

The common law has, for centuries, insisted that a lease must be granted for a certain term. In *Say v Smith* [1563] 1 Plowd 269 at 272, Anthony Brown J said that the beginning, the continuance and the end of the term, which really are 'but one matter', ought to be known before the start of the lease, and words which do not make this clear 'are but babble'. (Consider Shakespeare's Sonnet 18, written some 30 years later, which includes the line, 'summer's lease hath all too short a date'.) The LPA 1925 recognised this authority as we have just seen, and it was applied in *Lace v Chantler* [1944] 1 All ER 305 where a tenancy for the duration of the war was invalid by reason of uncertainty of the term since at the time the tenancy was granted no one, of course, knew when the war would end. The Court of Appeal in *Ashburn Anstalt v Arnold* [1988] 2 All ER 147 held that such uncertainty was not fatal to the validity of a lease since the tenancy in that case could be terminated by notice. This heterodox view was overruled by the House of Lords in *Prudential Assurance Co Ltd v London Residuary Body* [1992] 3 All ER 504 where all five law lords concurred in restoring orthodoxy. Quite simply, '[a] grant for an uncertain term does not create a lease' said Lord Templeman at 511. (With all due respect, one could say that the expression 'uncertain term' is self-contradictory, but the expression conveys what is meant.) Significantly, though, Lord Browne-Wilkinson, with whose comments Lord Mustill agreed, said (at 512) that he could see no reason for this 'ancient and technical rule of law', and hoped the Law Commission would see if there was any reason for maintaining it.

3.5 Parties to a lease

Normally, the parties to a lease are the landlord and the tenant. These are sometimes referred to, respectively, as lessor and lessee, but 'landlord' and 'tenant' are preferable terms as being more distinct. Additionally, there may be a guarantor (or surety). The landlord and the tenant mean not only the original parties to the lease but also their successors. When a landlord assigns its reversion, the assignee becomes the landlord; when a tenant assigns its lease (strictly, in the case of a fixed term, *the residue of the term* – that is, the time left of the contractual term), the assignee becomes the tenant. The description of these parties in the lease will normally say that the expressions 'landlord' and 'tenant' include their respective assignees and successors in title. In more modern language, the lease may say that 'landlord' means the person entitled for the time being to the reversionary interest, and that 'tenant' means the person entitled for the time being to the interest under the lease.

3.5.1 Competence

Both landlord and tenant must have legal competence respectively to grant and hold a lease. Each must have a legal persona. It must be remembered that the law draws a distinction between an individual and a person: an individual is a 'flesh and blood' human being, sometimes called a 'natural person', whilst the word 'person' includes additionally other legal entities, as companies (limited companies and plcs) and other corporate bodies such as local authorities and universities. Limited liability partnerships (LLPs) are legal entities as provided for by s 1(1) of the Limited Liability Partnerships Act 2000, and can hold and deal with real property like any body corporate.

When acting for a company, whether as landlord or tenant, and where the company is part of a group, care must be taken to ensure that the right company is chosen since, in groups of companies, there may be several companies with very similar names: see **1.4.2**. It is always best to check the company number as well as the name.

Some forms of association do not have a legal persona. Unincorporated associations (such as most working men's clubs, other social clubs, sports clubs, and the like) and most charities must hold property through trustees. Partnerships (other than LLPs) similarly hold partnership real property in the names of up to four of the partners as trustees for the partnership. It must be remembered that a legal estate may be held by a maximum of four people: s 34 (2) of the Trustee Act 1925. (Note that this does not apply to charities: s 34(3).)

Companies and other corporate entities only have the powers of holding and dealing with land conferred upon them by statute or their means of incorporation. For example, a limited company must act within its memorandum and articles, and a charity according to its trust deed.

Minors (those under the age of 18: Family Law Reform Act 1969, s 9, and formerly called 'infants') cannot hold a legal estate in land: ss 1(6), 20, 205(1)(v) of the LPA 1925; Sch 1, para 1(1)(a) of the Trusts of Land and Appointment of Trustees Act 1996.

An individual who is either a landlord or a tenant may come to lack legal competence through mental illness. In such cases, the Court of Protection assumes control of the individual's property and solicitors acting in relation to the patient's property must liaise with and follow closely the instructions of the Court of Protection.

3.5.2 Co-ownership

Where a landlord or a tenant comprises more than one person (up to a maximum of four as to the legal title unless the party is a charity), the rules relating to joint tenancy and tenancy in common apply. The legal title may only be held on a joint tenancy: s 1(6) of the LPA 1925. The right of survivorship applies as to other individuals, so that on the death of one individual, the legal title automatically is then held by the survivor(s). There may be any number of co-owners of the beneficial interest, and they may hold their interests as joint tenants or as tenants in common (that is, with distinct shares). In business, for example in a partnership, it is normal for co-owners to own the beneficial interests as tenants in common so that individual shares may be left by will; a business or professional partner cannot intend that his share on his death should go to the surviving partners but to his family.

3.5.3 Guarantors

Landlords are in business to make money, and if they are not totally satisfied as to the ability of a prospective tenant to pay the rent and to perform the other obligations under the proposed lease, they may require someone to act as guarantor to the tenant. Tenants are considered according to what is termed their 'covenant strength'; sometimes a 'good' tenant will be called simply a good 'covenant'. Where covenant strength is perceived to be weak, or the standing of the tenant is unknown, the landlord seeks a sufficiently financially robust guarantor. Clearly, it is for the landlord to make a sensible assessment of the need for a guarantor. Where the tenant is to be, for instance, one of the top supermarket companies or one of the big banks, there should be no question of asking for a guarantor (though a limited company within the group of a plc may prompt a requirement for a guarantor). But where the tenant is to be a limited company, the directors of that company will commonly be asked to stand as guarantors. Where the tenant is to be an individual with no track record in business, some person of substance will be required to act as guarantor or to take the lease on behalf of the defacto tenant: see, for example, *Chartered Trust plc v Davies* [1997] 2 EGLR 83, where a father (who was a businessman) was guarantor for his daughter. A guarantor in the jurisdiction of England and Wales will normally be required where the tenant is to be a foreign company or individual; this further avoids the possibility of having to take action in another jurisdiction.

Guarantors should be separately advised because of the obvious conflict of interest between a guarantor and the tenant being guaranteed.

3.5.3.1 Extent of liability

The liability of a guarantor is (or should be made to be) co-extensive with that of the tenant. The extent of liability will depend upon whether the lease is one governed by the Landlord and Tenant (Covenants) Act 1995: see **Chapter 6**. Under a lease entered into before the 1995 Act, a guarantor may be liable not only for the tenant he originally guaranteed but for that tenant's successors as well, unless the guarantor's liability was expressly limited to the time that the lease was vested in the tenant he originally guaranteed. Under the 1995 Act, a guarantor is released from liability to the same extent as the tenant: (s 24(2)), but consideration must be given as to whether the guarantor's liability continues under an authorised guarantee agreement.

The guarantee given may not be unilaterally withdrawn and is normally expressly made to extend to all the tenant's obligations under the lease and not just payment of rent or other sums due (such as a service charge).

3.5.3.2 Drafting points

Consideration must be given to the following:

(a) Should the guarantee apply where the landlord has 'given time' to the tenant, ie let the tenant have time to pay the rent late (which might otherwise release the guarantor)?

(b) Should the guarantor be protected from material variations of the lease? Clearly, a guarantor should be advised to insist on this otherwise he does not know the future extent of his liability.

(c) Should the guarantor be able to participate in any rent review process?

(d) Should the landlord be obliged to notify the guarantor of breaches complained of against the tenant, and to copy all notices to the tenant, formal and informal, to the guarantor?

(e) Should the guarantor be required to accept a lease where the tenant's liquidator or trustee in bankruptcy (as the case may be) disclaims the lease?

(f) Should the guarantor have the right to require an assignment of the lease from the tenant where the tenant is in default, thus giving the guarantor the chance then to assign to an assignee of good covenant strength?

(g) Should the tenant be obliged to provide a replacement guarantor where a guarantor ceases to exist?

(h) Should the landlord have a right of re-entry (and so be enabled to claim forfeiture) when an individual as guarantor dies or is adjudicated bankrupt, or when a receiver or liquidator is appointed in respect of a corporate guarantor?

3.6 Types of leases

3.6.1 Fixed term lease

Most business leases will be of this type: the lease is granted for a defined period of time (the 'contractual term') which may be as short as a year or as long as 99 years. The trend has been for business leases to become shorter, and since leases of more than seven years require substantive registration at the Land Registry (LRA 2002, s 4(1)), there is an incentive for the granting of leases of seven years or less. Existing leases for longer periods will be encountered, eg say, 25 years. Institutional landlords such as insurance companies and pension funds need long-term leases for the purposes of their investment strategy.

A fixed term lease cannot be created until the lease is executed, but the start of the term may be – and commonly is – before the date of execution of the lease, usually to coincide with the previous quarter day. Equally, the term may start at a date *after* the date of execution, though not more than 21 years after (LPA 1925, s 149(3)). Such a lease is called a *reversionary lease*. Note that a reversionary lease, granted out of unregistered title, which is to take effect more than three months from the date of the grant must be registered: s 66(2)(a) of the LRA 2002.

A fixed term can be brought to an end before the end of the contractual term ('effluxion of time') by forfeiture or a break clause. Otherwise, a business lease ends, not at the end of the contractual term, but only in accordance with the provisions of Pt II of the LTA 1954, which give qualifying tenants security of tenure so that their leases may, subject to the provisions for recovery of possession by the landlord, continue after effluxion of time. However, the 1954 Act provides for contracting out of these security of tenure provisions. See generally **Chapter 15**.

Given the requirement to register leases of more than seven years, there may be an increase in the use of short leases with an option to renew. This option is a proprietary right and must be protected, as a class C(iv) land charge or on the land register. Liability to Stamp Duty Land Tax will also be reduced or negatived by the grant of a short term with an option to renew (as opposed to a longer term with a break clause).

3.6.2 Concurrent leases

A concurrent lease arises when a landlord grants to a tenant a lease which is longer than an existing lease of the same premises. The tenant of the longer lease is, in effect, the immediate landlord of the tenant with the shorter lease and takes possession when the shorter lease ends. Such is the basis for the overriding lease for which the Landlord and Tenant (Covenants) Act 1995 provides.

3.6.3 Periodic tenancies

Such tenancies are granted for a short period such as a year, quarter or month, and such period is repeated, forming one continuous tenancy, until ended by notice. If the tenancy is created expressly, then the period of notice will be specified. If it is not, then the period of notice is by reference to the period of the tenancy: thus, a quarterly tenancy requires a quarter's notice. However, a yearly tenancy needs only six months' notice. Periodic tenancies may arise impliedly. Periodic tenancies enjoy security of tenure under Pt II of the LTA 1954.

3.6.4 Other types of tenancy

Land law books and books on the general law of landlord and tenant will refer to other types of tenancy: tenancies at will, tenancies at sufferance. These are technically not tenancies at all, but a tenancy at will may frequently arise in the commercial context. A *tenancy at will* is not a term of years but does confer possession. It fits awkwardly between a licence and a periodic tenancy, and can arise when a tenant enters into possession rent free before the start of a fixed term, and where a tenant holds over from the end of a fixed term. For judicial consideration of a tenancy at will, see *Javad v Aqil* [1991] 1 All ER 243.

3.7 Formalities for the creation and assignment of a lease

Land law text books such as Gray and Gray deal with formalities in detail.

'Formalities' means the legal requirements with which documents must comply to have effect at law. Thus, s 52(1) of the Law of Property Act 1925 provides that '[a]ll conveyances of land or of any interest therein are void for the purpose of conveying or creating a legal estate unless made by deed'. This begs the question, 'what does a document have to be like to be a deed?'. The answer is found in s 1 of the Law of Property (Miscellaneous Provisions) Act 1989.

The creation and the assignment of a lease are included in s 52(1) of the LPA 1925. But not all leases have to be created by deed (though all assignments do have to be). Section 54(2) of the LPA 1925 provides that a lease may be created orally ('by parol') if it takes effect in possession (that is, immediately and not in the future) for a term not exceeding three years at a full market rent and without payment of a premium (lump sum purchase price). A periodic tenancy may also arise without there having been a deed or any writing. It is important, however, to note that an assignment of an orally-created lease and of a periodic tenancy must be by deed even though one was not needed to create it. This is the effect of s 52(1) of the LPA 1925: see *Crago v Julian* [1992] 1 WLR 372.

In practice, a deed will be used on the grant of a lease; indeed, the word 'grant' assumes a deed. Where the lease is not within s 54(2) of the LPA 1925 and is not a periodic tenancy, it must be made by deed: s 52(1) of the LPA 1925.

To be a deed, a document must comply with the formalities for content and execution set out in s 1(2) of the Law of Property (Miscellaneous Provisions) Act 1989 as amended by the Regulatory Reform (Deeds and Documents) Order 2005 (SI 2005/1906) ('the 2005 Order').

Section 1(2) of the 1989 Act says:

An instrument shall not be a deed unless—

(a) it makes it clear on its face that it is intended to be a deed by the person making it or, as the case may be, by the parties to it (whether by describing itself as a deed or expressing itself to be executed or signed as a deed or otherwise); and

(b) it is validly executed as a deed—

(i) by that person or a person authorised to execute it in the name or on behalf of that person, or

(ii) by one or more of those parties or a person authorised to execute it in the name or on behalf of one or more of those parties.

Section 1(2A) provides:

For the purposes of subsection (2)(a) above, an instrument shall not be taken to make it clear on its face that it is intended to be a deed merely because it is executed under seal.

The 2005 Order also amended the provisions for execution of deeds by companies contained in s 74 of the LPA 1925 and added s 74A; the Order amended s 36A of the Companies Act 1985 (inserted by the Companies Act 1989) and added s 36AA. The Department for Constitutional Affairs, in its guidance notes on the rules for making deeds and documents by and on behalf of companies, described the key changes thus:

(a) merely sealing a document will not make it a deed;

(b) a third party can rely on the signatures of two directors to attest a company seal on a deed, as well as the signatures of one director and the company secretary, and similarly with other corporations;

(c) directors and secretaries of more than one company entering into a deed will have to sign separately for each company they represent;

(d) companies are given the same flexibility as individuals to complete the formalities of signing a deed in advance of being bound by it;

(e) third parties will be able to rely on a solicitor having authority to complete a transaction in all transactions and not just when land is being sold;

(f) companies will have power to delegate the task of execution;

(g) third parties can rely on the attestation of companies acting as director or secretary of another company when that company executes a deed.

It is essential that deeds and documents are drafted and executed correctly. If a document intended to be a deed is formally defective, it will not take effect as a deed, and this is likely to create difficulties for the client.

It must be borne in mind that if the required formalities for a contract for a disposition of land are not complied with, then doubt may arise as to whether any purported contract or lease exists at all. However, equity may have a remedy in the form of a constructive trust or proprietary estoppel (see *Yaxley v Gotts* [2000] Ch 162). In *Cobbe v Yeomans Row Management Ltd* [2005] EWHC 266, it was held that an oral agreement between the parties, that the defendant would buy certain property from the claimant if he got planning permission to develop the property, was binding on the defendant by way of proprietary estoppel; the defendant had encouraged the claimant to spend time and money on getting planning permission and in the belief that contracts would be exchanged when the permission was obtained.

Where there is a specifically enforceable contract but a defective grant (and so, really, no grant), the lease may take effect in equity under the rule in *Walsh v Lonsdale* (1882) 21 ChD 9. The parties should be advised to rectify any such error, but in any event, either party may seek an order for specific performance which is, it should be remembered, a discretionary remedy. In the meantime, the equitable lease is vulnerable as against third parties unless it is successfully argued that it is an interest under Sch 3, para 2 of the LRA 2002 (interests which override registered dispositions).

If a grant of a lease should be registered at the Land Registry and is not, it will exist in equity, but under Sch 3 (1)(b) of the LRA 2002, it does not have overriding status. There are difficult questions as to whether, in these circumstances, the tenant in actual occupation has an overriding interest under Sch 3, para 2 but the solicitor acting should make every effort to avoid the situation arising in which the question needs to be asked. It should be borne in mind that the Land Registry has requirements regarding the plans to leases. Where a grant or an assignment of a lease triggers registration, the requirements for plans must be complied with: see Land Registry Practice Guide No 40.

All assignments have to be by deed: see **1.4.3**.

4 Leases and licences

4.1 Importance of the distinction

There has been for some years a debate about the nature of leases and licences and how they are to be distinguished (see eg Megarry & Wade, 4th edn (1975), p 776 and 6th edn (2000), 14–011). That debate, aired in both academic journals and in the courts, goes deep, even into considerations of the very nature of property and the meaning of the terminology used.

For some time, the focus of this debate has been the decision of the House of Lords in *Street v Mountford* [1985] AC 809 and the controversial decision of the House of Lords in *Bruton v London & Quadrant Housing Trust* [2000] 1 AC 406. This decision is controversial because not only did the House overturn the decision of the Court of Appeal (which included a compelling – for some – speech by Millett LJ), but because Lord Hoffman, with whose speech the other law lords on the panel agreed, described as a tenancy an arrangement which some commentators say is really a contractual licence. It is not within the scope of this book to review, much less add to, that debate, but the distinction is important in practice as well as in theory: it is not possible to give proper advice to a client without some knowledge of the issues relating to the distinction between leases and licences: 'it is . . . crucial to know whether rights to use or occupy land give rise to a lease or licence, particularly in the business sector where tenancies enjoy significant statutory protection' (S Murdoch, (2005) Estates Gazette, 5 February, 201).

The basis of the distinction between leases and licences rests on the nature of proprietary and of personal rights. The reasons why this distinction is important have to do with creation, alienation, the effect of the arrangement on third parties and termination (including security of tenure) in relation to leases and licences. The possible cost of wrongly identifying a lease as a licence was seen in *Pankhania v Hackney London Borough Council* [2004] 1 EGLR 135. In that case, the local authority sold to the claimant land comprising a factory and a car park, representing that the car park was subject to a licence. It was found that the licence was really a lease which was protected under Pt II of the Landlord and Tenant Act 1954. Though the claimant eventually got possession of the car park (by paying off the tenant), damages were assessed and awarded to the claimant of £500,000.

Stamp duty land tax (SDLT), introduced by the Finance Act 2003 with effect from 1 December 2003, is potentially payable on leases (the transaction, not the document) but not on licences. HM Revenue & Customs, however, will be alert to attempts to use a licence to evade SDLT.

4.2 Licences

Before turning to look at the law relating to the distinction, the nature of licences must be examined. The basic concept of the licence is familiar: everyone knows that without a licence it is, for example, unlawful to drive a car, sell alcoholic drinks or watch television. Such instances illustrate the classic statement of Vaughan CJ in *Thomas v Sorrell* (1673) Vaugh 330 at 351, that a licence 'properly passeth no interest nor alters or transfers property in any thing, but only makes an action lawful, which without it had been unlawful'. In relation to land, a licence avoids the grantee of the licence being a trespasser but '[a] licence does not create any estate or legal or equitable interest in the property to which it relates': *Hill and Redman's Law of landlord and Tenant* (Butterworths) (hereafter '*Hill and Redman*'), Issue 34 A 205 para [629].

4.2.1 Types of licences

4.2.1.1 Bare licence

This is also called a gratuitous licence. This is mere permission to be on someone's land without any payment and so is not contractual. It is this which gives the right to, for instance, walk into a store to browse at the goods, or be present as a guest in someone's house. Such licence is revocable at any time on the licensee being given reasonable notice, the licensor not being liable in damages (see, for instance, *Babar v Anis* [2005] EWHC 1384). Clearly, such licences are not likely to engage the interest of the commercial property professional in practice. Here, at least, there is no argument that such a licence confers any proprietary interest in land – it is purely a personal right of the slenderest kind.

4.2.1.2 Contractual licence

For the commercial property professional, this is where the problems arise and where the debate lies mentioned above. At its simplest, a contractual licence is like a bare licence but for which valuable consideration is paid by the licensee. It is the licence someone has who pays for a seat in a theatre or for a hotel room for the night. Commercially, there are many situations in which a contractual licence is entirely appropriate to the circumstances: for example, for someone running a stall in a shopping centre mall; for a manufacturer of luggage selling its goods in a defined area of the floor of a department store (franchise agreements), or for a tradesman storing equipment (as in *Dresden Estates v Collinson* [1987] 1 EGLR 45). In some cases a tenancy will not be possible such as where a chattel is the subject matter, eg a houseboat as in *Chelsea Yacht and Boat Club Ltd v Pope* [2001] 2 All ER 409. Problems arise where the grantee claims to have not a licence but a tenancy with all the rights, particularly of security of tenure, which that gives. How to decide whether the grantee has a licence or a tenancy is the question referred to at **4.3** below.

4.2.1.3 Other types of licences

A licence coupled with an interest is an implied right to exercise a *profit à prendre*; since a *profit à prendre* binds a successor in title, so will the licence necessary for its enjoyment. A licence by estoppel (also called a licence coupled with an equity) generally arises in the context of informal domestic arrangements. Both types are unlikely to interest the commercial property professional.

4.3 Law relevant to the lease–licence distinction

4.3.1 Proprietary and personal rights

Land law distinguishes between *proprietary* and *personal* rights in land. Proprietary rights are protected by being enforceable against third parties (typically purchasers and mortgagees). The lease has been described above (see **3.2** and **3.3**): it grants the tenant an estate in possession in the land. Being an estate in land, the lease is clearly a proprietary right and therefore it will bind a third party. So, if A grants a lease to T and A transfers its estate to B, then B is bound by T's tenancy. This is emphasised by the fact that under s 4(1)(c) of the Land Registration Act 2002, a grant of a lease for more than seven years is subject to compulsory registration (the period had been more than 21 years) and it will be noted on the register of the title out of which it was granted (A's in the example given).

Personal rights, on the other hand, are held against a person without qualifying that person's estate, and so are not enforceable against third parties dealing with that person's estate. In other words, personal rights arise from agreements which merely give permission in relation to the land without creating any interest in that land. 'A licence . . . does not create an estate in the land': *Street v Mountford* [1985] 2 All ER 289, 291 *per* Lord Templeman. In *Ashburn Anstalt v Arnold* [1988] 2 All ER 147, Fox LJ (with whose speech Neill and Bingham LJJ agreed) reasserted the orthodox view that a licence does not create an estate in land, following the decisions of the House of Lords in *Edwardes v Barrington* (1901) 85 LT 650 and *King v David Allen & Sons Billposting Ltd* [1916] 2 AC 54. (This reassertion was felt necessary after the decision of Denning LJ in *Errington v Errington* [1952] 1 All ER 149 which suggested that a contractual licence, as such, may be binding on a third party.) Not being an interest in land, a licence is not proprietary – it is not protected by being enforceable against a third party even if that third party knows of the licence: see *Lloyd v Dugdale* [2002] 2 P & CR 167.

In short, a lease confers a proprietary right and so will bind third parties: a licence confers only a personal right and so will not bind third parties. That is the conventional wisdom. A legal lease of a shop for five years is undoubtedly an estate in land enjoyed by the tenant for the term and will bind all others. If A grants a licence to L in respect of its (A's) land, and A transfers its estate in that land (or, indeed, grants a lease out of such estate) to B, then B is not bound by L's licence: *Clore v Theatrical Properties Ltd and Westby & Co Ltd* [1936] 3 All ER 483, CA (see **4.3.5**). The grantor (A in the example) may, of course, be liable in damages to the licensee for breach of contract.

4.3.2 Exclusive possession

This has been mentioned earlier (see **3.4.1**). The classic view is that 'exclusive possession has tended . . . to mark out the borderline between the leasehold estate and the mere personal permission to be present on land' (Gray and Gray, 489). Exclusive possession (and the word 'exclusive' does not seem to add anything to the meaning of 'possession') includes the right to exclude all others during the owner's tenure of his estate: indefinitely in the case of the freehold estate; for a period of time in the case of the leasehold estate.

Exclusive possession is one of the characteristics of an estate in land and the degree of control it gives has been used to distinguish between leases and licences. Where the degree of control crosses a certain threshold, exclusive possession cannot be said to have been granted and a licence will be found, not a tenancy. This has been recognised for a very long time: see *Wells v Kingston-upon-Hull Corporation* (1875) L.R 10 CP 402. More recent cases illustrate the point.

In *Shell-Mex v Manchester Garages* [1971] 1 WLR 612, the Court of Appeal had no difficulty in finding that the document called a licence really granted a licence and not, as the defendant claimed, a tenancy. This was because the document provided that the licensee was '[n]ot to impede in any way . . . the company's [Shell's] rights of possession and control of the premises'. Such extensive control by the grantor is inconsistent with exclusive possession. In *Esso Petroleum Co Ltd v Fumegrange Ltd* [1994] 2 EGLR 90, Neill LJ said (at 93), '[t]here is no dispute as to the correct test to be applied. The question is whether on the proper construction of the licence agreements exclusive possession of the service stations was granted to Fumegrange'. Esso in that case had similar rights and powers to those of Shell in the *Manchester Garages* case, and Neill LJ (at 93) found that such 'rights and powers are quite inconsistent with an exclusive right to possession'. The degree of control retained by the grantor will often, therefore, be of decisive importance; an owner may be found to have retained a degree of control over the premises which is incompatible with and negatives a tenancy.

Also, exclusive possession cannot be found in any arrangement in respect of undefined premises: *Interoven Stove Co Ltd v Hibbard* [1936] 1 All ER 263. As Glidewell LJ commented in *Dresden Estates v Collinson*, '[y]ou cannot have a tenancy granting exclusive possession of particular premises subject to a provision that the landlord can require the tenant to move to somewhere else'.

Where, however, the arrangement is found not to be a licence but an easement which went with the demise, some variation of the right may not negative the right. In *Pointon York Group plc v Poulton* [2006] EWCA Civ 1001, the tenant was permitted to use certain car parking spaces subject to the right of the landlord to substitue other spaces. It was held that these spaces were part of the tenant's holding (for the meaning of which, see **15.2.4**), no point being taken as regards the landlord's right to substitute others.

In *Clear Channel UK Ltd v Manchester City Council* [2004] EWHC 2873, Ch, a draft agreement between the parties (Clear Channel being better known by its previous trading name of More O'Ferrall) related to 13 sites for the construction of advertising hoardings but the specific locations (as opposed to general addresses) were not defined. In particular, there were no plans of the sites. This was but one of a number of factors which led Etherton J to hold, with 'no hesitation', that a licence had been granted and not a tenancy. This judgment was upheld by the Court of Appeal in that case: see [2005] EWCA Civ 1304. As Jonathan Parker LJ made clear (at para 12), 'it is of the essence of a right of exclusive possession, and hence of a tenancy, that the area or areas of land over which the right is said to exist should be capable of precise identification *at the date when the right is said to be created*' (emphasis supplied).

Rights and powers which negative exclusive possession may be cumulative: a series of rights, each of which in itself would not negative exclusive possession, may do so when taken together. This was so in *Esso Petroleum Co Ltd v Fumegrange Ltd*.

In a lease, exclusive possession is emphasised by the fact that the landlord must reserve any rights it wants, such as, for example, to enter the premises to inspect them to check their state of repair. In *National Car Parks Ltd v Trinity Development Co (Banbury) Ltd* [2001] EWCA Civ 1686, NCP had a licence (from the original grantor, Standard Life Assurance Company) to operate a shopping centre car park in Banbury. The court noted that the agreement was framed as a series of obligations on NCP and that the lack of any grant of exclusivity, of a covenant for quiet enjoyment and of any rights of re-entry – the sort of terms one would expect to see in a lease – tended to suggest a licence and not a lease. (For a very useful comment on this case, see: M Haley, *'Licences of Commercial Premises: a return to form'* (2002, May), JBL 310–16; E Richards, *'Tenancy Tests'* SJ Vol 145, No 44, 1088.) This was a further reason for the decision relating to the 13 sites in the *Clear Channel* case: in the first instance hearing, Etherton J thought it was 'telling' that no express rights of way to the sites were granted in the draft agreement; rather, Clear Channel had been given express permission to enter the sites and this tended to the nature of a licence (see para 82).

Whereas in the 'domestic' cases such as *Street v Mountford* the courts were concerned to expose shams which sought to deprive innocent residents of then-existing Rent Act rights, commercial cases acknowledge that those in business are generally less likely to need such protection. Glidewell LJ in *Dresden Estates v Collinson* (at 47) contrasted *Street v Mountford* with commercial cases where there is no lodger, and so the factors which were so important in the residential cases may be less relevant to business tenancies. In *Esso Petroleum Co Ltd v Fumegrange Ltd*, Neill LJ said there was no foundation for the suggestion of a sham in that case because of the commercial justification for the arrangements. *Street v Mountford* stressed that the court must look at the substance and not the form of the agreement – that is, the test must be objective and not subjective.

However, in a commercial context, it is proper to have some regard for the intentions of the parties as expressed in the agreement. In *National Car Parks Ltd v Trinity Development Co (Banbury) Ltd*, Arden LJ said that she thought that what the parties said may be relevant: the parties' choice of wording and their contractual freedom should not be disregarded where those involved were commercial parties who received appropriate advice, were aware of the importance of the terms used and appreciated the significance of the agreement into which they were entering. In other words, where a case concerns experienced business people with the benefit of advice from specialist lawyers and surveyors, they may be taken to have known what they were doing, and any cry of 'sham' must be heard with circumspection. In *Stewart v Scottish Widows and Life Assurance Society plc* (QBD, 22 June 2005), HH Judge Eccles QC, construing an agreement for occupation for just eight days, was prepared to look 'at the label' as well as the purpose and period of occupation. His Honour declined to hold that the absence of a provision allowing the owner to share possession with the occupant compelled the inference of a tenancy.

This point was made forcefully by Jonathan Parker LJ in the Court of Appeal in *Clear Channel UK Ltd v Manchester City Council*. His lordship reiterated (at para 12) the well-established principle that 'whether a contractual relationship governing the use and occupation of land creates a tenancy or a licence depends not on the label which the parties have applied to it but rather on their substantive rights and obligations under it'. But, at para 28, his lordship said, 'I find it surprising and (if I may say so) unedifying that a substantial and reputable commercial organisation like Clear Channel, having (no doubt with full legal assistance) negotiated a contract with the intention expressed in the contract . . . that the contract should not create a tenancy, should then invite the Court to conclude that it did'. His lordship continued, at para 29:

> the fact remains that this was a contract negotiated between two substantial parties of equal bargaining power and with the benefit of full legal advice. Where the contract so negotiated contains not merely a label but a clause which sets out in unequivocal terms the parties' intention as to its effect, I would in any event have taken some persuading that its true effect was directly contrary to that expressed intention.

Though two cases are rarely identical, in the light of such comment practitioners should advise a grantee client in similar circumstances to consider carefully whether to press a claim that a tenancy was created.

The retention of keys to premises by the grantor is not very helpful in determining whether exclusive possession exists; it depends on the reason why keys were retained: see *Aslan v Murphy* [1990] 1 WLR 766. Where keys are retained so that the grantor can gain unimpeded access, this will help to suggest a licence, but the mere fact of retention of keys by the grantor is not inconsistent with a tenancy.

Exclusive possession has always been regarded by property lawyers as indicating an interest in the grantor's estate. What if the grantor has no estate? In *Bruton v London & Quadrant Housing Trust*, the House of Lords found that Mr Bruton had a tenancy even though his 'landlord' had only a licence because, as against his 'landlord', he had control of the premises. Mr Bruton was said to enjoy exclusive possession and so as between himself and the trust, he had a tenancy. It is not clear exactly what interest Mr Bruton had: it has been called a 'non-proprietary lease' (by Gray and Gray, 465–6), but Martin Dixon has called that a contradiction in terms (see M Dixon, *'The Non-Proprietary Lease: The Rise of the Feudal Phoenix'* [2000] CLJ 25). John Paul Hinojosa has argued ([2005] Conv 114–22) that Mr Bruton did indeed have a proprietary tenancy, though that argument is open to the criticism that it takes too narrow a view of what 'proprietary' means. Neuberger J, in *PW & Co v Milton Gate Investments Ltd* [2004] Ch 142, in holding that parties cannot contract out of the rule of law that termination of a head tenancy destroys any subtenancy (except by surrender), maintained the nature of a tenancy as an estate in land which can only be created by a grant out of a larger estate. This decision has been hailed as 'a welcome return to orthodoxy': see M Pawlowski, 'Contractual Intention and the Nature of Leases', (2004) 120 LQR 222–26. Those (including this writer) holding to the orthodox view that a tenancy can only arise from a greater estate than that granted, would argue that Mr Bruton had either exclusive possession without this amounting to a tenancy, or he had a contractual right to enforce exclusive occupation.

What is now clear is that a 'Bruton tenancy' is not binding on a third party. In *Kay v London Borough of Lambeth* [2006] UKHL 10, in which Lord Scott discussed the 'Bruton tenancy' in most detail, the House held that the rights of the occupiers could not survive the ending of the agreement between Lambeth and the housing trust and those rights were not binding on Lambeth.

It seems, however, that exclusive possession in the narrow sense of control over access can be found to a degree in a licence arrangement. Recent cases have shown that a licensee may have rights against third parties not formerly thought to be available to licensees, including actions in nuisance and trespass. Thus, when a licensee found others on the land in question, it successfully sought an order for possession: *Manchester Airport plc v Dutton* [1999] 3 WLR 524, a Court of Appeal decision criticised by E Paton and G Seabourne ([1999] Conv 535). (See further, Gray and Gray, 495 et seq.)

It has to be borne in mind that *exclusive possession* is not the same as *exclusive occupation*. Excusive possession connotes a right so extensive that it confers on the grantee an interest in the land which qualifies the estate of the grantor of the right. A tenancy clearly is such a right. Equally clearly, the lodger, the care home resident, the student in hall, and the homeless person in a council-run hostel has no such right: see *Westminster City Council v Clarke* [1992] 2 AC 288. Such people may have exclusive occupation of their 'personal space', but their rights cannot sensibly add up to an estate which could be defended and alienated. For a discussion of the difference between possession and occupation and application of the conclusion of that discussion, see *Akici v LR Butlin Ltd* [2005] EWCA Civ 1296, paras 17–36 per Neuberger LJ.

All this might be grist to the academic mill but it is not helpful to the practising lawyer who has to try to advise his client. *Bruton* has added 'complexity' and 'hazard' to this area of law. There is a lack of certainty, and, as has been said, '[i]n matters relating to title to land, certainty is of prime importance' (*Ashburn Anstalt v Arnold* [1988] 2 All ER 147 at 167 per Fox LJ). As far as commercial property is concerned, the decisions in *National Car Parks Ltd v Trinity Development Co (Banbury) Ltd* and *Clear Channel UK Ltd v Manchester City Council* have provided some certainty and so arguably have made the granting of licences of commercial property safer, though see **4.4**.

4.3.3 Creation

The creation of leases has been discussed in detail in Chapter 1. The usual business tenancy is created by deed because s 52(1) of the LPA 1925 says that a deed is required to create or convey a legal estate in land. Section 54 provides for the creation of a tenancy orally in the terms of that section, but even so, in practice, a deed will normally be used.

A licence is not an estate in land and so a deed is not required, nor, in fact, is any writing at all: see *Trustees of Grantham Christian Fellowship v The Scouts Association Trust Corporation* [2005] EWHC 209, Ch where the defendant occupied land for more than 30 years on the strength of a casual conversation. In practice, where it is intended to grant a licence, there will be a written agreement which will be drafted to avoid any suggestion that the arrangement is, in reality, a lease. Instead of rent, there will be mention of a licence fee. The grantor will not reserve rights since this tends to suggest the nature of a lease (see *National Car Parks Ltd v Trinity Development Co (Banbury) Ltd*); rather it will retain significant control (as in *Esso Petroleum Co Ltd v Manchester Garages*), including, where possible, the ability to move the grantee from one location to another (as in *Dresden v Collinson*).

Street v Mountford famously made clear that what the parties call the document does not determine its legal nature; the courts will apply an objective test to see what the reality of the arrangement is. Though as already suggested (see **4.3.2.**), labels cannot always be ignored, an agreement is what the court says it is, not what the parties say it is. If the agreement has all the characteristics of a lease then it is a lease though the parties may have called it a licence.

A licence may be granted for a fixed term or indefinitely until terminated by notice.

4.3.4 Alienation

At common law, a lease is freely alienable but, of course, most business tenancies contain an alienation clause modifying the common law position (see **Chapter 11**).

Bare licences are not alienable. A contractual licence, following the normal rules of contract, may have the benefit assigned. In accordance with contractual rules, the burden of a contractual licence may not be assigned. In practice, a licensee will be expressly prohibited from assigning the benefit.

4.3.5 Effect on third parties

Reference has already been made (see **4.3.1**) to the fact that proprietary rights bind third parties and personal rights do not. To reiterate, if L grants a lease to T and L then assigns its estate to A, T's lease is binding on A (except, it seems, in the case of a *Bruton* tenancy). This is not the case with licences. Such is the general law.

In *Clore v Theatrical Properties Ltd and Westby & Co Ltd*, a document which described itself as a lease was found by the Court of Appeal to be a licence, and an assignee of the grantor of the licence was held not to be bound by it (to the regret of Romer LJ). Lord Wright MR noted the lack of 'contractual nexus' between an assignee of the grantor and the licensee. *Ashburn Anstalt v Arnold*, as indicated above at **4.3.1**, confirmed this orthodox position but Fox LJ did consider the possibility that where assignee A purchases land with notice of a claimant C's personal right and A's conscience is affected, then, by means of a constructive trust, C's personal interest may bind A. Such circumstances had arisen in *Lyus v Prowsa Developments Ltd* [1982] 1 WLR 1044. For further analysis, see *Lloyd v Dugdale* (the leading judgment in which has been described as 'a thoroughly orthodox and convincing approach to the problem': M Dixon, *Modern Land Law* (5th edn, 2005) 335).

4.3.6 Termination

The termination of leases is a substantive topic and is dealt with in **Chapter 13**. Only the termination of licences is therefore considered here. Licences are excluded from the security of tenure provisions in Pt II of the Landlord and Tenant Act 1954 which is the main reason why it is so important to have ways of distinguishing leases and licences.

4.3.6.1 Bare licences

As said above (see **4.2.1.1**), a bare licence is revocable at will on giving notice which is reasonable in the circumstances. Failure to give reasonable notice may give rise to liability in damages: *Aldin v Latimer Clarke, Muirhead & Co* [1894] 2 Ch 437.

4.3.6.2 Contractual licences

Hill and Redman describes the revocability of contractual licences as 'abstruse and uncertain': Issue 45 A 221 para [687]. The basic position is that termination will be effective if done in accordance with the terms of the contract. Difficulties arise where there are purported revocations in breach of the terms of the licence. For a complete analysis of this area, see *Hill and Redman*, paras [687]–[747].

Where there is a termination in breach of the terms, then the summary provided in *Hill and Redman* (Issue 29 A 225 para [729]) is a guide to ascertaining what the position might be:

(a)   it is a matter of construction of the contract to determine whether or when the licence is revocable;

(b)   if the licence is revoked in breach of contract in all cases the licensee has a remedy in damages for breach of contract;

(c)   if the licence is revoked in breach of contract, and it is a specifically enforceable contract, the purported revocation is without effect and the licensee may remain without becoming a trespasser;

(d)   if the licence is revoked in breach of contract, and it is not a specifically enforceable contract, probably the revocation is valid and the licensee, if he does not leave within a reasonable time, becomes a trespasser.

4.4 Drafting

It will be obvious from the above that very careful consideration must be given not only to the actual drafting of a licence but to whether it is the correct medium to use at all. As already said at **4.2.1.2**, there are cases where a licence is entirely appropriate or even the only medium to use. In other cases, if a licence is indeed desired, then the following points should be borne in mind;

(a) advise the client of the risks;

(b) avoid specifically defined premises: if the case allows, include provision for the grantee to be moved about;

(c) avoid terms which tend to the nature of a lease, eg the grant and reservation of rights;

(d) for the grantor, retain extensive rights and powers of control to negate exclusive possession;

(e) try to avoid a fixed term.

In many cases, there will be a simple alternative to granting a licence in the commercial context: grant a lease of the desired length with security of tenure excluded (see **Chapter 15**).

5 Form and content of business leases

5.1 Introduction

Every lease must contain certain essential formalities and terms: date; names of parties; operative words, sometimes called words of grant, which effect the letting, eg 'lets' or 'demises'; the parcels clause, a sufficient description of the premises being let; the habendum which is the length of the term; the reddendum which means the rent reserved; covenants of the landlord and the tenant; provisos, especially the landlord's right of re-entry; execution.

A business lease may be very short or very long. Its length and complexity should be governed by the value of the transaction and the length of the term. Clearly, a lease of a small lock-up storage unit for three years requires the minimum necessary provisions. A 30-year lease of a major development consisting of, say, shops, a hotel, and offices needs a lease of sufficient complexity to manage the scheme. More substantial leases have to include complex clauses relating to matters such as rent review and service charges. A key difference determining length and complexity is that between a lease of whole and a lease of part. A lease of part of property, such as a unit in a shopping centre or part of a factory, may need an elaborate description of the premises and provision for the grant and reservation of easements and rights.

As mentioned at **1.3.3**, most solicitors will use their firm's precedents, so the form of the lease is already determined. There are two basic forms: either the clauses are set out in full with each containing all the required provisions, or the clauses are little more than headings with substantive content being set out in schedules at the end. The second of these forms is more popular for longer leases.

Any lease which will require to be registered must set out the required Land Registry details at the front. Leases granted on or after 13 October 2003 for more than seven years must be registered at the Land Registry. Furthermore, most leases granted on or after 19 June 2006 must contain the prescribed clauses: Land Registration (Amendment) (No 2) Rules 2005. The prescribed clauses, 14 in number, are: date; any relevant title number; parties; property; prescribed statements (eg disposition by a charity); term; any premium; prohibitions or restrictions on disposition; rights of renewal and surrender; restrictive covenants affecting other land; easements granted and reserved; any estate rent charge; restrictions to be entered; any declaration of trust. This important matter has been dealt with more fully at **1.4.6**.

5.2 A typical business lease

This may contain clauses covering the matters set out below. The list is not exhaustive, and reference may be made to precedent works such as the *Encyclopaedia of Forms and Precedents* and Ross, *Commercial Leases* (Butterworths, 1998) for further details. For a sample lease with explanatory notes, see the British Property Federation lease available at www.bpf.org.uk/publications/documents. Note that covenants may be absolute (there is a complete bar), qualified (not to do something without consent) or fully qualified (not to do something without consent, such consent not to be unreasonably withheld). For further consideration of covenants, see **Chapter 6**.

Date: this is the date on which the lease is delivered as a deed. It is rarely the date from which the term starts.

Parties: the correctly-named landlord, tenant and any guarantor with their addresses.

Definitions: basic definitions may be set out here. More detailed definitions are better dealt with in an interpretation clause. The following three items must be clearly defined.

Premises – also called the parcels clause. In a lease of the whole, an address may be enough. In a lease of part, a plan is highly desirable and is, in fact, required if the lease is to be registered at the Land Registry which issues guidance as to its requirements for plans (currently in Practice Guide 40). Plans should not be 'for identification purposes only', and plans and verbal descriptions must be consistent. See further at **1.4.6**. Care must be taken to define the premises fully and accurately including boundaries, services and fixtures. This includes, in the case of a lease of part of a building, describing exactly the extent of the premises including which surface finishes are and are not included, and whether windows and window frames are or are not included. Thought must also be given as to whether the case needs the exclusion of air space: see *Haines v Florensa* [1990] 1 EGLR 73.

Term – the term of the lease must be unambiguously defined. The convention is that where the lease specifies a date from which the term runs, that date is not included but the next date is. So, a term of five years 'from 29 September' will start at the first moment of 30 September and will end at the end of 29 September five years later. For the avoidance of any doubt, the definition should say, 'from and including . . . until and including [date]'. Making the dates clear is vital because the service of notices can be extremely date-sensitive, and getting it wrong by one day can cause disaster. One making a mistake will cry, like the Earl of Salisbury, 'One day too late, I fear me, noble lord, hath clouded all thy happy days on earth: O, call back yesterday, bid time return' (Shakespeare, *Richard II*, Act 3, scene 2). See further on dates at **1.3.4**.

Rent – where there is no rent review, this will simply state £X a year from the date from which rent is first due. Where there is rent review, the rent will be defined as the initial rent. See **7.2.5**.

Operative words: there must be words of grant. It is better to use the word 'lets' than 'demises'. In the case of a lease of part, there may also be mentioned here the right granted to the tenant and those excepted and reserved to the landlord. It may also be necessary to grant the lease subject to third party rights (eg of providers of services).

Payment of rent: it is common for rent to be made payable by equal quarterly payments in advance on the usual quarter days. These are 25 March, 24 June, 29 September and 25 December. For further details, see **7.1.6**. It is likely that the first payment will need apportioning since, as already said, the date of delivery of the lease will not be on a quarter day.

Rent Review: this is a hugely important area, and is considered in detail in **Chapter 7**.

Tenant's major covenants.

User: see **Chapter 8**.

Iterations: see **Chapter 9**.

Repairs: see **Chapter 10**.

Alienation/Disposition: see **Chapter 11**.

Service charges: see **Chapter 12**.

Other tenant's covenants.

Compliance with laws: there will be a broad obligation on the tenant to comply with all statutory provisions relating to the property and its use. This will include reference to such matters as the Disability Discrimination Acts, Defective Premises Act 1972, and health and safety legislation.

Planning: there will be detailed provisions here aimed at restricting the tenant's ability to apply for planning permission and to notify the landlord about all matters. There may be an absolute covenant against applying for planning permission.

Insurance: either the tenant will be responsible for insuring the premises (in a typical FRI (full repairing and insuring) lease) or the landlord will insure and require reimbursement from the tenant. This clause may be long in an effort to cover all possibilities, and should include provision for suspension of rent when insured damage occurs, for reinstatement, and for early termination in the event of destruction of the premises.

Outgoings: the tenant usually pays rates and taxes on the property, and also pays charges for the supply of services.

VAT: the landlord has an option to waive the exemption from VAT, and the VAT position must have been part of the pre-lease negotiations.

Access for the landlord: the landlord will oblige the tenant to permit access for a number of purposes such as to check the tenant's compliance with covenants.

Signs: landlords are very keen to restrict the putting up of signs and there may be detailed restrictions on this, the landlord specifying size, colour and location of signs. See *Heard v Stuart* (1907) 24 TLR 104.

Interest: to pay interest at a certain rate on any sums overdue to the landlord.

Costs: the tenant to pay all the costs and expenses incurred by the landlord.

Nuisance and annoyance: some modern precedents do not include this but there may be a covenant by the tenant not to cause any nuisance or annoyance to any adjoining or neighbouring owners or occupiers. See *Heard v Stuart* and *Hampstead & Suburban Properties Ltd v Diomedous* [1968] 3 All ER 545.

To yield up: to give back the premises in repair and decorative order and with tenant's fixtures and fittings removed on the landlord's request.

Landlord's covenants: there will be a covenant for quiet enjoyment (in any case implied). This preserves the tenant's exclusive possession, and includes physical interference by the landlord but not freedom from ordinary noise. For breach, the tenant has remedies in damages and injunction.

Forfeiture: if the landlord is to have the right to forfeit the lease for non-compliance by the tenant of tenant's covenants, there must be a right of re-entry reserved by the landlord. This clause will say what may be called 'forfeiting events'. See **Chapter 14**.

Break clause: if there is a landlord's or a tenant's break clause, this will be set out towards the end of the lease.

Provisos, options and declarations: a proviso for re-entry may appear here to enable an action for forfeiture by the landlord. An option to renew will also be placed here as will likewise an option to purchase the reversion (and see the next paragraph).

Enforcement of the covenants of other tenants: in a property of multiple occupation such as a shopping centre, the user clauses of all the leases may be balanced to ensure a good mix of trades in order to make the centre attractive to the public by providing variety. This is good estate management. Where the user clauses fit together, there may be a letting scheme. This will enable one tenant to sue another for breach of the user clause: *Williams v Kiley* [2002] EWCA Civ 1645. No special covenant is therefore needed where such a letting scheme is found to exist. There may, however, be a landlord's covenant with each tenant to enforce tenant covenants against the other tenants. Landlords may wish to avoid a letting scheme, and a declaration to that effect may be inserted. Specifically, tenants may be expressly disentitled from enforcing the covenants of other tenants. There may be a declaration instead that disputes between tenants are to be decided by the landlord or its surveyor.

Exclusion of the Landlord and Tenant Act 1954: where it is agreed that the tenant will not have security of tenure under the Act, the agreement must be set out in compliance with the provisions of the Regulatory Reform (Business Tenancies England and Wales) Order 2003 (SI 2003/3096). See **Chapter 15**.

It is a question of judgment and of following a firm's normal practice as to what to include in a lease. A perusal of the available precedents will show some variation in what is considered necessary.

6 Enforceability of leasehold covenants

6.1 Introduction

We saw at **3.5** who may be the parties to a lease, and we saw in **Chapter 5** that in a business lease both landlord and tenant have rights and obligations. It is true, however, that, given the number of tenant's covenants, much the greater burden of obligations rests on the tenant.

A covenant, it should be remembered, is a contractual promise contained in a deed. Consideration is not necessary to support such a promise: entering into the deed counts as consideration. The landlord and the tenant enter into covenants with each other and as between the original landlord and tenant, these covenants bind them like any contract. Contractual remedies, such as injunction, are available in the usual way. Covenants relating to land may be treated as interests in land because they affect an estate in land, whether freehold or leasehold. Here, of course, we are looking at covenants affecting leasehold land. This means that certain proprietary remedies such as an action for forfeiture of the lease are available.

Given that such covenants are contractual but affect the leasehold estate also, it is not surprising that this duality is reflected in two doctrines, one of contract and one of land, which apply to the enforceability of covenants. These are, respectively, 'privity of contract' and 'privity of estate'. The word 'privity' is archaic in normal language, but in legal language it means a relationship between parties to some agreement to the exclusion of others, and therefore 'privy' or 'private' as between those parties. In a judgment which Lord Templeman described as 'impeccable' (*City of London Corporation v Fell* [1993] 4 All ER 968 at 973), Nourse LJ, in *City of London Corporation v Fell* [1993] 2 All ER 449, 454, put the position thus:

> A lease of land, because it originates in contract, gives rise to obligations enforceable between the original landlord and the original tenant in contract. But because it also gives the tenant an estate in the land, assignable, like the reversion, to others, the obligations, so far as they touch and concern the land, assume a wider influence, becoming, as it were, imprinted on the term or the reversion as the case may be,

enforceable between the owners thereof for the time being as conditions of the enjoyment of their respective estates. Thus landlord and tenant stand together in one or other of two distinct legal relationships. In the first it is said that there is privity of contract between them, in the second privity of estate.

The Law Commission in 'Landlord and Tenant: Privity of Contract and Estate' (Law Com No 174, 1988), at para 1.1 describes the doctrines of privity of contract and privity of estate as follows:

> In the law of landlord and tenant privity of contract means that the original landlord and the original tenant normally remain liable to perform their respective obligations for the whole of the period for which the lease was granted, even if they have parted with all interest in the property. Privity of estate means that the landlord and the tenant for the time being automatically assume responsibility for the lease obligations which relate directly to the property for the period during which they own an interest in it . . .

As between the original landlord and tenant, the position is straightforward: both privity of estate and privity of contract exist, and so there is no question but that the parties can enforce all the covenants in the lease against one another. The position becomes less straightforward when one or both of the original parties assigns its interest. Privity of estate clearly exists between whoever are the landlord and the tenant at any given time, but since the law of contract provides that privity of contract may only exist between the contracting parties, means had to be found of establishing a contractual relationship between those who were not party to the original lease. As Lord Templeman put it in *Fell* [1993] 4 All ER 968 at 972:

> Common law, and statute following common law, were faced with the problem of rendering effective the obligations under a lease which might have to endure for a period of 999 years or more beyond the control of any covenantor. The solution was to annex to the term and the reversion the benefit and burden of covenants which touch and concern the land . . . The system of leasehold tenure requires that the obligations in the lease shall be enforceable throughout the term, whether those obligations are affirmative or negative.

The solution to which Lord Templeman refers had become expressed in rules which governed the law on enforceability of covenants for centuries.

These rules were replaced with effect from and including 1 January 1996. Thus, there are two sets of rules, the old and the new. The old rules continue to relate to leases created before 1 January 1996, called 'old leases'. The second, new set of rules relates to leases created on or after that date, called 'new leases'. The new set of rules was introduced because the old rules as they related to privity of contract were capable of leading to such injustice that reform was seen to be needed. That reform was provided by the Landlord and Tenant (Covenants) Act (L&T(C)A) 1995 which came into force on 1 January 1996.

Before going on to look at the two sets of rules, we need to consider the possible permutations of relationships that can exist. In the beginning, there are L1 and T1, the original parties, but either can assign its interest. And there is also the position of any guarantors to take into account.

L1 may assign its freehold reversion to L2 who may in turn assign to L3, and so on.

T1 may assign the residue of the term to T2 who may in turn assign to T3, and so on.

Any tenant may have had to provide a guarantor.

There is, as we have said, no problem about L1 and T1. The questions that arise are whether the following parties can enforce covenants against the other:

(a) L2 and T1;

(b) T1 and L2;

(c) L1 and T2;

(d) T2 and L1;

(e) L2 and T2;

(f) T2 and L2, and so on;

(g) in any event, where does any guarantor of any tenant stand?

The picture looks like this:

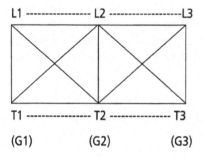

L1 ---------------- L2 -------------------L3

T1 ---------------- T2 ---------------- T3

(G1)   (G2)   (G3)

6.2 The old rules

The old rules – the solution referred to by Lord Templeman – still apply to any lease created before 1 January 1996, and there will be a number of these old leases about for some time. The rules are a mixture of common law and statute.

It must be noted that it is necessary for both the 'benefit' and the 'burden' of the covenant to pass. In other words, the right of one party to sue for breach of the covenant (benefit) and the obligation on the other party to perform the covenant (burden) must both pass according to the old rules. In any action, the position will be:

(a) claimant: acquired the benefit of (right to sue on) the covenant;

(b) defendant: acquired the burden of (obligation to perform) the covenant.

Privity of contract means not only that the original landlord and tenant are liable on the covenants they entered into, but that each remains liable after it has parted with its interest: assignment does not relieve the original party of liability. In most cases, this liability creates much the greater risk to the original tenant than to the original landlord. Suppose T1 takes a lease from L1, and covenants, of course (among other things), to pay the rent. T1's assigning to T2 does not relieve T1 of that liability. In fact, that liability to pay rent remains with T1 until the end of the lease term. This is not the result of the old rules but of the law of contract. The old rules deal with the further passing of the benefit and burden of covenants.

The key phrase in the quotation from Lord Templeman's speech in *Fell* (see **6.1**) is 'touch and concern the land'. The idea is this: since it is not sensible for privity of contract to cause covenants to lose their force after the original parties have assigned their interests, there must be some rationale for saying that the covenants should continue, even as between those who were not original contracting parties. That rationale is that those covenants which, in the archaic jargon, 'touch and concern the land', do continue to bind successors to the original parties. These are those covenants which are annexed to the term and to the reversion. Of course, this raises the question, 'which are they?'. Covenants which 'touch and concern the land' are those which relate to the landlord and tenant relationship. Covenants to pay rent and to repair are obviously within this relationship. In reality, most of the covenants in a lease touch and concern the land. Which covenants would not? Essentially, those which are personal to the parties, such as an option granted to the tenant to buy the freehold reversion: that is a not a landlord and tenant relationship but a relationship of potential seller and buyer: see below **6.2.6**. Where a landlord takes from a tenant a sum of money as a deposit to secure payment of rent or against damage to the property, that landlord will covenant with that tenant to repay the deposit: such a covenant is personal between those parties and does not touch and concern the land (see: *Hua Chiao Commercial Bank Ltd v Chiaphua Industries Ltd* [1987] AC 99, PC). Also, a covenant by an assignor not to trade in a defined area for a defined period of time is a personal covenant.

The law on 'touching and concerning' goes back to *Spencer's Case* [1583] 5 Co Rep 16a. Statute later completed the pattern. The position was set forth by Lord Templeman in *Fell* ([1993] 4 All ER at 972) thus:

> At common law, after an assignment, the benefit of a covenant by the original landlord which touches and concerns the land runs with the term granted by the lease. The burden of a covenant by the original tenant which touches and concerns the land also runs with the term: see *Spencer's Case* . . .

> By statute, the benefit of a covenant by the original tenant which touches and concerns the land runs with the reversion. Section 141 of the Law of Property Act 1925 . . . provides:

> '(1) Rent reserved by a lease, and the benefit of every covenant or provision therein contained, having reference to the subject matter thereof, and on the lessee's part to be observed and performed, and every condition of re-entry and other condition therein contained, shall be annexed and incident to and shall go with the reversionary estate in the land . . . immediately expectant on the term granted by the lease . . . '

> By statute, the burden of a covenant by the original landlord which touches and concerns the land also runs with the reversion. Section 142 of the 1925 Act . . . provides:

> '(1) The obligation under a condition or a covenant entered into by a lessor with reference to the subject matter of the lease shall, if and as far as the lessor has power to bind the reversionary estate immediately expectant on the term granted by the lease, be annexed and incident to and shall go with that reversionary estate . . . and may be taken advantage of and enforced by the person in whom the term is from time to time

vested . . . and . . . the obligation aforesaid may be taken advantage of and enforced against any person so entitled . . . '

So, as regards any landlord and any tenant for the time being, the position as to covenants which touch and concern the land can be illustrated like this:

(a) L has the benefit of T's covenants plus the burden of L's covenants: ss 141, 142;

(b) T has the benefit of L's covenants plus the burden of T's covenants: *Spencer's Case*.

Privity of contract is thus made to continue after any assignment, whether of the landlord's reversion or of the tenant's term. So, when L1 and T1 covenant with each other when they enter into a lease, L1 remains liable to T1 *and its successors* even after L1 has assigned its reversion to L2, and so on. Likewise, T1 remains liable to L1 *and its successors* even after T1 has assigned the lease to T2, and so on. For how long liability lasts depends on what was agreed in the lease. Normally, it will last for the length of the contractual term. Liability could continue during any extension of the term if the tenant had been so ill-advised as to accept such a burdensome covenant. There may be some old leases in which tenants may have tried to reduce their liability by way of a proviso in either of the following ways: (a) that liability shall cease after assignment, or (b) that liability shall cease after the assignee shall assign. Whether a tenant had been able to negotiate such a concession from the landlord would have depended on their respective bargaining strengths at the time the lease was negotiated. Where liability continues for the term of the lease then, given that the greater covenant burden lies on the tenant, particularly as to payment of rent, the risk to the tenant is great.

Under the old rules, the longer the term, the greater the risk, especially if the rent was subject to review. In *Scottish & Newcastle plc v Raguz* [2006] EWHC 821, Ch, Scottish & Newcastle (S&N) took two underleases in 1967 and 1969 for terms to expire in 2062 subject to upwards-only rent reviews. S&N assigned the underleases to the defendant, R, in 1982, taking an indemnity covenant (see **6.2.3**) from R. After some assignments, the underleases became vested in HSJ which went into receivership in 1999 and fell into substantial rent arrears. In 2001, National Car Parks Ltd (NCP) (by now the landlord under the underleases) served statutory notices (under s 17 of the L&T(C)A 1995 – see **6.3.2**) on S&N, claiming from it all arrears of rent; S&N, in turn, sought to pass on the liability to R under the indemnity covenant. Hart J noted (at para 350) that such facts 'dramatically illustrate how severely the rule [concerning original tenants' liability] can impact on the original tenant'.

The impact is unfortunate for a substantial public limited company but it would be catastrophic for an individual who might, years into retirement, receive from an unknown landlord a demand for rent, the level of which had been lifted by review, which was unpaid by an unknown tenant. Such is the force of privity of contract, and it was this legal but iniquitous scenario – played out in well-publicised cases where people had been ruined – which led to the call for reform.

There was little the courts could do to mitigate the rigour of the old rules. In *Centrovincial Estates plc v Bulk Storage Ltd* [1983] P & CR 393, an original tenant was liable for arrears of rent incurred by an assignee, the rent having been reviewed under the rent review clause in the lease. The rent review clause was part of the bargain to which the original tenant had contracted. However, where the original tenant has assigned and the landlord and tenant for the time being enter into a variation of the lease so that the varied term is not what the original tenant contracted to, then the original tenant is not liable for the greater liability created by the variation, though does remain liable under the term without the variation. So the Court of Appeal decided in *Friends Provident Life Office v British Railways Board* [1996] 1 All ER 336, reversing, on this point, the decision of Harman J in *Selous Street Properties Ltd v Oronel Fabrics Ltd* [1984] 1 EGLR 50. There, Harman J decided that an assignee of a lease could vary its terms (by agreement with landlord) because the assignee was in the shoes of the original tenant who would be bound by the variation. In *Friends Provident*, rent payable under a lease without a rent review clause was £12,000. This was varied by successors to the original parties to £35,000, and there was relaxation of the user and alienation clauses. Sir Christopher Slade, assisted, as he said he was, by a note by Patrick McLoughlan in [1984] Conv 443, set out four propositions:

(1) The assignment of a lease does not destroy the privity of contract which exists between the landlord and the original tenant; in the result, the original tenant remains liable on all his covenants contained in the original lease, notwithstanding the assignment.

(2) If the contract embodied in the original lease itself provides for some variation in the future of the obligations to be performed by the tenant (eg by a rent review clause), the original tenant may be bound to perform the obligations as so varied, even though the variations occur after the assignment of the lease – this will depend on the construction of the relevant covenant(s) in the original lease.

(3) The actual decision in *Centrovincial Estates* is justifiable on ground (2) above, though the decision in *Selous Street Properties* is less easily justifiable on that ground because there the assignee had altered the premises in breach of covenant , arguably so as to increase their value, before the rent review.

(4) If, on the other hand, an assignee of the lease by arrangement with the landlord agrees to undertake some obligation not contemplated by the contract contained in the original lease, the estate may be altered, but the variation does not affect the obligations of the original tenant . . .

Beldam LJ, with whom Sir Christopher Slade and Waite LJ agreed, decided that 'extensive though the changes were to the user and alienation covenants and to the rent reserved, they did no more than vary the obligations of the covenants touching and concerning the land which were "imprinted" on the term; they did not vary the term itself'. Because the changes affected the terms of the lease but not the legal estate, it followed that the British Railways Board was liable for the rent at £12,000 but not at the higher level set by the variation. Where changes affected the legal estate by, for example, altering the extent of the premises or the term of the lease, there would be a surrender and regrant of the lease – in effect a new lease – and this would release the original tenant from all liability since the contract into which it had entered would no longer exist.

It is noteworthy that *Friends Provident* was decided less than six months before the coming into force of the L&T(C)A 1995, and anticipated s 18 of the Act.

6.2.1 How the rules work

6.2.1.1 L2 and T1 – passing of benefit to L2

When L1 assigns its reversion to L2, privity of estate then exists between L2 and T1 because they are now landlord and tenant. There is, however, no privity of contract since L2 was not party to the original contract. Section 141(1) of the LPA 1925 applies to make the rent payable and the benefit of all covenants in the lease 'having reference to the sub-ject-matter thereof' (which is how s 141 describes touching and concerning) pass to L2. This means that L2 could sue T1 for breaches of covenant committed, not only after L2 became landlord but for breaches which occurred when L1 was landlord since L1 cannot sue after assignment to L2. Gray and Gray (14.274) assume that L2 can even sue T1 for breaches committed when T1 has assigned to T2; this is doubted by P Luxton and M Wilkie, *Comercial Leases* (1998), 104–5 though the argument in favour is considered.

6.2.1.2 T1 and L2 – passing of burden to L2

Section 142(1) of the LPA 1925 is the other side of the coin from s 141(1). Landlord's covenants which have 'reference to the subject-matter of the lease' bind L2. Where the lease is of part of property, this is especially important. Typical landlord's covenants in such a case are to insure and repair the building and common parts. If L2 is in breach of such covenants, T1 can sue L2.

L2's liability is limited to the time that L2 is landlord, and so L2 is not liable for breaches committed by L1: *Duncliffe v Caerfelin Properties Ltd* [1989] 2 EGLR 38. But if there is a breach of a continuing nature such as outstanding disrepair, L2 may be liable to T2. Indeed, where T1 had an action against L1 because of L1's breach, and T1 had withheld rent against damages claimed – known as the equitable right of set-off – L2 may be bound by that right: see *Muscat v Smith* [2003] 1 WLR 2853.

6.2.1.3 L1 and T2

As between these, L1 may sue T2, and T2 may sue L1 (though not for breaches committed by T1) by the simple application of *Spencer's Case*.

6.2.1.4 L2 suing T2

Here, neither was party to the original contract, and so there cannot be any privity of con-tract. There is, of course, privity of estate simply because these parties are landlord and tenant. Section 141(1) of the LPA 1925 operates to pass to L2 the benefits of the tenant's covenants as in L2 and T1 (see **6.2.1.1**). The burden of the tenant's covenants passes to T2 under *Spencer's Case*. So, L2 may sue T2 for any breach by T2, whether before or after L2 became landlord.

6.2.1.5 T2 suing L2

Section 142(1) of the LPA 1925 passes to L2 from L1 the burden of landlord's covenants as in T1 and L2 (see **6.2.1.2**). T2 acquires the benefit of such covenants under *Spencer's Case*. T2 can therefore sue L2 but only for breaches since T2 became tenant.

6.2.2 Direct covenants by assignees with L

It must be remembered that, in old leases, the rules were usually varied. Landlords did not rely only on the old rules concerning the liability of tenants other than the original tenant; they attempted, and often succeeded, in getting any assignee to covenant directly with the landlord. Landlords would normally insist that the alienation clause contained a covenant by the tenant to procure that any assignee entered into a covenant directly with the landlord to observe all the tenant's covenants and all other provisions in the lease. This liability would be co-extensive with the liability of the original tenant, which would normally be for the contractual term (though great care must be taken to see if liability has been made to enure during any extension of the term). By such a direct covenant with the landlord, every new tenant of an old lease is put under the same obligation to the landlord as the original tenant.

For example, L1 granted a lease to T1. T1 assigns to T2. In the licence to assign, T2 covenants directly with L1 and its successors to perform the covenants in the lease, probably for the residue of the term, though possibly for only as long as T2 is tenant if T2 had been able to negotiate that. Then T2 assigns to T3. Again, L1 (or its successor) takes a direct covenant from T3 similarly. If T3 breaches a covenant, then L (or its successor) has the full range of remedies against not only T1 but also T2. L can sue whichever person looks most solvent.

6.2.3 Indemnity covenants

Each tenant seeks to protect itself by taking a covenant from its assignee to indemnify the assignor against claims brought by the landlord for breach of covenant. Thus, if T1 is sued, it can claim from T2 under the indemnity covenant which T2 gave to T1: see *Scottish & Newcastle plc v Raguz* [2006] EWHC 821, Ch. T2 may in turn claim from T3, and so on. Such a chain of indemnity covenants is vulnerable to being broken if any intermediate tenant is insolvent or cannot be found. L is thus protected if one former tenant in the chain becomes insolvent. Indeed, liability of an intermediate tenant ceases if the liquidator or trustee in bankruptcy (as the case may be) disclaims the lease, so leaving T1 and any other intermediate tenant exposed to L's action.

One crumb of comfort for T1 when sued by L for a breach by, say, T3, T2 being insolvent, is that T1 can sue T3 under the rule in *Moule v Garrett* [1871] LR 7 Exch 101. This will be of no comfort, though, if T3 is insolvent.

6.2.4 Guarantors

The position of guarantors and some of the circumstances in which they may be required was considered at **3.5.3**. If a tenant's liability extends to the end of the term, its guarantor should try to agree with the landlord that its liability will enure only whilst the lease is vested in the tenant. The point is not necessarily historical: an old lease with still some years to run may give rise in practice to the situation where an assignee is required by the landlord to provide a guarantor, and the extent of liability sought by the landlord will then have to be negotiated.

If a guarantor agreed to be liable for the original tenant, then since that tenant's liability extends to the end of the term, if, after a number of assignments, L chooses to sue the original tenant, the guarantor may be sued as well. If a guarantor has been so ill-advised as to guarantee a tenant 'and its successors in title', the guarantor has exposed itself to the risk of being liable for the default of future tenants. If the guarantor agreed to be liable for only so long as the term was vested in the tenant it guaranteed, then its liability cannot extend any further: *Johnsey Estates Ltd v Webb* [1990] 1 EGLR 80.

Where G agreed with L1 to stand as guarantor for T and L1 assigns its reversion to L2, the question may arise whether L2 may sue G for T's default. This question was considered in *Kumar v Dunning* [1987] 2 All ER 801 by Sir Nicholas Browne-Wilkinson V-C, who, giving the judgment of the Court of Appeal, decided in favour of the landlord and held the guarantor to be liable. This decision was approved by the House of Lords in *P & A Swift Investments v Combined English Stores Group plc* [1988] 2 All ER 885. There, Lord Oliver said (at 887) that the question was whether the benefit of a surety's – or guarantor's – covenant ran with the reversion so that L2 had the benefit of it even though there was no express assignment of that benefit from L1. He noted (at 888) that there can only be privity of contract between the landlord and the guarantor, and no privity of estate. In the absence of express assignment, the covenant could only run with the reversion if it touched and concerned the land according to the usual rules for determining whether a covenant touched and concerned the land (Lord Oliver clarifying that a reversion is land). Being a liability to pay money, it did run, and so L2 could sue the guarantor for rent unpaid by the tenant. The House of Lords later made it clear that a guarantor is liable under the 'touching and concerning rules' for all its obligations: see *Coronation Street Industrial Properties Ltd v Ingall Industries* [1989] 1 WLR 304.

A guarantor may be required in the covenant with the landlord to take a fresh lease if the tenant's lease is disclaimed by a liquidator (or trustee in bankruptcy in the case of an individual). Such a lease will be an old lease if the guarantor entered into its guarantee before 1 January 1996. If the guarantor guaranteed a tenant (necessarily not the original tenant) of an old lease but entered into the guarantee after that date, the lease taken by the guarantor will be a new lease under the L&T(C)A 1995.

6.2.5 Overview

It will be apparent from the authorities that landlords enjoy considerable protection under old leases. The original tenant is liable for the whole of the term. They usually take direct covenants from assignees. They may require a guarantor from the original tenant or any assignee. A landlord with such protection may, where a tenant for the time being defaults on the rent (say), sue the defaulter, its guarantor, the original tenant or its guarantor, or any intermediate tenant and its guarantor. A non-defaulting tenant may be able to recover under an indemnity covenant or under the rule in *Moule v Garrett*. A guarantor may, by way of indemnity, recover from its principal or from the tenant in default or its guarantor. But as is so often the case, such rights may be hollow where the object of a claim has no money.

6.2.6 Options and rights of pre-emption

A head lease may include a right for the tenant to buy the freehold on terms. This may be by way of an option or a right of pre-emption.

An option is a contract under which the grantee is given the opportunity to buy the interest of the grantor. The grantee may or may not have to pay for the benefit of the option. It is granted for a period of time, say, five years, on terms as to purchase price and other matters. Typically, it gives a tenant the opportunity to buy the landlord's freehold reversion. The option is a contract for the sale of land and must comply with s 2 of the Law of Property (Miscellaneous Provisions) Act 1989. As a contract, an option must be protected as a Class C (iv) land charge under the Land Charges Act 1972 if the grantor's title is unregistered, or by a notice on the register in the case of registered title. Such an option is called a 'call option' since the grantee can exercise it by calling on the grantor to comply with it. Where the grantor has the right to require the grantee to exercise the option, it is called a 'put option'. Call options are more normal in the context of a lease.

Options do not touch and concern the land: the parties contract as seller and buyer, not landlord and tenant. Accordingly, where L1 grants an option to T1 to last for the term of the lease, T1 may exercise the option after it has assigned the lease, and T2 cannot exercise it as not being a party to it. T1 then becomes L2. If, having granted an option to T1, L1 assigns its reversion to L2, T1 will be able to exercise the option against L2 provided T1 protected it as mentioned in the previous paragraph. Where title is unregistered, the option is lost, if unprotected, when L1 assigns its reversion to L2. Then, L1 is liable for breach of contract and L2, if it knew of the option, may be liable for the tort of conspiracy (having induced L1 to break its contract with T1): see *Midland Bank Trust Co Ltd v Green* [1981] AC 513. If the option is unprotected but the title is registered, then, T1 may have an overriding interest under Sch 3 of the Land Registration Act 2002.

A right of pre-emption is effectively an agreement under which, where the grantor decides to sell its interest, the grantee is given a right of first refusal. The same matters apply as with options.

6.2.7 Landlord and Tenant (Covenants) Act 1995

It must be remembered that ss 17-20 of this Act apply to old leases: see **6.3.2** for the effect of these sections.

6.3 The new rules

6.3.1 Background

There is no shortage of comment on the Landlord and Tenant (Covenants) Act 1995, not all of it complimentary. It has been said that the Act was rushed through Parliament and was subject to modifications and additions during its passage as the views of those in the industry, notably landlords, were taken into account. In *First Penthouse Ltd v Channel Hotels & Properties* (UK) Ltd [2004] 1 EGLR 16, para 16, Lightman J said that the 1995 Act was 'the product of rushed drafting' and that its provisions 'create exceptional difficulties'. Commenting on this case, Sandi Murdoch commented that in this rush, 'the legislation suffered a lack of clarity': 'Personal Remarks', (2004) Estates Gazette, 6 March.

There have so far been few reported cases on the 1995 Act but in those few cases there is much judicial description of the 1995 Act and its history: see *BHP Petroleum Great Britain Ltd v Chesterfield Properties Ltd* [2001] 2 EGLR 11, paras 13–20 *per* Lightman J at first instance, and in the Court of Appeal [2002] 2 EGLR 121, paras 18–41 *per* Jonathan Parker LJ; *Avonridge Property Co Ltd v Mashru* [2004] EWCA Civ 1306, paras 13–27 *per* Jonathan Parker LJ and, in the House of Lords, *sub nom London Diocesan Fund v Phithwa* [2005] UKHL 70, paras 10–20 *per* Lord Nicholls of Birkenhead, paras 37–40 *per* Baroness Hale of Richmond (who was a member of the Law Commission which produced report No 174 (see **6.1**) whose recommendations, though modified, were implemented by the Act).

The new law was prompted by concern that L1 was unduly protected, and T1 was unduly prejudiced by being liable throughout the whole term. The Act gives effect to the recommendation that the basic principle governing the running of covenants in leases should be that they ought to be enforceable only as between the persons who are L and T for the time being.

The new rules relate only to leases created from and including 1 January 1996, except that the provisions in ss 17-20 apply to all leases: see **6.3.2**.

6.3.2 The 1995 Act

The long title of the Act is:

> An act to make provision for persons bound by covenants of a tenancy to be released from such covenants on the assignment of the tenancy, and to make other provision with respect to rights and liabilities arising under such covenants; to restrict in certain circumstances the operation of rights of re-entry, forfeiture and disclaimer; and for connected purposes.

This states that the basic aim of the Act is to release parties from their obligations after they have assigned their interest. That basic aim is, however, qualified as will be seen below.

6.3.2.1 Section 28

It is useful to look next at parts of the definition section, s 28(1). This sets out the terms used in the earlier sections.

> 28.—(1) In this Act (unless the context otherwise requires)—

> 'covenant' includes term, condition and obligation, and references to a covenant (or any description of covenant) of a tenancy include a covenant (or a covenant of that description) contained in a collateral agreement;

> 'landlord' and 'tenant', in relation to a tenancy, mean the person for the time being entitled to the reversion expectant on the term of the tenancy and the person so entitled to that term respectively;

'landlord covenant', in relation to a tenancy, means a covenant falling to be complied with by the landlord of premises demised by the tenancy;

'tenant covenant', in relation to a tenancy, means a covenant falling to be complied with by the tenant of premises demised by the tenancy.

The 1985 Act introduced the terms 'landlord covenant' and 'tenant covenant' which, by their wide meaning, indicate that the 'touching and concerning' concept is abandoned. The effect is that only landlord covenants and tenant covenants are transmissible under s 3. Personal covenants are not transmissible.

6.3.2.2 Section 2

2.—(1) This Act applies to a landlord covenant or a tenant covenant of a tenancy—

(a) whether or not the covenant has reference to the subject matter of the tenancy, and

(b) whether the covenant is express, implied or imposed by law.

Combined with s 28(1), s 2(1)(a) makes it clear that the Act aims to shed all reference to 'touching and concerning'.

6.3.2.3 Section 3

3.—(1) The benefit and burden of all landlord and tenant covenants of a tenancy—

(a) shall be annexed and incident to the whole, and to each and every part, of the premises demised by the tenancy and of the reversion in them, and

(b) shall in accordance with this section pass on an assignment of the whole or any part of those premises or of the reversion in them.

(2) Where the assignment is by the tenant under the tenancy, then as from the assignment the assignee—

(a) becomes bound by the tenant covenants of the tenancy except to the extent that—

(i) immediately before the assignment they did not bind the assignor, or

(ii) they fall to be complied with in relation to any demised premises not comprised in the assignment; and

(b) becomes entitled to the benefit of the landlord covenants of the tenancy except to the extent that they fall to be complied with in relation to any such premises.

(3) Where the assignment is by the landlord under the tenancy, then as from the assignment the assignee—

(a) becomes bound by the landlord covenants of the tenancy except to the extent that—

(i) immediately before the assignment they did not bind the assignor, or

(ii) they fall to be complied with in relation to any demised premises not comprised in the assignment; and

(b) becomes entitled to the benefit of the tenant covenants of the tenancy except to the extent that they fall to be complied with in relation to any such premises.

(4) In determining for the purposes of subsection (2) or (3) whether any covenant bound the assignor immediately before the assignment, any waiver or release of the covenant which (in whatever terms) is expressed to be personal to the assignor shall be disregarded.

(5) Any landlord or tenant covenant of a tenancy which is restrictive of the user of land shall, as well as being capable of enforcement against an assignee, be capable of being enforced against any other person who is the owner or occupier of any demised premises to which the covenant relates, even though there is no express provision in the tenancy to that effect.

(6) Nothing in this section shall operate—

(a) in the case of a covenant which (in whatever terms) is expressed to be personal to any person, to make the covenant enforceable by or (as the case may be) against any other person . . .

Section 3 builds upon s 2 and works with s 5 to abolish the old rules. Section 3(1) provides for the shifting of the entirety of the burden of covenants from landlord to landlord and from tenant to tenant as their respective interests are assigned. Section 3(2) and (3) deal in more detail with the position on an assignment by the tenant and by the landlord respectively.

Section 3(6), with s 15, was predicted to cause problems: see Luxton and Wilkie, 116–18; P Luxton, 'The Landlord and Tenant (Covenants) Act 1995: Its impact on Commercial Leases', [1996] JBL 388, 390–1. These predictions were fulfilled in *First Penthouse Ltd v Channel Hotels & Properties Ltd* [2003] EWHC 2713. Lightman J, at para [48], held that the term 'personal' 'does not mean non-transferrable, but means not intended to bind the person from time to time entitled to the tenancy'. His Lordship had to consider the meaning of s 3(6) and s 15 which 'make plain that a covenant is not to be regarded as personal (and therefore disqualified from being a landlord or tenant covenant) unless it is "in whatever terms" expressed to be personal to any person'. He went on to say:

the language of tenancy, read in its context, expresses or otherwise conveys the intention that the covenant shall be personal in the sense that it is not to be annexed to the tenancy or reversion. There is no requirement as to how the intention is to be expressed: the tenancy does not have to spell it out in terms that the covenant is to be personal. The intention may be stated in terms or it may be deduced from the language used read in its proper context.

If judges have to look at the form of covenants and interpret them, rather than look at their substance, the question arises whether they will always be able to do so without recourse to the old 'touching and concerning' principle.

6.3.2.4 Section 5

5.—(1) This section applies where a tenant assigns premises demised to him under a tenancy.

(2) If the tenant assigns the whole of the premises demised to him, he—

    (a) is released from the tenant covenants of the tenancy, and

    (b) ceases to be entitled to the benefit of the landlord covenants of the tenancy, as from the assignment.

(3) If the tenant assigns part only of the premises demised to him, then as from the assignment he—

    (a) is released from the tenant covenants of the tenancy, and

    (b) ceases to be entitled to the benefit of the landlord covenants of the tenancy, only to the extent that those covenants fall to be complied with in relation to that part of the demised premises.

(4) This section applies as mentioned in subsection (1) whether or not the tenant is tenant of the whole of the premises comprised in the tenancy.

Section 5 abolishes the old doctrine of privity of contract. On an assignment, tenants are released from the burden of tenant covenants and lose the benefit of landlord covenants. Section 5 must be read with s 11 which says what assignments are excluded from the operation of s 5. In particular, assignments in breach of covenant are excluded.

Also, s 5 must be read with s 24(1) which provides that s 5 does not operate to release a tenant from liability for a breach of covenant occurring before the release. Section 24(2) operates similarly to release a tenant's guarantor.

6.3.2.5 Section 6

Section 6 contains provision for the release of a landlord from landlord covenants. However, this release is not automatic on the assignment of the reversion. Instead, the landlord has to apply for a release from its covenants in accordance with the procedure in s 8.

When L1 assigns its reversion, the burden of the landlord's covenants and the benefit of the tenant covenants pass to the assignee, L2. But L1 is not released from its liability. Instead, L1 has to apply to T1 for a release from its liability. T1 has to respond in four weeks. If T1 fails to do so, L1 is released. If T1 responds and releases L1 then of course L1 is released. If T1 responds and refuses to release L1, L1 can appeal to the court which will decide if it is reasonable to release L1.

If L1 is in breach of covenant, for example to repair, what happens when L1 assigns to L2? The burden of landlord covenants pass, so L2 becomes liable – but not for breach of covenant before the assignment of the reversion from L1. L1 remains liable for breaches it committed before assignment to L2.

This release procedure for landlords only relates to landlord covenants, not to personal covenants. In *BHP Petroleum Great Britain Ltd v Chesterfield Properties Ltd*, the defendant landlord C agreed to refurbish a building in London SW1 and then grant a lease of it to BHP which is what happened. C covenanted with BHP to remedy any defects in the premises. This agreement, though by its nature 'touching and concerning' the land (in the old language), was expressly stated to be personal to C. C assigned its reversion to an associated company, and sought release from its obligations to BHP as provided under ss 6 and 8 of the L&T(C)A 1995. Two years later, glass panels cracked and one of them fell off and injured a passer-by. The local authority, Westminster City Council, served a dangerous structure notice on BHP which asked C to comply with its obligations. C argued that it had been released by its s 6 notice. BHP argued that it had not because the statutory release did not apply to personal covenants. Both the High Court and the Court of Appeal held that even though C's covenant was not on its face personal in nature, the agreement said that it was and was capable of making it so, and the parties had been free so to agree. 'Landlord' in the 1995 Act means the landlord for the time being, and a landlord covenant was an obligation on that person. Personal covenants could not bind anyone but the covenantor and are not covered by ss 6 and 8. Since the notice it had served on BHP was inapt, C's obligation thus survived. The result is that developers cannot escape personal obligations via the release procedure.

The release procedure for landlords would seem to be plain enough. Taken with the anti-avoidance provisions of s 25, one might think that here is a statutory scheme which strikes a fair balance between landlords and tenants. The decision of the House of Lords in *London Diocesan Fund v Phithwa* indicates that this is not so. The facts, briefly, were as follows. Avonridge (A) had a headlease from LDF. It granted six underleases for large premiums and at peppercorn rents. In these underleases A had a clause, cl 6, which said that after it (and only it) had parted with its reversion, it would not be liable to the underlessees to pay rent under the headlease. Being very much in its interest to do so, A assigned to Phithwa (P) who failed to pay the rent under the headlease (and who disappeared, though not before he had granted a seventh underlease in return for £50,000). L sued A as well as P, and because the underleases could be forfeit, the underlessees sued A and P for failing to pay the rent under the headlease.

A argued that cl 6 was personal to it and so it had escaped liability. The judge at first instance and the Court of Appeal held that this was an attempt to avoid liability and fell foul of s 25(1). Clause 6 was by its nature transmissible and so a landlord covenant and its nature could not be changed by seeking to make it personal. This case was different from the *BHP* case where the covenant to refurbish was capable by its nature of being made personal. Section 25(1) was clear and cl 6 was an attempt to exclude liability: L can only avoid liability by following the procedure in s 8. A was liable.

The House of Lords, though acknowledging that A's course of dealing had all the appearance of a scam, reversed the Court of Appeal's decision (though Lord Walker of Gestingthorpe dissented). The House of Lords said, in effect, that there was a difference between an agreement to limit future liability (which parties had always been able to do) and an agreement to evade the procedure for release from liability (however ample or restricted that liability). There was nothing in the Act to proscribe the former, and by ss 8 and s 25, it made provision for the latter. Furthermore, cl 6 in the underleases was a landlord's covenant, and not personal: it would bind A's successors. This did not help the hapless underlessees because cl 6 operated to limit A's liability to the time when it held the reversionary interest of the immediate landlord. The release procedure under ss 6 to 8 was a way of releasing landlords from liability but it was not the only way since, to reiterate, the Act did not stop parties from agreeing on some limit to liability. Indeed, since such limitation of liability was rare, the Act had provided the release mechanism. A had not found a loophole: as Lord Nicholls observed (at para 21), '[t]he risks involved were not obscure or concealed. They were evident on the face of the subleases. The sublessees were to pay up-front a capitalised rent for the whole term of the subleases. But clause 6 enabled Avonridge to shake off all its landlord obligations at will. Any competent conveyancer would, or should, have warned the sublessees of the risks, clearly and forcefully'. Lord Nicholls headed a section of his speech, 'A trap for the unwary?' – it might have been called, 'a trap for the ill-advised'. For further comment, see [2006] 70 Conv 79.

6.3.2.6 Section 16

16.—(1) Where on an assignment a tenant is to any extent released from a tenant covenant of a tenancy by virtue of this Act ('the relevant covenant'), nothing in this Act (and in particular section 25) shall preclude him from entering into an authorised guarantee agreement with respect to the performance of that covenant by the assignee.

(2) For the purposes of this section an agreement is an authorised guarantee agreement if—

   (a) under it the tenant guarantees the performance of the relevant covenant to any extent by the assignee; and

   (b) it is entered into in the circumstances set out in subsection (3); and

   (c) its provisions conform with subsections (4) and (5).

(3) Those circumstances are as follows—

   (a) by virtue of a covenant against assignment (whether absolute or qualified) the assignment cannot be effected without the consent of the landlord under the tenancy or some other person;

   (b) any such consent is given subject to a condition (lawfully imposed) that the tenant is to enter into an agreement guaranteeing the performance of the covenant by the assignee; and

   (c) the agreement is entered into by the tenant in pursuance of that condition.

(4) An agreement is not an authorised guarantee agreement to the extent that it purports—

   (a) to impose on the tenant any requirement to guarantee in any way the performance of the relevant covenant by any person other than the assignee; or

   (b) to impose on the tenant any liability, restriction or other requirement (of whatever nature) in relation to any time after the assignee is released from that covenant by virtue of this Act.

(5) Subject to subsection (4), an authorised guarantee agreement may—

  (a) impose on the tenant any liability as sole or principal debtor in respect of any obligation owed by the assignee under the relevant covenant;

  (b) impose on the tenant liabilities as guarantor in respect of the assignee's performance of that covenant which are no more onerous than those to which he would be subject in the event of his being liable as sole or principal debtor in respect of any obligation owed by the assignee under that covenant;

  (c) require the tenant, in the event of the tenancy assigned by him being disclaimed, to enter into a new tenancy of the premises comprised in the assignment—

    (i) whose term expires not later than the term of the tenancy assigned by the tenant, and

    (ii) whose tenant covenants are no more onerous than those of that tenancy;

  (d) make provision incidental or supplementary to any provision made by virtue of any of paragraphs (a) to (c).

Section 16 is a compromise, in favour of landlords, on the original proposal for a 'clean break' when assignments take place. It preserves privity of contract to a limited extent by means of the authorised guarantee agreement (AGA). Where a tenant assigns its interest, the landlord can require, as a condition of giving consent to the assignment, that the out-going tenant guarantees the incoming tenant's obligations under the lease. It must be reasonable for the landlord to require an AGA, but doubtless all landlords will include in their leases a proviso that the tenant enter into an AGA on assignment. Tenants cannot be made liable after their immediate assignee has assigned on. An assignment in breach of covenant is effective to pass the legal estate but is an excluded assignment, and under s 11 the assignor's liability continues. If the tenancy is disclaimed by a trustee in bankruptcy or liquidator of the immediate assignee, the assignor may be required to take a new lease on similar terms for the residue of the disclaimed lease. Whether a guarantee of an AGA will be effective is a question which awaits case law guidance.

6.3.2.7 Sections 17–20

These sections apply to all leases, old and new.

Section 17(2) requires a landlord to serve notice on any former tenant or guarantor (whether liable under an old lease or under an AGA) that it claims payment from it of any fixed charge. 'Fixed charge' means rent, service charge or other liquidated sum due as a result of failure to comply with a tenant covenant. It does not include an unliquidated sum such as would be payable as a result of a breach of covenant. The notice must be served within six months of the charge becoming due, but the landlord can then start proceedings at any time during the six-year period allowed under s 19 of the Limitation Act 1980. If the landlord fails to comply with the time limits, the tenant or guarantor is freed from liability. The effect of s 17 is that a former tenant or guarantor cannot be taken by surprise by a claim for accumulated sums. Where there is a long-drawn-out rent review outstanding at the time the notices need serving, the sums for which the former tenant is liable cannot be known until completion of the review. Section 17(4) allows the landlord to serve a further notice telling the former tenant that the claim may involve a greater amount. Protective notices should be served within six months of the former tenant's liability arising, rather than waiting until the revised rent is known: *Scottish & Newcastle plc v Raguz* [2006] EWHC 821, Ch.

Section 18 was anticipated by the decision in *Friends Provident Life Office v British Railways Board* as mentioned in **6.2**. A former tenant's liability cannot be increased by a variation of the tenancy terms provided the variation has been effected since 1 January 1996: s 18(6). Section 18 does not exclude liability for rent due at a higher level under a rent review clause included in the original lease terms.

Sections 19 and 20 provide a new remedy for a former tenant, T, or guarantor, G, who has had to pay a fixed charge unpaid by some assignee, A. T (or G) may require L to grant it an overriding lease. This is granted for a term equal to that of the existing tenancy plus three days and so is a lease of the reversion. Becoming thus the immediate landlord of the defaulter, T now has rights of re-entry and forfeiture, which, if exercised, cut short A's breach, and give T possession and thus an asset which can be assigned or sublet. T must make a claim for an overriding lease within 12 months of the payment being made and L must respond in a reasonable time. Since L can claim against a possible array of persons, there may be competition for an overriding lease; in that case, the first to apply will have the right.

6.4 Use of insolvency law to avoid liability

Early in 2006, a retailer, PowerHouse, sought to use a company voluntary arrangement (CVA) to avoid its obligations under the leases of a number of its unprofitable stores. CVAs were introduced by the Insolvency Act 1986 to allow qualifying companies to come to arrangements with their creditors to avoid administration or liquidation. PowerHouse intended to use this device to avoid large amounts of rent payable to its landlords and to shield its parent company from liability under its guarantees. This use of CVAs was being challenged by a group of institutional landlords but PowerHouse collapsed in August 2006, and the proposed testing of this use of CVAs in the court is unlikely now to take place. There are suggestions that if such moves by retailers were to succeed, there would be dire consequences for values in the commercial property sector. For comment, see EG 20 May 2006, p 66 and 12 August 2006, p 36. In any event, the collapse of PowerHouse must mean a significant amount of retail space coming onto the property market.

7 Rent and rent review

7.1 Rent

7.1.1 Introduction

In *Street v Mountford* [1985] AC 809, Lord Templeman apparently suggested that rent was an essential feature of the landlord and tenant relationship. That it is not was affirmed by the Court of Appeal in *Ashburn Anstalt v Arnold* [1988] 2 All ER 147. Though not essential, rent is obviously usual in the commercial context since landlords are in business to make money from rental income.

Rent historically related to tenure but now the contractual character of leases is emphasised and rent is regarded as part of the contractual bargain between the landlord and the tenant. The usual case is that rent is payable in pounds sterling at regular intervals. In a very few special situations where there is, in effect, no rent payable, the rent may be stated to be a peppercorn, hence the expression 'peppercorn rent'; it was and still may be stated to be rent by those drafting leases who are nervous about a lack of any consideration. Rent is not the only way a tenant can pay for a lease; it is possible, though probably unwise, to pay a lump sum at the start of the lease as a kind of purchase price. In other words, the rent is capitalised. For an example of this – and why it may be unwise – see *London Diocesan Fund v Phithwa* at **6.3.2.5**.

7.1.2 Definition of rent

In a lease, the rent is usually defined in a definition section at the beginning of the lease. It will often simply state the annual rent due under the lease. Where there is a rent review clause, it will refer to the 'initial rent' which means the rent payable from the beginning of the lease until the first time it is reviewed. Then the 'rent' will be defined as the initial rent and thereafter the rent as ascertained in accordance with the rent review clause.

7.1.3 Certainty

The rent must be certain or ascertainable with certainty – not normally a problem when a specific sum is mentioned. If a sum is not stated, the formula for ascertaining the rent must avoid uncertainty. Rent may be based on the turnover of the tenant's business. This means a percentage of the tenant's trade in a year.

7.1.4 Reservation

The 'reddendum' is the actual reservation of rent, which it is necessary to reserve expressly, and in a typical lease it will be incorporated in the demise clause with wording such as:

> The landlord lets to the tenant the premises to hold the same for the term yielding and paying therefor to the landlord by banker's standing order direct debit or such other means as the landlord shall determine to such bank account as the landlord shall from time to time determine the rent without deduction or set-off by equal quarterly payments in advance on the usual quarter days the first such payment being a proportionate sum for the period from and including the rent commencement date to and including the day before the quarter day next after the rent commencement date to be paid on the date of this lease.

7.1.5 When and how rent is payable

The definition clause may also say at what intervals the rent has to be paid: monthly or quarterly. Rent is normally paid in advance. By far the most common interval is quarterly on what are called the 'usual quarter days'. Leases involve many calculations of time, and the payment of rent is linked with certain age-old events in the calendar. The quarter days are based on Christian festivals which mark the quarters of the year and correspond approximately to the equinoxes and solstices. Centuries ago this would have helped tenants remember when their rent was due. So, 25 March (sometimes called 'Lady Day' – a reference to the Feast of the Annunciation) is the first quarter day; the second is 24 June (Midsummer Day and the Feast of the Nativity of St John the Baptist); the third is 29 September (Michaelmas or the Feast of the Archangel Michael and also the start of the legal year and of the university terms at Oxford, Cambridge and some other universities); and, finally, Christmas Day.

It is now usual for the tenant to be required to pay rent by standing order or direct debit to a bank nominated by the landlord.

The traditional quarterly payment of rent is currently being challenged by retail tenants. In the current difficult trading climate for retailers, quarterly payments of rent in advance can cause or add to cash flow pressure. The British Retail Consortium (BRC), which describes quarterly payments in advance as 'an archaic practice', has orchestrated a campaign on behalf of retailers to pressure landlords into accepting monthly payments. The BRC claims that very many retailers have collapsed because of this practice. Landlords are not in a hurry to give in to this pressure, but monthly payments for retailers would be a mark of the greater flexibility which the government would like to see in the commercial leases market. For more information, see www.brc.org.uk

7.1.6 Apportionment

The clause at 7.1.4 provides for rent to be apportioned on the grant of the lease. It will also be apportioned at the end of the tenancy. It is unlikely that the lease will be completed exactly on a quarter day (if that is the payment interval), so the annual rent is calculated on a daily basis and the relevant proportion payable from the date of completion of the lease until the next quarter day. Say the annual rent is £10,000 and the lease is completed on 1 March. From 1 March to 24 March inclusive is 24 days. The apportionment will be:

$$10,000 \div 365 \times 24 = £657.53$$

Then, of course, on 25 March, £2,500 will be payable.

7.1.7 Deductions

The clause at **7.1.4** includes the words, 'without deduction or set-off'. The landlord's aim is that the rent payable should be net. The word 'deduction' by itself may not achieve this aim entirely. The meaning of 'set-off' was considered by Bean J in *Edlington Properties Ltd v JH Fenner and Co Ltd* [2005] EWHC 2158. The lease in that case provided that rent was payable 'without deduction or abatement'. Set-off was not mentioned. In a claim to set off rent against an alleged breach by the landlord's predecessor in title (which claim was unsuccessful), Bean J referred to *Connaught Restaurants Ltd v Indoor Leisure Ltd* [1994] 1 WLR 501 as confirming that clear words were needed to exclude a tenant's equitable right to set-off, Waite LJ having said (at 505) '[t]here is however a starting presumption that neither party intends to abandon any remedies for breach arising by operation of law, and clear language must be used if this presumption is to be rebutted'.

7.1.8 Interest

Only if there is an express tenant covenant to pay interest on overdue payments of rent and other payments due under the lease will the landlord be able to charge interest. Such a clause will be found in any well-drawn lease. It is likely to provide that the tenant must pay interest at a certain rate – often a fixed amount such as 4% over base lending rate – on sums not paid within 14 days. It is characteristic of some leases that 'interest' will be defined in the definition section, likewise the interest rate, and the covenant to pay it else-where in the lease. There is, therefore, the inconvenience of looking in several places to put together the whole provision.

7.2 Rent review

7.2.1 Introduction

> There is really no dispute that the general purpose of a provision for rent review is to enable the landlord to obtain from time to time the market rental which the premises would command if let on the same terms on the open market at the relevant review dates. The purpose is to reflect the changes in the value of money and the real increases in the value of the property during a long term.

Thus did Sir Nicholas Browne-Wilkinson V-C state the purpose of rent reviews in *British Gas Corp v Universities Superannuation Scheme Ltd* [1986] 1 All ER 978 at 981. Rent review clauses are, simply, an anti-inflationary device to preserve for the landlord the value of rental income over the longer term. Such clauses did not become common until the severe inflation of the late 1960s and 1970s. In the 1950s, inflation was virtually unknown in the UK. But between 1967 and 1992, the average rate of inflation was 9% though it was at its worst during the early and mid-1970s, peaking in August 1975 at 27%. Such a rate of inflation actually causes significant negative returns on investment, ie losses in real terms. In the 1970s and 1980s, it was common for a rent review clause to provide for the rent to be reviewed every three years, even when the rate of inflation had fallen to an average of 7% as it did in the 1980s. The last decade has seen low inflation (about 2%) and price stability in the UK, meaning that inflation does not impact on commercial decision-making. Rent review clauses now commonly provide for review every five years. Furthermore, as lease terms have become shorter, fewer leases now have rent review clauses at all. This does not mean that the topic has reduced in importance; there are many long leases still current which have rent review clauses, and new leases are still granted with rent review clauses, especially in certain parts of the retail market.

While it is for the lawyer to draw up the terms of the rent review clause, the parties must be urged, especially where the rent is significant and the term will involve several rent reviews, to take advice from a chartered surveyor with specialist expertise in rent reviews. The same advice applies where a person is proposing to take an assignment of either the freehold reversion or of the lease.

7.2.2 Upwards and downwards review

During times of inflation, even if the rate of inflation is low, prices and rents alike go up and so what is called the open market rental (OMR) would go up. OMR means the rent which the premises would attract if let in the usual way on the open commercial property market. Rent review clauses are nearly always drafted as 'upwards only' and are called 'upwards only rent reviews' or UORRs (called 'ratchet clauses' in Australia and New Zealand). However, recent history shows that rents can go down as well as up. In the recession of the late 1980s and early 1990s, some rents halved. When this happens, there can be unfairness.

Take a simple example. Suppose the initial rent in 2000 was £10,000 a year. There is a review after five years. The OMR in 2005 is £12,000. The rent would have been increased to £12,000. But if there had been a recession, the OMR might be £8,000. Yet the review clause says the reviewed rent cannot be less than it was before the review, so it stays at £10,000. The tenant is paying £2,000 more than the OMR. On one view, this creates bad feeling on the part of the tenant and it contradicts the purpose of the rent review which was only to maintain the real value of the landlord's income stream, not to lift it above OMR. The British Property Federation, however, contends that UORRs are an important feature of the property market: see its report; *Commercial Property Leases*, (September, 2004).

The perceived unfairness of UORRs to tenants has been debated by the government and the property industry. In April 2004, a report on commercial leases produced by the University of Reading said that, despite the debate (which had taken place since 2001), UORRs were the norm, and rent review clauses which provided for the reviewed rent to be truly the OMR – be that more or less than the rent payable before review – were rare. The

Government contemplated legislation to outlaw UORRs. This was opposed by the British Property Federation. In March 2005, the Government said that it would not, for the time being, bring in legislation to outlaw UORRs but it would keep the matter under review.

Where a clause is found which does provide for upwards or downwards review, it is clearly important that the tenant as well as the landlord should have the right to initiate review. A rent review clause which provides for an open review – that is, upwards or downwards – is not inconsistent with the rent review being operable only by the landlord. In other words, there is no presumption that such a clause ought to be operable by either the landlord or the tenant: clear words are needed if the tenant is to have the right to operate the review. Such was made clear in *Hemingway Realty Ltd v Clothworkers' Company* [2005] EWHC 299, Ch following the decision of the Court of Appeal of New Zealand in *Australian Mutual Provident Society v National Mutual Life Association of Australia Ltd* [1995] 1 NZLR 581.

7.2.3 When rent is reviewed

As mentioned in **7.2.1**, it is usual currently for the rent to be reviewed every five years. The review will normally be effective from the anniversary of the start of the term. So, in the case of 5-yearly reviews of rent in a 15-year lease granted for a term starting on 25 March 2002, reviews are due to take place on 25 March 2007 and 25 March 2012. The date of the start of the term is almost always not the same as the date of the lease, and care must be taken by both parties to understand the effect where there is (unusually) any appreciable gap of time between the two dates, especially where the start of the term is backdated, so advancing the date of the first review. For example, if a lease is completed on 1 July 2006 for a term starting on 29 September 2005, the first review date is nearer four years away than five.

Sometimes, where the tenant will have security of tenure, landlords stipulate a rent review date the day before the end of the contractual term. This has the effect of giving the landlord the benefit of higher rent during any holding over by the tenant. It is very likely that such a reviewed rent will be higher than an interim rent set by the court during renewal proceedings.

Alternatively, the rent review clause may be drafted so as to achieve the same effect more obliquely. For example, in a lease for a term of 11 years from 25 March 2005, the clause might provide that the rent is to be reviewed every 5 years on the anniversary of the contractual term. Reviews would be due on 25 March in 2010 and 2015, but the term ends on 24 March 2016, so giving the landlord the benefit of a review just a year before the end of the term. The landlord could, instead, stipulate rent reviews on each five-yearly anniversary of the term but define the term as including any holding over under the security of tenure legislation; the landlord then will argue that the starting date of the holding over is the occasion of a review. Tenants should resist such stipulations.

7.2.4 How the rent is reviewed

Over the years, the inventiveness of draftsmen has led to there being a variety of types of review clauses, some of such complexity with their intricately interlocking formulas and provisions for alternative possibilities that it might even be advisable for the less experienced or less specialist legal practitioner to take advice on the meaning and effect of the clause. Clearly, the type of clause used should be reflected in the type of property. For a 15-year lease of office premises, for example, the simplest type of clause is likely to be appropriate. For a 25-year lease of a department store in a large shopping centre, the more complex type will be used. There are three types of clauses commonly found: index-linked, turnover rent, and OMR.

7.2.4.1 Index-linked

Index-linking is not common but may be found in older leases. The Office for National Statistics issues data on price inflation for each month. There are two common indexes: the Retail Price Index (RPI) and Retail Price Index excluding mortgage interest repayments (RPIX). These are obviously more appropriate to leases of retail premises. However, these indexes essentially track consumer price inflation, and landlords may see little relevance in this to their commercial property market concerns.

7.2.4.2 Turnover rent

Turnover rents have become much more common recently in the retail sector of the commercial property market. Turnover means the value of goods or services sold before the deduction of business expenses. In other words, it is the gross income of the tenant's business. The revised rent is determined by the actual turnover of the tenant. This method is especially appropriate for a captive market tenant (such as an airport shop), shopping centre tenants and factory outlet retail premises.

There are two sorts of turnover rent: rent based entirely on turnover, and that based on a mixture of turnover and a basic minimum rent. Unlike other types of rents, turnover rents may be payable monthly in arrears. Given this mechanism, the more usual rent review clause is not needed.

With turnover rents, the landlord shares in the commercial success (or otherwise) of the tenant. Some landlords may want to guard against any downturn in the tenant's fortunes. This writer recalls, in a rent review clause of a unit in a large shopping centre, a provision that if the tenant's turnover was less than the landlord thought it ought to be, the landlord could substitute a higher figure according to a complex accounting process.

A recent case highlights the importance of precision in drafting the terms of a turnover rent clause. In *Debenhams Retail plc v Sun Alliance & London Assurance Co Ltd* [2005] EWCA Civ 868, it was held that VAT was included in turnover because the tax was in succession to the old purchase tax. It must be made clear that turnover is exclusive of VAT.

For a very full and helpful description of turnover rents, see the website of the Valuation Office Agency at http://www.voa.gov.uk/instructions/chapters/rating_manual/vol4/sect5/pn1-15.htm accessed 1 May 2006.

7.2.4.3 OMR

Still much the most common type of rent review clause is that in which the rent is reviewed by reference to the open market rental value.

7.2.5 OMR as the basis of review

Even a straightforward rent review clause using OMR as the basis of review may be five pages long. There are, of course, many variations on the theme, but most will contain the following provisions:

(a) the initial rent will be payable until the first review date (the initial rent and the intervals (say, every fifth anniversary of the term) will have been defined in the definition clause);

(b) the rent from each successive review date to be the same as the rent previously payable or the revised rent, whichever is the greater. This means the clause is 'upwards only';

(c) the revised rent can be agreed at any time between the parties – it often is. There are two ways that agreement can be reached: either 'informally', meaning negotiated within a certain time frame, or 'formally' by the service of notice and counter-notice. The use of a notice – called a 'trigger notice' – to start the review has been the subject of much case law: see **7.2.6**.

What then follows is the machinery for determining the revised rent in the absence of agreement:

(a) the parties to appoint a suitably experienced chartered surveyor to determine what the OMR should be, with provision that if the parties cannot agree who that surveyor should be, one should be appointed by the President of the Royal Institution of Chartered Surveyors;

(b) the surveyor to act as expert or as arbitrator: see **7.2.7**;.

(c) what is meant by OMR: see **7.2.8**.

The provisions which need further comment are trigger notices, the difference between expert and arbitrator and the meaning of OMR. Each of these is now considered.

7.2.6 Trigger notices

An example of this formal method of agreeing the revised rent could be that the landlord may serve on the tenant a notice (usually called a 'rent notice') not less than six months and not earlier than twelve months before the relevant review date specifying what the revised rent should be. The tenant may then be required to serve a counter-notice within one month either agreeing with the landlord's proposal or proposing its own revised rent. The question that often arises is, what happens if either party fails to serve its notice within the time stated? In other words, is time of the essence? If time is of the essence, then missing the date makes the late notice voidable; if time is not of the essence, then lateness does not affect the validity of the notice.

This question was considered by the House of Lords in *United Scientific Holdings Ltd v Burnley Borough Council* [1977] 2 All ER 62. The council had been two months late in serving its notice. Equity does not regard time as being of the essence in contracts, and this is reflected in the LPA 1925 where s 41 states this rule. Of course, it would be simple just for the draftsman to say in clear words whether or not time is of the essence; as Lord Simon said (at 86):

> Such clauses could easily be drafted so that they state expressly whether time is or is not to be treated as of the essence. So drafted they would present no difficulty. Unfortunately, they rarely are. They should be, for if they were, a great deal of expensive litigation would be avoided.

(Why some draftsmen do not do what is simple and obvious is one of life's mysteries.) The House of Lords held that time is not of the essence in relation to time limits in a rent review clause. This is a presumption which can be rebutted in two ways: by express provision, or what are called 'contra-indications', though delay does not rebut the presumption.

7.2.6.1 Express provision

If the clause expressly says that time is to be of the essence in relation to any time limits, then that is conclusive. The consequences of missing a date cannot be avoided. In *Fox & Widley v Guram* [1998] 3 EG 142, the landlord served a notice on the tenant stating that the rent was to be £14,000. This was a fanciful figure, given that the OMR was £3,500, but there is nothing to stop a party from proposing any figure. The tenant should have served a counter-notice within three months as to which time was of the essence. In failing to comply with the time limit, the tenant was fixed with the figure of £14,000.

7.2.6.2 Contra-indications

Where there is no express provision, there may be contra-indications which rebut the presumption that time is not of the essence. The House of Lords did not suggest what such contra-indications might be. A line of case law has shown that a clear timetable and what are called 'deeming provisions' may be found to rebut the presumption that time is not of the essence.

In *Henry Smith's Charity Trustees v AWADA Trading and Promotion Services Ltd* [1984] 1 EGLR 116, a landlord's failure to comply with a stipulation as to time meant that the rent was as stated in the tenant's counter-notice because the Court of Appeal (unanimously) held that the effect of an elaborate timetable with 'deeming provisions' made time of the essence. Yet some six months later, in *Mecca Leisure Ltd v Renown Investments* (Holdings) Ltd [1984] 1 EGLR 137, a differently-constituted Court of Appeal, considering facts similar to those in the *Henry Smith's Charity* case, held that time was not of the essence, though there was a robust dissent by Browne-Wilkinson LJ.

The conflict was resolved by the Court of Appeal in *Starmark Enterprises Ltd v CPL Distribution Ltd* [2001] EWCA Civ 1252. There, the landlord could serve a rent notice on the tenant at any time during a period of six months before the relevant anniversary date of the term of the lease, saying what the new rent should be. The tenant, within one month of receipt of such notice, could serve on the landlord a counter-notice calling for negotiations. If the tenant failed to serve such counter-notice, then it was deemed to have accepted the rent proposed by the landlord. Three rent reviews had occurred without any problem. At the fourth, the landlord served a notice proposing a rent of £84,800 a year. The tenant served a counter-notice six weeks late and proposed a rent of £52,725. At first instance, Neuberger J was obliged to follow the *Mecca Leisure* case but his lordship made it clear that the conflict in the law should be resolved and he hoped the parties would go to the Court of Appeal which they did. The Court of Appeal unanimously followed the decision in the *Henry Smith's Charity* case, and held *Mecca Leisure* to have been wrongly decided, Kay LJ stating (at para 63) that the approach of Browne-Wilkinson LJ in that case had been the 'only proper approach'. Arden LJ considered the meaning of a deeming provision and noted that the clause in *Starmark* made no provision as to what was to happen if the tenant served a counter-notice late.

Starmark was applied in *Monella v Pizza Express (Restaurants) Ltd* [2003] EWHC 2966. There, a lease of 30 October 1997 granted a term of 25 years from the date of the lease subject to 5-yearly rent reviews. The rent review clause was in standard form, and provided (amongst other things) that if the rent had not been agreed and the landlord had not applied to the President of the Royal Institution of Chartered Surveyors (RICS) for the appointment of a third party to determine the rent, then the tenant could serve on the landlord a notice proposing a figure for the rent (not being less than that previously payable) and this proposed rent would be deemed to be the revised rent unless the landlord made an application to the President of the RICS within one month after the tenant's notice. The landlord had earlier suggested a rent of £37,000. On 30 October 2001, the tenant proposed £21,000 under the provision just mentioned. The landlord served a notice for the appointment of a third party on 9 December – nine days late. The court held that *Starmark*, though only recently decided, should apply and the landlord could not plead that the effect of this case must be taken to have been out of the contemplation of the parties. On the contrary, changes in the law are to be expected. The figure of £21,000 had to stand.

Where time is not of the essence, a tenant cannot make it so by serving a notice and unilaterally declaring time to be of the essence: *Barclays Bank plc v Saville Estates Ltd* [2002] EWCA Civ 589. There, a lease of 1969 had an early form of rent review clause. When the landlord, Saville Estates, did nothing to initiate review, the tenant bank tried to force their hand by serving a notice requiring them to appoint a third party in 28 days and making time of the essence. The judge at first instance held that nothing in the rent review cause entitled the tenant to do that. Reversing this decision, the Court of Appeal said that it is important for tenants to know what level of rent they face, both for the purposes of their business and for facilitating any assignment. The landlord must apply for a third party determination within a reasonable time which in this case would be three months.

7.2.6.3 Other words as contra-indications

There may be words which lead the court to conclude that the presumption is rebutted and time is of the essence. In *First Property Growth Partnership LP v Royal & Sun Alliance Property Services Ltd* [2002] EWCA Civ 1687, the rent review clause said that the landlord's rent notice could be given at any time not more than 12 months before every fifth year of the term but not at any other time. The Court of Appeal held that on its ordinary and natural meaning this provision created a period of time with a clear beginning and a clear end, namely, 12 months before the expiry of the relevant 5-year period. The expression 'but not at any other time' reinforced the probable intention of the parties to fix firmly the start time and the end time for the giving of the notice.

7.2.6.4 Delay

Delay in the service of a notice does not of itself rebut the presumption. This was not clear at the time of *Telegraph Properties (Securities) Ltd v Courtaulds* (1981) 257 EG 51, CA where it was held that a delay of five years caused the landlord to lose the right to review. In *Amherst v James Walker (Goldsmith and Silversmith) Ltd* [1983] 2 All ER 1067, a case also involving a five-year delay, Oliver LJ said *Telegraph Properties* was wrong and mere delay, however long, cannot rebut the presumption. In fact, said Oliver LJ, even hardship to the tenant caused by delay was insufficient to rebut the presumption unless the delay induced the tenant to act to its detriment – in effect there had to be an element of estoppel.

7.2.6.5 Effective date of review

What is now clear is that arguments as to whether time is of the essence relate to the machinery for review but not to the date from which the reviewed rent is payable. In *Riverside Housing Association Ltd v White* [2005] EWCA Civ 1385, a residential case rather than a commercial case, there was a formula for increasing the rent and the increase was to take effect on 1 June each year. The landlord then changed that date to 1 April. That was not a valid implementation of the rent review procedure. The Court of Appeal agreed with counsel for the tenants that the presumption that time is not of the essence applies only to the machinery for fixing the rent on review, but cannot apply to the date from which the increase is to take effect. The reason is that this date is clearly stated and fixed and there is no scope for applying the presumption that time is not of the essence; a tenant cannot be made to suffer uncertainty as to this date since this would enable a landlord to choose a date most advantageous to it.

7.2.7 Expert or arbitrator

Where the parties have not agreed the new rent and the machinery for determining it is used, a chartered surveyor (appointed by agreement or, in default of agreement, by the President of the RICS) will decide the new rent. He is to act either as expert or as arbitrator. The question is how to decide in which of these two capacities the surveyor should act.

In the first place, the clause should make clear exactly the capacity of the third party. It is not enough to say, 'surveyor', and terms which have no precise meaning such as 'umpire' must be avoided: see *Safeway Food Stores Ltd v Banderway Ltd* (1983) 267 EG 850. Assuming no such problems of construction arise, it is important to know the difference between an expert and an arbitrator.

7.2.7.1 Expert

An expert:

(a) acts in a professional capacity;

(b) need not hear argument from the parties;

(c) cannot compel witnesses or production of documents;

(d) decision cannot be appealed against – the decision is final and binding;

(e) can be sued for negligence;

(f) procedure is quicker and cheaper.

7.2.7.2 Arbitrator

An arbitrator:

(a) acts in a quasi-judicial capacity;

(b) hears argument from the parties;

(c) can compel witnesses and production of documents (under the Arbitration Act 1996);

(d) decision can be appealed (to the High Court on a point of law);

(e) cannot be sued;

(f) procedure is longer and more expensive.

It follows that arbitration will only be used in particularly complex or very high value cases.

7.2.8 OMR

In the absence of agreement between the parties as to the revised rent, the third party chartered surveyor is to determine what the revised rent should be. The wording may be as follows (the parts underlined being examined below):

[2] The revised rent payable from any review date may be agreed at any time by the landlord and the tenant or in the absence of agreement determined not earlier than the relevant review date at the landlord's option by an independent valuer (acting as an expert and not as an arbitrator) to be nominated in the absence of agreement by the President of the Royal Institution of Chartered Surveyors on the application of the landlord or the tenant made not earlier than six months before the relevant review date so that in the case of such determination the revised rent shall be such as the independent valuer shall decide should be the Open Market Rent at the relevant review date.

[3] For the purposes of this clause 'Open Market Rent' means the annual rent exclusive of VAT at which the premises might reasonably be expected to be let on the relevant review date assuming:

[3.1] that <u>the premises</u>:

[3.1.1] are available to be let on the <u>open market</u> <u>without a fine or premium</u> with <u>vacant possession</u> by a <u>willing landlord</u> to a <u>willing tenant</u> for a <u>term of 10 years or the unexpired residue of the term of this lease whichever shall be the longer</u>

[3.1.2] are <u>to be let as a whole</u> <u>subject to the terms of this lease</u> other than the amount of rent but including the provisions for review of that rent

[3.1.3] are <u>ready and fit for immediate occupation and use</u>

[3.2] that if the premises or any part thereof shall have been destroyed or damaged the same have been fully restored

[3.3] that no work has been carried out by the tenant on the premises which has diminished the rental value of the premises

[3.4] <u>that the tenant's covenants in this lease have been fully performed</u>

but disregarding:

[3.5] the fact that the tenant its sub-tenants or their respective predecessors in title have been in <u>occupation</u> of the premises

[3.6] any goodwill attaching to the premises by reason of the carrying on thereat of the business of the tenant, its sub-tenants or their respective predecessors in title

[3.7] any effect on the rental value of the premises attributable to the existence at the relevant review date of any improvement to the premises or any part thereof carried out with consent where required otherwise than in pursuance of an obligation to the landlord or its predecessors in title except obligations requiring compliance with statutes or with the directions of the local authority or any body acting with statutory authority.

Such provisions define what the valuer must value and how to find the OMR. It is important to realise that what is being valued is a leasehold interest and not the premises. The basis of valuation must exclude factors which would distort the OMR; such factors would include the actual tenant because it has a special reason for wanting the premises. So what is valued is a hypothetical lease of real premises to be let by a hypothetical landlord to a hypothetical tenant. This may seem like a strained pretence but it is necessary to maintain objectivity, and the reasoning behind this approach was explained in *FR Evans (Leeds) Ltd v English Electric Co Ltd* (1978) P & CR 185: see comment by H Williamson QC, (2004) Estates Gazette, 12 June, 143. Those parts of the provisions underlined are now examined. Some of the commentary is taken from the judgment of Donaldson J in the *FR Evans* case.

The premises
The premises should be correctly defined so that the valuation is precise.

Open market
It should be assumed that there is a market and that the premises are not unique, even if they really are. The real premises cannot exist in a vacuum or in the abstract. The market will be determined by location: High Street Rotherham and Brompton Road Knightsbridge are two very different markets.

Without a fine or premium
Any upfront lump sum payment must be discounted because that would reduce the OMR.

Vacant possession
The tenant is deemed to have moved out or never to have occupied the premises so that any special need of the real tenant is removed.

Willing landlord
The valuer must assume that there are parties prepared to negotiate meaningfully for the hypothetical lease. Neither party's position is distorted by such matters as problems of cash flow. The landlord is an abstraction with the right to grant the lease. It is neither desperate to grant the lease nor indifferent as to whether to grant it or not.

Willing tenant
There is at least one willing tenant who is similarly an abstraction who is keen but not anxious to take the hypothetical lease, but not so casual about it as not to care whether it takes the lease or not.

Term

Both parties should get specialist advice about the hypothetical term when the lease is being negotiated. This provision is of prime importance since the length of the hypothetical term clearly has an impact on the level of rent. The longer the term of a lease, the lower the rent. As the trend is now towards shorter terms, long terms are unattractive and the discount effect of a long term is likely to be all the more marked. If there has been a letting incentive in the form of an initial rent-free period, this must be taken into account since a hypothetical term which has no rent-free period might lead to a discounted rent.

The use in the example given is a hybrid of the residue and a fixed period, thus combining two possibilities. It is a common choice which is attractive for landlords. However, bearing in mind that a rent review clause aims to maintain not only the value of rental income in real terms but to reflect movements in the market, such a formula is a compromise.

A new and simple formula has been proposed. If the wording says, 'a letting for a term of a length which produces the best rent in the open market at the relevant review date' then, it is said, the value of landlords' assets is protected and tenants do not benefit unfairly from discounting: see M Hull, 'Landlords go back to the future' (2005), Estates Gazette, 16 July, 118.

Let as a whole

This means that sublettings are excluded. This is better for the tenant since it leaves out of account the value of sublettings. Where premises are sublet in part or as a whole, the rental income for the tenant makes the lease more valuable and so would inflate the rent.

Subject to the terms of this lease

This is really the heart of the clause since it determines what interest is being valued. Although the lease to be valued is hypothetical, it mirrors the terms of the actual lease. This means that the terms of the actual lease must have been studied carefully since they largely determine the level of rent. Furthermore, the valuer must take into account any variations of the lease, noting the terms of any deeds and licences effecting variations. The most important terms will be clauses dealing with alienation and user. The more restrictive a clause from the tenant's point of view, the more depressing the effect on the rent. Any unusual terms may also cause deviation from the OMR. Some precedents include an assumption that the premises may be used for any of the purposes permitted by the lease as varied or extended by any licence. Such a provision should be resisted by a prospective tenant since it extends the use beyond that authorised for the time being. With regard to user, the relevant case law provides guidance on a number of points.

Where the user is expressed to be that of a named tenant (as opposed to the tenant for the time being), it must be assumed that there is a market and so a number of potential tenants otherwise the hypothetical nature of the exercise is made meaningless: see *Law Land Co Ltd v Consumers' Association Ltd* [1980] 2 EGLR 109.

If a user clause is absolute, which has a depressing effect on rent, the landlord cannot argue that account should be taken of the ability of the landlord to relax the clause, nor can the landlord unilaterally vary the user clause in order to make it less onerous and so have a less depressing effect on the rent: see, respectively, *Plinth Property Investments Ltd v Mott Hay & Anderson* [1979] 1 EGLR 17; *C & A Pensions Trustees Ltd v British Vita Investments Ltd* [1984] 2 EGLR 75.

Ready and fit for immediate occupation and use

This assumes no need for the hypothetical tenant to have a fitting-out period. Sometimes the clause will say that no reduction of rent is to be made to take account of any rental concession for fitting-out works.

Tenant's covenants have been fully performed

Suppose that the premises are in a less good state than they would have been if the tenant had complied with its covenant to repair or to decorate: such state would tend to reduce the level of rent. That would mean that the tenant gained an advantage due to its failure to comply with its covenants. This provision counters this possibility.

Conversely, if the landlord has not complied with its covenants (eg to repair in a lease of part), it would be unfair on the tenant to have an assumption that the landlord had complied with its covenants because the rent would be higher than it would have been despite neglect on the part of the landlord. Therefore, the tenant should not accept an assumption that the landlord has complied with its covenants.

Occupation

This is to be disregarded because the real tenant would pay more to get back into its own premises whereas the hypothetical tenant must be one with no especial need to do so.

Goodwill

Goodwill is the reputation of the tenant's business (see **11.5**) and it has value. It is, however, not part of the lease interest and so is disregarded.

Improvements

If the tenant improves the premises it increases their rental value. Since the tenant has paid for the improvements, it would be unfair for the tenant to be penalised by a higher rental level. This disregard should extend to any improvements carried out by any previous tenants and also by any subtenants.

It has been known for the landlord, in its licence to carry out improvements, to take a covenant from the tenant to carry out the works, and then claim that they were carried out under an obligation to the landlord, so taking them out of the disregard. Such an attempt was made in *Historic Hotels Ltd v Cadogan Estates* [1995] 1 EGLR 117, but the Court of Appeal rejected it.

It is right that this disregard should extend to works the tenant is required to do. An example would be works required by some competent authority in order to bring the premises into compliance with statute.

7.2.9 OMR and the presumption of reality

In *Basingstoke and Dean BC v Hose Group Ltd* [1988] 1 WLR 348 at 353, Nicholls LJ gave guidance on the proper construction of rent review clauses as follows:

> . . . what the Court is seeking to identify and declare is the intention of the parties to the lease expressed in that clause. Thus, like all points of construction, the meaning of this rent review clause depends on the particular language used, interpreted having regard to the context provided by the whole document and the matrix of the material

surrounding circumstances. We recognise, therefore, that the particular language used will always be of paramount importance. Nonetheless, it is proper and only sensible, when construing a rent review clause, to have in mind what normally is the commercial purpose of such a clause.

So far as the hypothetical lease and its term are concerned, the hypothesis should be as close to reality as possible. The purpose of a rent review clause is to maintain the value to the landlord of rental income during the term of the lease. In relation to the term of the hypothetical lease, this should mean that such term, subject to balancing as in the example given above, should be construed as starting from the rent review date. But difficulty can arise if there is no balancing out of the hypothetical term but a reference to the original term of the real lease. The difficulty is in deciding whether such a term is to be regarded as running from the commencement date of the real lease, or from the rent review date. Two cases illustrate the difficulty.

In *Canary Wharf v Telegraph Group Ltd* [2003] EWHC 1575, the relevant clause said that the hypothetical term was 25 years. The clause did not say from what date that term was to run. The landlord argued it should be from the date of the original lease, 1 April 1992, which would result in a higher level of rent than if the term were to be from the rent review date, 1 April 2002 as the tenant argued. Neuberger J said that the natural meaning, and the meaning to a lawyer and a surveyor, was that the term was from the review date. The natural meaning of the words used may not accord with commercial reality.

Chancebutton Ltd v Compass Services UK & Ireland Ltd [2005] 1 P & CR 8 concerned a rent review clause which used the expression 'Current Market Rent' rather than OMR but no point was taken on that. The definition of the Current Market Rent included a hypothetical term 'equal to the term originally granted under this lease'. The original term was 25 years less one day. Was the hypothetical term, being the same as the original term, to be taken as starting from 24 June 1982, or from the relevant review date, namely 24 June 2002? Lawrence Collins J noted that authority favoured the view that a 'term equivalent to the original term' or some such wording meant that the hypothetical term was to commence on the same day as the original term. He distinguished the expression, 'a term of 25 years' which had been construed by Neuberger J as meaning such a term as from the relevant review date, and held that a hypothetical term 'equal to the term originally granted under this lease' meant a term of 25 years from the commencement date of the actual term.

Whilst it possible to see the distinction semantically between the two expressions in these cases, it is clearly undesirable that such fine distinctions should lead to opposite results. Clients are entitled to better clarity of language than that so often used by those drafting leases who, even if they know what they mean, seem unable to look at their handiwork objectively and so to consider whether the wording they choose is capable of bearing another meaning from that which they have in mind and so cause ambiguity.

Where the wording is clear and the clause is, in the court's opinion, capable of implementation, the court will not be able to apply the presumption of commercial reality. In *Earl Cadogan v Escada AG* [2006] 05 EG 272, CS, the rent review clause required certain specific assumptions to be made regarding works the tenant had to carry out. At the time of the lease, the premises were two separate units, but the landlord argued that the context made it clear that the premises were to become one unit. The court agreed that the clause did not make the best commercial sense but the clause did not require the valuer to assume that the premises were one unit, and the court could not rewrite the clause for the parties.

In *Beegas Nominees Ltd v Decco Ltd* [2003] 3 EGLR 25 (Ch), an otherwise normal rent review clause required the valuer to assume that comparable rents several miles away were to be taken into account in valuing the lease, thus ignoring the actual location of the premises. This would result in a higher OMR. The tenant argued that this went against commercial reality. Finding for the landlord, the court accepted that commercial reality was the starting point for the consideration of a clause but if clear drafting were used to alter the valuation principles to be applied then this would be evidence of the parties' intention to adjust the assumptions used for review. The case is an instance of the rent review clause not only saying what interest was to be valued but how it was to be valued; the commercial objective was, however, clear.

7.2.10 After the review

7.2.10.1 Payment of backdated rent
The rent review clause is likely to provide that if the review is completed some time after the relevant rent review date, the tenant is to pay the difference between the rent it was paying and the reviewed rent together with interest. In the case of a downwards review, the tenant will claim the difference with interest.

7.2.10.2 Recording the review
A memorandum of the rent review should be endorsed on the lease and counterpart, both signed by both parties. The rent review clause is likely to provide for this but to do so is good practice anyway.

8 User

8.1 Introduction

The user clause in a lease is normally one of the key terms which will be specifically mentioned in the heads of terms which will form the basis of the landlord's solicitor's instructions. A number of factors affect the user clause and its drafting:

(a) landlord's and tenant's concerns;

(b) whether the clause is to be absolute, qualified or fully qualified;

(c) whether the clause is to be positive or negative;

(d) how the use is to be defined;

(e) factors outside the lease;

(f) other clauses in the lease.

As with other covenants, the case law gives guidance on the interpretation of user clauses.

8.2 At common law

If there is no user clause in the lease, the tenant may use the premises for any lawful purpose, which would include any use permitted by the planning legislation. If the premises are used for an illegal purpose, then the lease is unenforceable. It is rare but not unknown for a commercial lease to contain no user clause: see *British Glass Manufacturers' Confederation v University of Sheffield* [2004] 1 EGLR 40. The doctrine of waste provides that any user of premises should not cause damage. Waste can mean one of three things: deliberate or negligent damage causing permanent harm (eg causing a floor to collapse by overloading it); unauthorised tenant's improvement (eg alterations); failure to maintain (eg allowing a building to collapse). The Law Commission has recommended the abolition of the doctrine of waste as being archaic and unnecessary: (Law Com No 238, 1996).

8.3 Express covenants

Normally, there will be an express covenant regulating user of the premises. The remaining parts of this chapter are concerned with where the parties have included an express covenant in the lease. An express user clause does not constitute a warranty by the landlord that the permitted use is authorised. In *Hill v Harris* [1965] 2 All ER 358, a user clause in a sublease which was inconsistent with the user clause in the headlease was not warranted by the immediate landlord; it was for the subtenant to satisfy himself that the head landlord consented to the use.

8.4 Landlord's concerns

As with other covenants, the landlord must decide how restrictive the clause is to be, balancing the need for control of the premises with the effect of the clause on the level of rent and, where applicable, on rent review. Therefore, the following need to be considered:

(a) maintenance of the market value of the premises to maximise rental income;

(b) where L owns neighbouring premises, the regulation of user in all premises. In a shopping centre, for example, a good mix of uses is necessary as part of good estate management; the right mix keeps up levels of trade and enhances the value of the centre;

(c) getting the best result on rent review.

8.5 Tenant's concerns

The tenant needs to consider:

(a) whether the permitted use accommodates T's business;

(b) whether the clause is too wide, leading to a higher than appropriate rent on review;

(c) how easy will it be to assign the premises with the permitted user. A clause which is wider than necessary not only inflates the rent, but also the premium that may be charged on assignment – these factors have to be balanced by T.

8.6 Drafting

8.6.1 Absolute, qualified, fully-qualified

Where the covenant is absolute (eg 'not to use the premises except as a food supermarket'), the tenant is at the mercy of the landlord who does not have to consider any application for a change or relaxation of the covenant, though, of course, could do so, doubtless for a payment. How limiting this may be depends on the wording of the covenant. An absolute covenant to use the premises only for a specific trade (eg 'shoe repairer') should clearly be resisted by a tenant. But an absolute covenant widely drawn (eg 'for retail trade') is clearly less problematic. Both parties need to be aware of the effect of a narrowly-drawn covenant: for the landlord, it depresses the rental level; for the tenant, assignment would be more difficult.

A qualified covenant (eg 'not without the landlord's previous written consent to use the premises except as a food supermarket') has a similar effect to an absolute covenant since there is no statutory implication that consent should not be unreasonably withheld. However, s 19(3) of the Landlord and Tenant Act 1927 provides that a landlord may not require any financial advantage for giving consent but may only claim its legal and other expenses provided that the change of use sought by the tenant does not involve structural alterations to the premises. It is not possible to contract out of this provision. *In Barclays Bank v Daejan Investments (Grove Hall) Ltd* [1995] 1 EGLR 68, a tenant wanted to sublet to a proposed subtenant whose use would be different from the use permitted under the head lease. The landlord was willing to give consent subject to the tenant accepting a landlord's break clause. This was held to be a financial advantage and so would be a breach of s 19(3). However, the proposed subtenant planned structural alterations and so, in fact, s 19(3) did not apply. Where the landlord demands a payment or 'fine', the tenant may go ahead with its change of use, disregarding the demand. If the tenant does (unwisely) pay the payment demanded, it cannot recover it: *Comber v Fleet Electronics Ltd* [1955] 1 WLR 566.

A fully-qualified covenant (eg 'not without the landlord's previous written consent such consent not to be unreasonably withheld to use the premises except as a food supermarket') clearly gives the tenant an advantage since the unreasonableness of a refusal of consent can be challenged. Whether the refusal of consent to a change of use is reasonable is a matter for the court to determine. The burden of proof is on the tenant to show the unreasonableness of the refusal though this is more easily discharged if the landlord gives no reason. Where the landlord's reason is to gain a collateral advantage this will be held to be unreasonable. In *Anglia Building Society v Sheffield City Council* [1983] 1 EGLR 57, the local authority landlord objected to a change of use to a certain service use, preferring a retail use which would have generated a higher rent. The landlord's motive was that it had a duty as a local authority to maximise its revenue. The Court of Appeal rejected this argument as seeking an advantage outside the landlord and tenant relationship.

8.6.2 Positive or negative

If the covenant is drafted positively (eg 'to use the premises as a food supermarket'), this places an obligation on the tenant actually to use the premises for that purpose, and any cessation of use is a breach of covenant. The tenant is, in effect, obliged to trade. The landlord will want such a covenant in certain cases such as that of a lease of a unit in a shopping centre where it is important for the centre as a whole that shops are open and trading. The tenant must be advised of the obligation assumed by such a covenant. A similar effect is created by a keep-open clause: see **8.11**.

A negative covenant is usual in a non-retail case (eg 'not to use the premises except as offices') and non-user is not a breach of covenant.

Ambiguous wording of course may lead to litigation. In *JT Sydenham & Co Ltd v Enichem Elastomers Ltd* [1989] I EGLR 257, a user clause said, 'not to carry on upon the premises any trade or business or occupation of an obnoxious or offensive character but to use the premises only for . . . '. The judge held that this was a negative covenant since the words were permissive and not obligatory.

8.6.3 Definition of use

There are several ways of defining the permitted use. The simplest way is to state the permitted use and word the covenant so that only that use is permitted (eg 'not to use the premises except as food supermarket'). Less common is to state that certain uses are expressly permitted and others prohibited.

A common method is to refer to the relevant Use Classes Order. Use Classes Orders are made in statutory instruments under the planning legislation. They set out uses which do not require planning permission if there is a change within a category of uses. Older leases may refer to the Use Classes Order of 1972 (SI 1972 1385). This was replaced by the Use Classes Order of 1987 (SI 1978 764) which was revised with effect from 21 April 2005 by the Town and Country Planning (Use Classes) (Amendment) (England) Order 2005 (SI/2005 84). The cumbersome title hints that the drafting is not to everyone's liking: see the article by H Williamson QC, (2005) Estates Gazette, 2 July. The Office of the Deputy Prime Minister (now DCLG) issued guidance notes in Circular 03/2005.

The parts, other than Part A, of the Schedule to the 1987 Use Classes Order were unaffected by the revision, and many business premises may have their use defined by reference to one of these. Thus, a lease of a warehouse may be defined by reference to B8, 'Use for storage or as a distribution centre'.

It is unwise to define the permitted use by reference to a named tenant's business since it gives rise to confusion.

8.7 Factors outside the lease

Factors outside the lease which may affect user are:

(a) restrictive covenants in the freehold title;

(b) restrictive covenants in the headlease in the case of a sublease;

(c) planning restrictions;

(d) licensing matters;

(e) restraint of trade;

(f) letting scheme;

(g) legislation affecting premises.

8.7.1 Restrictive covenants in the freehold

Leases for more than seven years should be registered at the Land Registry, and so investigation of the freehold title out of which the lease is granted is necessary. If restrictive covenants which could affect user under the lease are found, they need to be considered. It cannot be assumed that old covenants will not pose a problem. However, any post-1925 covenant depends for its survival on having being registered, as a class D(ii) land charge in the case of unregistered land or as a notice in the charges register of the title in the case of registered land. Pre-1926 restrictive covenants depend for their survival on the doctrine of notice. A common way of dealing with older covenants whose impact is uncertain is to insure against their being enforced. Where appropriate, a prospective tenant should ask for a copy of the restrictive covenant indemnity insurance policy.

8.7.2 Restrictive covenants in the headlease

Covenants in a headlease should be repeated in the sublease so that the tenant has a way of ensuring compliance with them after it has granted the sublease. Since the covenants in the headlease are binding on any derivative estate, the subtenant may be sued directly by the head landlord for breaches.

8.7.3 Planning restrictions

It is the tenant's responsibility to make sure the use permitted under the lease has planning permission. The usual searches at the local authority will establish the planning position. If there is no planning permission for the proposed use, the tenant must obtain it. It is not in the landlord's interest to delay a grant of a lease or risk putting off a prospective tenant by marketing premises which lack planning permission for the proposed use.

8.7.4 Licensing matters

Firms of solicitors of any size will have a solicitor, normally one experienced in litigation and advocacy, who specialises in this important area of law. Many premises cannot lawfully be operated without a licence. Related to licensing are provisions requiring the registration of certain activities; thus, for example, scrap metal dealing must be registered under the Scrap Metal Dealers Act 1964.

It is well known that premises whose use includes selling alcohol need a licence. The licensing laws were revised by the Licensing Act 2003 which came into force on 24 November 2005. This Act provides a regime for various licensable activities including entertainment (theatres, cinemas, etc) and the provision of refreshments, as well as the serving and supply of alcohol. Responsibility for licensing lies with the licensing authorities which means the local authorities. Details are available from the website of the Department of Culture, Media and Sport and from the local licensing authority.

Obviously, premises used for gambling in various forms (casinos, betting shops, bingo halls, pubs with gaming machines) need a licence for such use. The governing legislation is the Gambling Act 2005. The Act established the Gambling Commission and provides for regulations to be made. At the time of writing, a consultation process is under way, and the full implementation of the Act is expected during 2007. Local authorities have the function of licensing authorities and are required to have a policy statement.

Licences are required for many other types of premises, including animal boarding establishments, butchers' shops, dealers in game (game birds such as pheasant, rabbits, and venison), caravan sites, pet shops, petrol stations, residential homes, and tattoo parlours. The police are responsible for licensing dealers in firearms.

Where a solicitor is acting for a prospective tenant or assignee, it is necessary to check whether the intended use requires a licence and to advise the client of the need to obtain the licence or a transfer of it in conjunction with the grant or assignment as the case may be.

8.7.5 Restraint of trade

If the user clause excessively restricts the trade which may be carried on at the premises, it may be void as being in restraint of trade. Apart from the application of the law of contract, restraint of trade may be in breach of Arts 81 and 82 of the Treaty of Rome. Cases concerning beer tie arrangements between pub landlords and breweries have illustrated the position. Where the supplier of beer was a large company with a significant share of the market, the tie was void, though the rest of the lease stood: *Inntrepreneur Estates v Mason* [1993] 2 CMLR 293. But where the supplier is a small regional brewery, such a tie may be valid: *Passmore v Morland plc* [1998] 4 All ER 468. It may be thought unhelpful for the pub landlord (actually, the tenant!) that the legal status of a tie should depend on the size of the supplier. For further details, see *Woodfall*, Chapter 11, paras 184 and 253.

8.7.6 Letting scheme

Where the landlord lets a number of properties, as in a parade of shops or a shopping centre, it will be concerned to ensure that the various uses complement each other to attract the public. Privately-owned shopping centres will ensure a tenant mix which maximises rental income. Many suburban shopping centres and parades are owned by the local authority which will have a policy governing its management of such premises. That policy will aim to provide a tenant mix which serves the community by the provision of appropriate trades and services. As part of its policy, a local authority may limit non-retail uses to, say, 20% of the available lettings in any one centre or parade.

Landlords may take the initiative to enforce the tenants' obligations. Otherwise, if one tenant, in breach of its covenant with the landlord, then trades competitively with another, that other will be concerned to know what action it can take. The Contracts (Rights of Third Parties) Act 1999 may be excluded and so be of no help, but where a letting scheme exists, it provides a way in which tenants can sue each other in such circumstances.

A letting scheme requires that there be not merely identical covenants, but an intention to impose a scheme of mutually enforceable covenants in a clearly defined area. That a letting scheme in relation to business tenancies could exist was not established until the decision of the Court of Appeal in *Williams v Kiley (t/a CK Supermarkets Ltd)* [2002] EWCA Civ 1645: see further at **8.9**.

8.7.7 Legislation affecting premises

Non-domestic premises are affected by a wide range of legislation regulating the carrying on of activities. Health and safety regulations and fire precautions are obviously especially important. The Health and Safety Executive has wide responsibilities in respect of places of work.

The Government has reformed the regulations on fire safety. Made under the Regulatory Reform Act 2001, the Regulatory Reform (Fire Safety) Order 2005 (SI 2005/1541) was approved by Parliament on 7 June 2005. Fire certificates are abolished. Compliance with the Order rests with the 'responsible person' who, in the case of let business premises, is the tenant. Premises to which the Order applies include not only the obvious business premises such as factories, offices and shops, but also care homes, places of entertainment, educational premises, community halls and even tents and marquees at open air events. The responsible person cannot wait for a visit from a fire officer; he must prepare a fire risk assessment and emergency plan. Those with an existing fire certificate are not exempt from the Order. Tenants must check their responsibilities under the Order. Information and guidance are available from the DCLG, the Health and Safety Executive and from the local fire and rescue service.

Other legislation affecting premises includes: the Environmental Protection Act 1990, the Factories Act 1961, the Hazardous Waste (England and Wales) Regulations 2005 (SI 2005/894), the Offices, Shops and Railway Premises Act 1963, the Pollution Prevention and Control (England and Wales) Regulations 2000 (SI 2000/1973) and the Water Resources Act 1991. For the effect of statutory control of advertisements, see **8.8.5**.

8.8 Other clauses in the lease

The user clause cannot be read in isolation since there are likely to be other clauses in the lease which have an impact on user. The way various clauses work together has to be considered.

8.8.1 Nuisance or annoyance

Most leases have a covenant by the tenant not to cause any nuisance or annoyance to any neighbours. Nuisance is the unreasonable interference with the utility of the claimant's land. Landlords include this covenant in case they are held liable by a third party for some act of nuisance by the tenant; the covenant gives the landlord rights against the tenant in those circumstances, including forfeiture.

Landlords, in fact, are not as vulnerable in this regard as they may fear. The law of nuisance is notoriously complex, but it seems clear that landlords may not be liable for the nuisance of their tenants because landlords are not in possession and control of the premises. An authorised use does not authorise the carrying on of the activity in a way which causes nuisance or annoyance to neighbours, and in such a case the landlord will not be liable, much less does it authorise nuisance unrelated to the tenant's status as tenant. But if the user clause authorises an activity which, when carried on reasonably, does cause a nuisance, then the landlord may be liable. The law in this regard was considered in *Hussain v Lancaster City Council* [1999] 4 All ER 125, and *London Borough of Southwark v Tanner* [2001] 1 AC 1. For comment, see S Bright, 'Landowners' Responsibility in Nuisance for Antisocial Behaviour', [2003] Conv 171, and M Davey, 'Neighbours in Law', [2001] Conv 31. See also **9.3.2**.

8.8.2 Noxious trades

A covenant against carrying on a noxious trade overlaps with nuisance, but is nowadays just as likely to be covered by environmental protection legislation.

8.8.3 Immoral and illegal user

Immoral user may depend on the opinion of the landlord but illegal user is clearly objective. Illegal user would mean any user which breached any statutory restriction, including planning legislation.

8.8.4 Loading of floors

Where the premises comprise more than the ground floor, or just an upper floor, there is likely to be a covenant not to overload the floor for obvious reasons. If the tenant's business involves using heavy machinery or storage of heavy items, a surveyor should be asked to report on the load-bearing ability of the floors.

8.8.5 Signs and advertisements

Landlords are typically very keen to have close control over what signs and advertisements are put on the premises. There is often a covenant against putting any signs and advertisements without the landlord's consent. Landlords will specify size types and colouring very often.

There is extensive statutory control of outdoor advertisements. The rules are the Town and Country Planning (Control of Advertisements) Regulations (SI 1992/666) as amended by SI 1994/2351 and SI 1999/1810. Guidance notes are available in the form of DoE circulars. Local planning authorities are responsible for deciding whether any advertisement should be permitted. There are further restrictions relating to advertisements in urban development areas, National Parks and in the Norfolk Broads. Since there will invariably be in the lease a tenant covenant to comply with statutory requirements relating to the premises, tenants must check with the local planning authority whether any proposed advertisements need permission, though many advertisements have deemed consent. 'Advertisement' is widely defined. (It seems that a Cross outside a church is an advertisement and requires permission or so Dudley Metropolitan Borough Council told a Methodist minister. See the report in the *Daily Telegraph,* 8 March 2006.) There is much information about advertisements on the website of the ODPM.

8.8.6 Applications for planning permission and building regulation approval

There is normally in a lease a tenant's covenant, whether absolute or qualified, not to apply for planning permission. One does not have to own land to apply for planning permission. Clearly, such a covenant restricts what the tenant can do under both the user and alienation clauses. Generally, the landlord may want this covenant to be absolute or qualified to guard against any planning permission resulting in an adverse effect on rental level. The tenant, on the other hand, may want the clause to be fully qualified.

Less common is a tenant's covenant against applying for building regulations approval. Such a covenant would be more restrictive than a bar on applying for planning permission, and a tenant would resist it unless the lease were short term and the nature of the premises and their authorised use made such a covenant acceptable.

8.8.7 Alterations

There is a clear connection between the user clause and the alterations clause. A very tight alterations clause could restrict even the authorised use (see **Chapter 9**).

8.9 Interpretation of user clauses

Litigation in the area of user clauses has largely been concerned with the interpretation of the expressions used. In older leases, terms may be used which have lost their original meaning as retail trends have changed. No modern user clause would use terms such as 'draper' or 'hosier' yet such terms may be found in older leases. It might be thought that there would be a clear rule as to whether a user clause has to be interpreted as at the date of the lease or whether regard could be had to changing retail trends. The following cases suggest there is a rule based on the former approach, though it seems to have been arrived at without much deliberation.

In *Basildon Development Corporation v Mactro Ltd* [1986] 1 EGLR 137, the defendant ran a small supermarket in Basildon under a lease granted by Basildon DC in 1980. The positively-worded user clause provided, in effect, for the premises to be used as a food supermarket. There was a further clause which provided that the premises were not to be used for the carrying on of any other trade or business. Soon after opening, the tenant started selling electrical goods and items usually found in a pharmacy. Other traders complained. Balcombe LJ declined to say whether he thought such covenants have to be interpreted as at the date of the lease since counsel for the defendant had conceded that they should be. Since the lease was only about one year old, that was not much of a concession, and the opportunity for guidance on the point was lost. In this case it was held that there was a partial breach of the covenant.

A similar point was at issue in *St Marylebone Property Co Ltd v Tesco Stores* [1988] 2 EGLR 40. There, Hoffmann J declined to agree with counsel for the defendant that changing retail trends should be taken into account when construing a user clause.

In *Mount Cook Land Ltd v Joint London Holdings Ltd* [2005] EWCA Civ 1171, the Court of Appeal had to construe the meanings of the words 'victualler' and 'coffee house keeper' contained in a lease granted in 1950 which prohibited use of the premises for these trades (among many others). There was no argument as to whether the terms had to be construed according to their meaning in 1950; it was assumed that they had. As a result, recourse was had to dictionaries (including Dr Johnson's dictionary of 1785). In the event, 'victualler' was given its wider meaning of supplier of food and drink, and 'coffee house keeper', originally meaning the keeper of a coffee house as known in the seventeenth and eighteenth centuries, in 1950 meant a place for the serving of food and drink on a more modest scale than a restaurant. The effect of the court's judgment was to favour the appellant landlord's contention that the proposed use by a prospective subtenant, Pret a Manger, would be a breach of the user clause.

It seems now beyond doubt that the terms used in a user clause must be given their meaning as at the time the lease was granted. Terms have to be construed according to the meaning the parties to the lease would have intended them to mean in a popular and not a technical sense. In *Williams v Kiley (t/a CK Supermarkets Ltd)* [2002] EWCA Civ 1645, Carnworth LJ (at para 37) agreed with the first instance judge that the correct test was to consider the character of the use as understood at the date of the lease. His lordship acknowledged (at para 28), as argued by counsel for the defendant, that this test froze the use at a fixed point in time, but pointed out that old covenants could be removed or modified by the Lands Tribunal under s 84 of the LPA 1925.

Even more recent terms, though, have called for interpretation, none more so than the word, 'supermarket'. In *Calabar (Woolwich) Ltd v Tesco Stores Ltd* [1978] 1 EGLR 113, Sir John Pennycuick thought that 'supermarket' had not yet become an ordinary English word, and that it certainly was not in 1961. Therefore, problems arose when the question, 'what goods are usually sold in supermarkets?', had to be answered. It later became clear to judges what a supermarket is but a user clause in a 1950s lease still had to be construed without reference to subsequent understanding of the nature of a supermarket.

Not only terms but even mere prepositions can lead to litigation. In *Atwal v Courts Garages* [1989] 1 EGLR 63, Nicholls LJ had to consider the meaning of the word 'with' in a user clause which prohibited any use 'except that of a garage with car sales and vehicle repairs'. Mr Atwal complained that his tenant, the defendant, was selling a wider range of goods than the user clause permitted, thereby competing with his own business. His lordship held that 'with' in the clause was descriptive only, as Mr Atwal argued, and did not mean 'additionally' as the defendant argued. This narrowed the meaning of the clause so that the defendant was partially in breach of the covenant.

8.10 Ancillary use

A retail tenant may be complying with the user clause but expand its trade to include sales which are not within the authorised use. Is this a breach of the user clause? As is so often the case, it is a matter of degree. A tenant selling items which are outside the user clause may argue that sale of such items are 'ancillary' to the permitted use and therefore not a breach of the covenant. If a tenant does expand its use, this may not cause a breach of the user clause.

In *Calabar (Woolwich) Ltd v Tesco Stores Ltd*, the permitted user provided for the sale of goods usually sold by supermarkets. Tesco started selling freezers. Calabar argued that this was not usual for a supermarket. The Court of Appeal said it was a matter of degree. The percentage of sales of freezers was 15%. This did not mean that the store was no longer a supermarket, and there was no breach of the covenant.

8.11 Keep-open covenants

As has been said (see **8.6.2**), a positively worded user clause obliges the tenant to keep trading and cessation of trade will be a breach of covenant. In many leases of retail premises, there is, in any event, a separate covenant to keep the premises open for trade – a 'keep-open covenant'. The purpose of keep-open covenants is to maintain the amenity of a shopping centre or parade of shops. Empty shops with dirty windows, fly posters and a pile of junk mail behind the door are obviously unappealing to the shopping public.

The remedy for a breach of covenant may be equitable, such as specific performance, or damages at common law. Equitable remedies are at the discretion of the court. In relation to a breach of a keep-open covenant, the settled practice is that specific performance will not be granted except in exceptional circumstances. The rationale behind the settled practice was explained in *FW Woolworth plc v Charlwood Alliance Properties Ltd* [1987] 1 EGLR 53. To force a business to trade at a loss may be oppressive, and a grant of specific performance would involve the court in supervising the order and would keep the parties locked together in litigation. Damages, on the other hand, effect a clean break between the parties, rather like a divorce. So settled was this practice that in *Transworld Land Co Ltd v J Sainsbury plc* [1990] 2 EGLR 255, the landlord did not even apply for specific performance but there was merely an inquiry as to damages to be paid.

The settled practice was affirmed by the House of Lords in *Co-operative Insurance Society Ltd v Argyll Stores (Holdings) Ltd* [1997] 3 All ER 297. Argyll operated a Safeway supermarket in the Hillsborough Shopping Centre in Sheffield. As part of a reorganisation, Argyll closed the Safeway store in breach of a keep-open clause. Influenced, it seems, by Argyll's behaviour, the Court of Appeal was prepared to grant an order for specific performance. This sent shock waves around the industry. The House of Lords restored the settled practice, Lord Hoffmann setting out in full the reasons for it. Only in exceptional circumstances would specific performance be granted. Lord Hoffmann thought such exceptional circumstances would be a case of a gross breach of personal faith or the threat of non-performance of the covenant. For further comment, see P Luxton, 'Are you being served?', [1998] 62 Conv 396.

8.12 Tenants' tactics

Tenants which are large companies will sometimes make use of the procedures for applying for planning permission to impose their business use. For example, a company which operates for the sale of soft drinks and snacks may open for business even if the use is not authorised by the local planning authority. They continue trading whilst a planning application is made and whilst any appeal against refusal of permission is made.

9 Alterations

9.1 Introduction

Landlords are typically very keen to have close control of the physical structure of their properties: they will wish to retain the character and appearance of the property; prevent damage; preserve the reversionary value of the premises and of their rental value, and, if the landlord owns neighbouring property, ensure the overall character and amenity of the entire holding. Invariably, therefore, commercial leases include a covenant which restricts tenants' ability to alter the layout and structure of the premises.

Tenants are likely to want the flexibility of being able to make such alterations as their business might need in the future. They also must consider how marketable the premises may be should it be decided to assign them: the less onerous the alterations clause, the wider will be the market of potential assignees.

The right balance between the parties will depend on how long the lease is. If the lease is short – say, three years – then even an absolute prohibition of alterations is reasonable. If the lease is long – say, 25 years – a compromise is needed which meets the concerns of the landlord and the tenant. As with other covenants, the parties should each bear in mind the effect of a given covenant on rent review – the more restrictive the covenant the more the depressing effect on rent; the more relaxed the covenant, the higher the rent (see **7.2**).

As with any clause, alterations covenants cannot be considered in isolation. When it is drafted, the covenant has to be made to fit the overall scheme of the lease and reflect the client's aims and wishes. The effect and construction of the covenant have to be looked at in relation not only to the overall scheme of the lease but also to factors outside it.

9.2 Factors outside the lease affecting alterations

9.2.1 Planning legislation

Certain alterations will need planning permission. Whether such permission is needed is best checked with the local authority's planning officer for the area where the premises are located. Advice can also be sought from a chartered surveyor or architect. If the premises are in a conservation area, there will be further restrictions relating particularly to the outside appearance of the premises.

Yet further restrictions apply to buildings listed as being of architectural or historic importance – 'listed buildings'. There are nearly half a million listed buildings in England and
Wales and so it is likely that the practitioner will encounter them regularly. Alterations to a
listed building need consent from the local planning authority: s 7 of the Planning (Listed
Buildings and Conservation Areas) Act 1990. This Act provides that non-compliance with it
is a criminal offence in respect of which a custodial sentence may be imposed. Tenants
need to take such restrictions into account before entering into a lease or taking an assignment of an existing lease, where appropriate getting advice, though it should be obvious
that there will be very little scope for altering, for example, office premises in a smart
Georgian square of listed buildings. On the other hand, certain tenants (such as, indeed,
solicitors and surveyors) may seek a listed building as an enhancement to their image.

9.2.2 Other legislation

9.2.2.1 The Building Act 1984

Under this Act, local authorities maintain building control departments. The aim is to
check that structural building work is done according to statutory specifications. Approved
inspectors visit premises where such work is being done to ensure compliance. It may be
necessary to get Building Regulations approval even when planning permission is not
needed. The need for Building Regulations approval is much less well known than that for
planning permission, and it is common for people to do structural work at a property
without getting this approval. When that property is later being disposed of, the absence
of approval may then cause delay or difficulty.

9.2.2.2 The Disability Discrimination Acts 1995 and 2005

The Disability Discrimination Act 1995 Act has been fully in force since 1 October 2004 and
is of great significance to commercial premises depending on their size and the sort of
business carried on there. Service providers, which expression means anyone who provides
goods and services (including all manner of commercial premises), are under a duty not to
treat the disabled less favourably than others. This means adapting premises though not
at unreasonable cost. The duty is placed on even the smallest service provider. The person
on whom the duty is placed is the one providing the service which, in the case of premises
let under a business lease, means the tenant and not the landlord. Requirements in the
Act may override the lease by providing that where certain tenants make alterations in
order to comply with the Act, the lease is deemed to contain a fully qualified covenant
under which such a tenant may apply to the landlord for consent. The tenant should apply
for landlord's consent for alterations required under the Act and then the landlord has
21 days in which to respond; failure so to respond is deemed to be a refusal of consent.
Whilst the landlord may reasonably refuse consent, refusal is likely only to be reasonable if
the landlord could show harm to the value of its reversionary interest.

The Disability Discrimination Act 2005 amends and extends the 1995 Act in respect of,
amongst other things, all activities in the public sector, private clubs with 25 or more
members, and lettings of residential and commercial premises. It also extends the meaning of 'disability' so as to include those who have HIV, cancer and multiple sclerosis from
the date of diagnosis.

Clearly, required alterations should have been carried out at premises, and prospective tenants and assignees of leases should be alert to ensure that premises which they are thinking of taking on comply with the Acts. Surveyors should advise in this respect. Landlords with empty premises they are looking to let and tenants seeking to assign need to be aware of the difficulty they may face in letting or assigning premises which fail to comply. Lawyers need to be able to give accurate, relevant and up-to-date advice on these matters to clients.

9.2.2.3 Other legislation

Other legislation which also may have an impact on a tenant's ability to carry out alterations includes the Factories Act 1961, the Offices, Shops and Railway Premises Act 1963, the Fire Precautions Act 1971, the Telecommunications Act 1984, and the Environmental Protection Act 1990. The basic effect of such legislation is to provide that where certain alterations are required by statute there is machinery to enable them to be done notwithstanding restrictions in leases which would otherwise prohibit such alterations.

9.2.3 Restrictive covenants in the superior title

In relation to freehold land, restrictive covenants are promises in deeds not to do something on the affected or *burdened* land for the benefit of the *benefited* land. For example, there may be a restrictive covenant on A's land not to use that land for any trade or business, and A's neighbour, B may have the benefit of that restrictive covenant. It would be an unusual freehold title which had no restrictive covenants at all.

Where a lease is granted out of a freehold title which has the burden of restrictive covenants, the prospective tenant should check whether these are likely to limit its enjoyment of the premises during the term of the lease, and whether they might adversely affect the marketability of the premises if it was decided to assign them. Where restrictive covenants are found which could adversely affect the tenant by restricting or prohibiting its ability to make alterations, it should not be assumed, perhaps because they are very old, that the covenants will not cause a problem.

Whether there is a problem at all should first be checked: a restrictive covenant created before 1 January 1926 may have been extinguished by a bona fide purchaser for value of the legal estate without notice of the covenant; one created on or after that date may not have been protected by registration as a land charge in the case of unregistered land, or by a notice in the case of registered land.

Where the lease is very short, the likelihood of the tenant wishing to make alterations will anyway be remote, and the tenant may take that view and not be concerned. The prospective tenant under a long lease should give careful thought as to what action to take in relation to any potentially troublesome restrictive covenant; clearly, a prospective tenant which intended to build would have to consider what action to take in relation to a covenant restrictive of building on burdened land included in the proposed lease. Where the person with the benefit of such a covenant is identifiable, it may be possible to negotiate. Where that person cannot be found, the answer in practice, very often, is to take out restrictive covenant indemnity insurance under which any successful claimant for breach can be paid out. In the case of an assignment, there may be existing insurance which an assignee can take over.

The discovery of restrictive covenants in a freehold title should be simple: most titles are registered and the register is open to public inspection (Land Registration Act 2002, s 66). In the case of an unregistered title, the prospective tenant should require production of the landlord's title.

9.2.4 Interference with easements

As with restrictive covenants in the superior title, so with expressly granted easements – there may be, for example, rights of way for the benefit of neighbouring owners through the premises of a tenant. There may also be easements granted to neighbouring tenants in their leases. Clearly, a tenant should not carry out alterations which interfere with any easements: for example, there should be no building over the route of a right of way or of underground pipes or cables which are the subject of easements for the benefit of neighbours. Equally, there should be no making of alterations which interfere with easements which may have been acquired other by express grant, such as rights of air and light acquired impliedly or by prescription. Further, there should be no interference with arrangements entered into by the freeholder with utility companies.

9.2.5 Trespass

For many reasons, it is vital that premises are precisely defined in the parcels clause of the lease. There could be situations where an alteration results in some addition to the premises which actually extends outside the premises as defined. To take an instance from practice, where a canopy was fixed to the side wall of premises and projected into the airspace (above a driveway) of the neighbour, the neighbour objected, pointing out that if in time it was successfully argued that some right for the canopy existed, this could prevent development of the neighbour's land up to the side wall (which the respective titles allowed). Though not concerning leasehold premises, similar facts arose in *Laiqat v Majid* [2005] EWHC 1305, QB; [2005] 26 EG 130, CS where it was held that an extractor fan which protruded into neighbouring premises constituted a trespass because it was at a height (4 m) which did interfere with the claimant's airspace. The point was made clear in *Taylor v Vectapike Ltd* [1990] 2 EGLR 12. There, certain alterations to improve premises would have involved taking pipe work outside the premises as strictly defined. Morritt J would not relax the covenant to permit this. In *Haines v Florensa* [1990] 1 EGLR 73, a tenant could extend into the airspace above the premises because the airspace had not been excluded from the lease; obviously, if it had been, then there would have been a trespass into the landlord's airspace. *Frederick Berry Ltd v Royal Bank of Scotland* [1949] 1 KB 619 concerned a third-floor tenant who put up a nameplate on a wall in the ground floor entrance of the building; this wall was clearly not part of the tenant's premises, and so the fixing of the plate there was a trespass. The principle in that case could obviously apply to something more substantial than a nameplate.

9.2.6 Nuisance

Alterations or the making of them could constitute an actionable nuisance. In *Owen v Gadd* [1956] 2 QB 99, scaffolding put up outside the tenant's ground-floor shop to enable the landlord to do repairs to his retained first-floor premises was held by the Court of

Appeal, affirming the decision at first instance, to be an interference with the tenant's quiet enjoyment of the shop. The case concerned repairs and only nominal damages (£2) were awarded, but it is clear that the principle is readily applicable to alterations by a tenant which, or the making of which, caused nuisance. A tenant should be advised that any licence for alterations from the landlord should, where necessary, include an appropriately drawn licence for access onto the landlord's adjoining land.

9.3 Factors in the lease affecting alterations

9.3.1 Planning permission

It is very common for a lease to include a tenant's covenant restricting or even prohibiting application for planning permission. Clearly, a fully qualified alterations covenant is not as generous as it seems if there is elsewhere in the lease an absolute bar on applying for planning permission. Tenants need to consider the combined effect of the alterations and planning permission covenants.

9.3.2 Nuisance and annoyance

Leases normally include a covenant by the tenant not to do anything which causes nuisance or annoyance to the landlord, its tenants, or the owners, occupiers or tenants of adjoining or neighbouring premises. There is little case law on this, but *Heard v Stuart* (1907) 24 TLR 104 illustrates the position. Heard had granted a lease of premises to Stuart who covenanted, amongst other things, 'not to do or suffer to be done any act or thing which might be or grow to the annoyance, damage, or disturbance of the lessors or the neighbourhood'. Stuart put advertisements (some of which were for alcoholic drinks) on a wall of the house facing a church. This annoyed the vicar and the congregation of the church. It was found that particular advertisements were objectionable, and, generally, they tended to lower the 'tone and character' of the neighbourhood. Joyce J held that there was a breach of the covenant (and, indeed, of many others). See also **8.8.1**.

9.3.3 Repairing covenant

Unauthorised alterations will be a breach of the repairing covenant in so far as a repairing covenant includes a duty not to cause disrepair by destruction. Only expressly and impliedly authorised alterations will avoid such a breach.

9.3.4 Covenants against specific alterations

In addition to the alterations covenant itself, there may be further covenants against specific alterations such as against altering external elevations of a building or its external appearance. In *London County Council v Hutter* [1925] Ch 626, a lease of premises in Piccadilly Circus, London, included a tenant's covenant not to alter the elevation of the building. Without the landlord's licence, the tenant fixed an iron framework round the whole frontage of the building and installed 'an electric light advertisement' on the framework (this was the beginning of such advertisements in Piccadilly Circus which are now well known). Tomlin J held this to be a beach of the covenant, and also of a covenant not to maim the walls.

The nature of the premises may prompt the landlord to include a covenant not to overload the floors of the premises; so, a prospective tenant which may want to install machinery or store heavy items must take this into account.

There may be a specific covenant against installing certain types of equipment such as aerials, satellite dishes, masts, and the like.

9.3.5 Covenants relating to signs

Landlords are very keen to have control over what signs are put up on their properties, and there will normally be an express covenant requiring landlord's consent for the putting up of signs and advertisements. Whether the covenant is absolute, qualified or fully qualified is a matter for negotiation. The number, size, colour, and style of signs and advertisements may be specified in the covenant, together with their location. See also **8.8.5**

9.3.6 Waste

Waste is an ancient and technical doctrine which ought to be abolished (see Law Com No 238). It refers to permanent damage to premises by some deliberate or negligent act of the tenant such as overloading a floor (called 'voluntary waste'), altering a building ('ameliorating waste'), or damage caused by neglect such as letting a building collapse through lack of repair ('permissive waste'). The tenant's obligations with regard to waste are implied, and a breach may give rise to tortious liability. In *Mancetter Developments Ltd v Garmonson Ltd* [1986] QB 1212, the removal of certain trade fixtures left holes in the walls of the premises and the Court of Appeal held that since there had been no reinstatement of the premises (by making good the holes) the landlord was entitled to damages for waste. There will usually be an express covenant, perhaps within the alterations covenant, not to commit waste, and an unauthorised alteration will be actionable under the doctrine of waste.

9.4 Scope and meaning of alterations: construction of covenants

The leading case which established basic principles of construction of alterations covenants is *Bickmore v Dimmer* [1903] Ch 158. This case concerned premises in Church Street, Liverpool. Dimmer had taken an assignment of the premises, a jeweller's and watchmaker's shop, without the landlord's consent. The landlord complained and that action was compromised, partly by Dimmer covenanting with the landlord directly to observe the covenants in the lease. The alterations covenant said that the tenant would not 'make or suffer to be made any alteration to the said premises, except as herein expressly provided, without the consent in writing of the lessors first obtained'. Dimmer decided to advertise his business of jeweller and watchmaker by fixing onto the outside wall fronting Church Street a large clock. He asked for landlord's consent; the landlord refused but Dimmer put up the clock anyway. It had Dimmer's name and business on both sides and was lit at night. It was 1.2 metres in diameter, looked 'like a drum', and was fixed to the stone wall by iron bolts driven in to a depth of 15 centimetres.

The landlord objected to the clock, and took action on the covenant. Giving the first judgment, Vaughan Williams LJ said that it was necessary to look at the whole lease, the purpose for which it was granted, and then to see what was the proper construction of the covenant. He thought that not every addition to premises would be a breach of the alterations covenant, and that alterations really meant affecting the form and structure of premises. It was a question of where to draw the line: 'we ought so to draw the line as that the covenant will not operate to prevent a tenant . . . from doing those acts which are convenient and usual for a tradesman to do in the ordinary conduct of his business'. Stirling LJ agreed and said that such alterations as are 'reasonable', as opposed to 'necessary' as counsel for the landlord argued, for a tenant's enjoyment of premises would not be a breach of covenant.

It is clear, then, that there is a significant limitation on the meaning of alterations, and a tenant will be able to do a range of works to premises before being in breach of covenant, depending on its wording. In *Joseph v London County Council* [1914] 111 LT 276, a tenant put up a framework and electric light advertisements on it. The landlord claimed this was a breach of a covenant not to make any alteration to the elevation of the building. Astbury J said 'elevation' meant the front view of a building, and 'alteration' meant what *Bickmore v Dimmer* had said it meant. Since the framework could easily be removed, the addition was not an alteration. This is in contrast to the decision in *Hutter* (see **9.3.4**) where there was a breach of the covenant because of the permanent nature of the work, as well as a breach of the specific covenant against maiming the walls. Yet in *Lilley & Skinner v Crump* [1929] 73 SJ 366 (which concerned a well-known shoe shop in London's Oxford Street), Rowlatt J decided that making two openings in a wall was an alteration and not a breach of an absolute covenant against cutting the walls.

The construction of a covenant is sometimes made difficult by bad drafting. *Westminster City Council v HSBC Bank plc* [2003] 1 EGLR 62 concerned a qualified alterations covenant in a lease of a bank building in London's Piccadilly built to a highly-praised design by the noted architect, Sir Edwin Lutyens. Mr Recorder Black QC, sitting as a deputy judge of the Technology and Construction Court (a division of the High Court), said the ambiguous clause, drafted in a 'convoluted manner', simply did not make sense if read in a literal and technical way; it had, rather, to be read in a way which was in 'accord with commercial reality'. The clause restricted the making of any alteration or addition to 'the structural or external elevation' of the building. The deputy judge found that the expression 'structural elevation' made no sense; he said that if the word 'structure' were substituted for 'structural' the clause would then have the likely intended meaning of restricting alterations to the structure or the external elevation of the building.

9.5 Landlord's consent

In *Bickmore v Dimmer*, the landlord's refusal of consent to an alteration was unreasonable because the work done by the tenant was not an alteration under the terms of the covenant as construed. A separate question is whether a landlord's refusal of consent may be reasonable where what the tenant proposes is an alteration. The court, in answering this question, considers (a) what was the reason for refusal of consent and (b) whether that reason was or was not reasonable.

One of the questions in *Lambert v FW Woolworth & Co Ltd* [1938] Ch 883 was whether a landlord had unreasonably withheld consent to alterations. Slesser LJ said (at 906) 'that the onus of proving that the withholding is unreasonable is on the tenant, but if the landlord gives no reason but merely refuses, that, in itself, I think, puts upon him the duty of showing that his action is reasonable'. In considering what may be reasonable grounds for refusal, his lordship went on (at 907):

> I agree . . . that many considerations, aesthetic, historic or even personal, may be relied upon as yielding reasonable grounds for refusing consent . . . In the present general decline of taste and manners, a shop-keeper, looking at the matter from a purely commercial point of view, may be right in saying that the removal of some beautiful casement and the substitution of a garish window or façade of false marble may prove to be an attraction to the public and so, from his point of view, be an improvement. It is most important that the landlord should be able to be heard to say that it may be reasonable that he should withhold his consent to the perpetration of contemplated atrocities.

The landlord, of course, can only decide how to respond if it has been given the necessary information by the tenant: *Kalford Ltd v Peterborough City Council* [2001] EGCS 42.

Two cases have provided an opportunity for a review of this area. *Iqbal v Thakrar* [2004] 3 EGLR 21 concerned premises consisting of first floor flats, and ground floor space which the claimant tenant wished to convert into an Indian restaurant. The tenant held the ground floor premises on a 999-year lease which had a fully qualified covenant as to alteration. Unusually, there was no user clause, but there was A3 planning permission. The tenant, having got planning permission and building regulations approval for the proposed conversion scheme, applied to the defendant landlord for consent, which was refused, mainly on the ground of concern that the structural works proposed could affect the structure of the building as a whole. The recorder at the local county court found that the landlord's refusal of consent was unreasonable.

Allowing the landlord's appeal, the Court of Appeal said that it had been for the tenant to make clear how issues of structural integrity would be dealt with, and since the proposals had not done this, the landlord was entitled to refuse consent. It is worth noting, however, that the Court of Appeal agreed with the recorder that had the landlord's real motive been to prevent a restaurant being run on the ground floor on the basis of a perceived loss of amenity to the flats above, that must fail as a ground: landlords cannot withhold consent for reasons outside the landlord and tenant relationship. Peter Gibson LJ set out what he believed to be the factors to take into account when considering whether a landlord had unreasonably refused consent. He said (at para 27) that the court considers two questions: what was the reason for refusing consent which is a subjective enquiry to discover what was in the landlord's mind; secondly, was the landlord's reason as so discovered reasonable or not, this being an objective enquiry.

Drawing on principles from cases (notably, *International Drilling Fluids v Louisville Investments* (Uxbridge) Ltd [1986] Ch 513) relating to landlord's consent to an assignment (see **Chapter 11**), he said (amongst other things) that (1) the purpose of the covenant is to protect a landlord's property interests; (2) consent cannot be refused on grounds unrelated to its property interests; (3) provided the tenant has put forward sufficiently clear proposals, it is for the tenant to show that the landlord has unreasonably withheld consent; (4) it might be reasonable, in some circumstances, to refuse consent on the grounds of a proposed use even if that is not forbidden by the lease; (5) consent cannot be refused on the grounds of financial loss, though compensation may be required. Peter Gibson LJ was moved to add that it was highly unfortunate that this matter had reached such an expensive impasse; clearly, every effort should be made by parties and their advisors to avoid this.

A condition attached to consent may render that consent unreasonable as in *Sargeant v Macepark (Whittlebury) Ltd* [2004] 3 EGLR 26. The landlord, Mr & Mrs Sargeant, owned a country club and leisure complex in Northamptonshire. They let adjoining land to the tenant, Macepark, which built a hotel on that land. Relations between landlord and tenant were not good. The lease contained an unqualified covenant against making alterations, and Macepark asked for consent to build a substantial addition to its facilities. Fearing competition for part of their own business, the landlord made consent conditional on a specific limitation as to use of the addition. Although this appears to have been an attempt to use financial loss as a ground for refusing consent (and so unreasonable), Lewison J thought that the landlord's property interests would be affected (a reasonable ground for refusal of consent). A landlord can impose a condition on consent to protect its legitimate concerns for its business. However, the actual condition sought to be imposed by the Sargeants went too far since it would have prevented the tenant from carrying on activities which would not have competed with those of the landlord.

The most common conditions of the landlord for granting consent are that plans and specifications for proposed alterations must first be approved, that the tenant must comply with the approved plans and specifications, that all necessary consents be obtained, and, if the lease does not contain an express provision, a requirement to reinstate (see **9.9**).

Where a tenant thinks that its landlord is unreasonably withholding consent, it may proceed without consent and counter any action for breach of covenant which the landlord may bring with an allegation of unreasonableness. A safer course is to seek the court's declaration that the landlord's withholding of consent is unreasonable.

9.6 Licence for alterations

Consent is given in a deed which is drafted by the landlord's solicitors. There may be some negotiation as to its terms, and when the deed is agreed, it is prepared in two parts like the lease itself, one part being executed by the landlord and the other by the tenant, the parties completing the process by each party keeping the part executed by the other.

Care must be taken that communications between the solicitors acting respectively for the landlord and tenant do not accidentally grant consent. In *Prudential Assurance Co Ltd v*

Mount Eden Land Ltd [1997] 1 EGLR 37, the heading 'Subject to Licence' on a letter saying that consent would be given subject to a formal licence was regarded by the Court of Appeal as in fact granting conditional consent.

All the matters in **9.5**, that is, what conditions will be attached to the consent, must be given careful thought when drafting the licence for alterations.

Furthermore, the landlord will consider whether to impose an obligation on the tenant to carry out the alterations. If the licence is granted for consideration, this would give the landlord the benefit of taking the alterations outside s 2(1) of Part I of the Landlord and Tenant Act 1927, which entitles the tenant to compensation for improvements (though see **9.10**). Also, such an obligation would countervail the normal provision that improvements should be disregarded on rent review: see s 34 of Part II of the Landlord and Tenant Act 1954, and at **7.2.8**.

Clearly, the tenant should resist any attempt by the landlord to make the alterations obligatory otherwise it will be prejudiced by both paying for the alterations and a higher level of rent in consequence of those alterations.

9.7 Alterations and improvements: qualified covenants and s 19(2) of the Landlord and Tenant Act 1927

As with some other covenants, alterations covenants may be absolute, qualified or fully qualified. Which it is to be must be part of the original lease negotiations. Qualified covenants against alterations are governed by s 19(2) of the Landlord and Tenant Act 1927. This provision converts a qualified covenant into a fully qualified covenant. However, the subsection does not use the word 'alterations', but refers to 'improvements'. Is an 'improvement' the same as an 'alteration'?

Section 19(2) says that a covenant against making improvements without consent – a qualified covenant – is deemed to be subject to a proviso that consent is not to be unreasonably withheld, thus making it a fully qualified covenant. It is expressly provided that there can be no contracting out of this provision. The landlord can, though, require:

(a) a reasonable sum of money to cover any damage to or diminution in the value of the reversion;

(b) payment of legal and other expenses (such as surveyor's fees), and

(c) an undertaking to re-instate the premises to how they were before the alteration.

In *Balls Brothers Ltd v Sinclair* [1931] 2 Ch 325, Luxmoore J decided that whether an alteration is an improvement must be regarded from the tenant's point of view. It almost always will be, and so the subsection will apply to alterations in all but the most exceptional cases.

This authority was relied upon by the Court of Appeal in the litigation involving the landlord (Mr GE and Mr WR Lambert) of shop premises in Bournemouth held under a lease by Woolworths. Woolworths had separate leases of two shops divided by a party wall. They wanted to remove the wall and make one shop. There was a qualified alterations covenant. In the first case, *F W Woolworth & Co Ltd v Lambert* [1937] Ch 37, the landlord would only consent on condition that Woolworths paid £7,000, and Woolworths could not show that this was unreasonable.

In the second hearing, *Lambert v F W Woolworth & Co Ltd* [1938] Ch 883, the Court of Appeal not only agreed (by a majority) that the alteration was an improvement for the purposes of s 19(2) but said that since the landlord had given no reason for refusal, it was the landlord who had to show that its refusal was reasonable, and this it failed to do. In fact, as Slesser LJ noted at the end of his judgment (at 908), the one ground that the landlord did have for refusing consent – damage or diminution to the value of their reversion – was not pleaded.

9.8 Drafting the covenant

In the light of the case law, it is clearly advisable for landlords to give detailed thought as to how to achieve the right amount of control for the protection of their interests.

The first consideration is whether to make the clause absolute, qualified or fully qualified.

Those drafting clauses in leases may know what they mean but have to ensure that the wording makes that meaning clear to others. Draftsmen should avoid the ambiguity and meaninglessness found in the clause in *Westminster City Council v HSBC Bank plc*.

Having regard to how the courts have construed alterations covenants – rather in favour of tenants it might be thought – landlords should consider very carefully the content of the covenant. Especially in the case of a lease of part of a building, the definition of the premises – preferably with a plan – is essential. Thought should be given as to whether to prohibit all works and define a class of permitted alterations. Alterations may be defined in greater detail, given the approach of the court in *Bickmore v Dimmer*. In particular, it should be decided whether a distinction should be made between non-structural and structural alterations, perhaps permitting the former and restricting the latter. In any case, 'structure' should be defined.

Such situations as those in *Lambert v F W Woolworth & Co Ltd* and *Sargeant v Macepark (Whittlebury) Ltd* can easily be avoided if the original parties to the lease agree to a provision in the alterations clause that the landlord should give reasons for any refusal of consent. Clearly, it is better if future intentions and aims can be identified at the time the lease is being drawn up so that conditions can be put into the clause itself and so avoid arguments about the validity of any licence.

In general, the clause should include provisions that the tenant is to carry out any works in a proper manner to an appropriate standard with suitable materials. What is required for a 1960s shop will be different from what is required for a building of recognised architectural merit.

All necessary consents should be required to be obtained such as planning permission, Building Regulations approval, and any others.

When drafting, the more that the covenant is made to deal with matters which are likely to arise, the simpler will be the arrangements for a licence for consent, and so the scope for argument and litigation may be greatly reduced.

9.9 Reinstatement

Where consent is given for alterations, the landlord may require the tenant to reinstate the premises at the end of the term. Such a requirement may be in the licence for alterations, and s 19(2) of the LTA 1927 allows the landlord to do this. However, it is more often contained in the lease itself since this reduces the risk of the requirement being found to be unreasonable and it will bind the tenant's successors in the case of a pre-1996 lease. The tenant should seek to limit the covenant to reinstate to doing that which is reasonable; clearly, it would be unreasonable to require reinstatement where the alterations had been done to comply with statute, and where the landlord intended to redevelop the premises.

Under the Landlord and Tenant (Covenants) Act 1995, a covenant for reinstatement will bind the tenant's successors as a 'tenant covenant'. There are limits on how far a landlord can go in claiming damages for breach of such a covenant. In *James v Hutton & J Cook & Sons Ltd* [1950] 1 KB 9, a landlord required that a new shop front should be replaced in accordance with a covenant for reinstatement contained in a licence. Lord Goddard LCJ, suspecting that the landlord merely would pocket any damages, said that reinstatement 'would be a sheer waste of money' (at 17); the landlord would recover her premises 'with a modern and convenient front' (at 17), and she was entitled to only nominal damages.

9.10 Compensation for improvements

Part I of the Landlord and Tenant Act 1927, introduced a scheme under which tenants could claim compensation for improvements. The idea was that landlords should not gain value in their premises as a result of work and expenditure by tenants. There is thus a statutory procedure for tenants to follow if the improvements are qualifying improvements. In reality, the procedure is little used, and the Law Commission has recommended its abolition (Law Com No 187).

10 Repairs

10.1 Introduction

Because of the sometimes great cost of repairs, there is no shortage of case law, ongoing since 1890, concerning repairing covenants. Any properly-drawn business lease will contain an express covenant to repair, and it is with these that this chapter is concerned. There is no doubt in the cases as to who is the covenantor (the party giving the benefit of and so bearing the burden of a covenant); the cases generally arise from disputes as to the extent of the liability of the covenantor.

Who is the covenantor will normally depend on whether the lease is of whole or of part. On the grant of a lease of whole, the landlord will expect the tenant to be liable, as under the usual 'full repairing and insuring lease'. The landlord's aim, after all, is to get rental income at no cost to itself. Where there is a lease of part, such as of a suite of offices in an office block or of a unit in a shopping centre, there may not be much for the tenant to repair; such leases of part are sometimes called 'binliner' leases or 'eggshell' leases. The premises let are merely space bounded by the surface finishes of the floor, walls and ceiling. The structural parts are retained by the landlord who enters into a landlord's covenant to repair though the cost of any repair will be recoverable from all the tenants, usually by way of a service charge.

10.2 Definition of the premises

All buildings need repair from time to time, but since repair can be a costly matter, there is every incentive to avoid responsibility for it if possible. The lease should leave no room for doubt which leads to argument and litigation. One way of avoiding doubt is to ensure that the premises are precisely defined. In the case of a lease of the whole, this ought to be easier though boundaries must be exact. One problem for the legal practitioner is that clients are sometimes reluctant to spend money on having good plans drawn. Where the lease is of a part of a building, the premises must be defined in every detail. It is not enough to refer to the 'interior'; it must be made clear which surface finishes, conducting media, and what parts of windows are part of the premises and which are not. In a multi-let building, there must be no 'gaps' of responsibility where it is unknown who is responsible for repair.

10.3 Before the lease is entered into

In commercial property, there is no equivalent to the NHBC scheme for domestic property and a tenant taking a lease or assignment of a lease where it will be responsible for repair must satisfy itself as to the physical state and condition of the premises. The tenant should commission a survey, and this is so whether the building is old or new.

10.3.1 Survey

A survey should alert the tenant to any problems. If the surveyor is negligent, then the tenant may be able to recover from the surveyor. In *Prudential Assurance Co Ltd v McBains Cooper (No 2)* WL 1421232, Prudential commissioned a survey which said that the roof needed minor repairs costing up to £1,500. Soon after Prudential acquired the premises (actually by purchase), the roof collapsed and repair was needed costing some £175,000. Furthermore, Prudential claimed and got further damages for the stigma now attaching to the building for having required such extensive repair.

In *Baxall Securities Ltd v Sheard Walshaw Partnership* [2002] EWCA Civ 9, the tenant sued the architect for an inherent design defect but the court held that the tenant's proper action was against the surveyor who should have seen and reported on the defect.

In an apparent exception to the rule that one party cannot claim damages for loss suffered by another, a company, the first claimant, which engaged a firm of chartered surveyors to supervise construction of a building, recovered damages for defects to the building measured by the loss to its controlling shareholder, the second claimant, to whom the building had been transferred: *Catlin Estates Ltd v Carter Jonas* [2005] EWHC 2315, TCC.

Landlords cannot, however, shift all responsibility to the tenant's surveyor. They must give full answers to the tenant's enquiries about the property. In *Clinicare Ltd v Orchard Homes & Developments Ltd* [2004] EWHC 1694 QB, the landlord was liable to the tenant because of misleading answers given to enquiries concerning dry rot in the premises, even though the tenant's surveyor had drawn attention to the problem.

10.3.2 Schedule of condition

In the case of an older building, there may also be a need for a schedule of condition. This is a complete survey which evidences the state and condition of the premises at that time. It is agreed by the parties and annexed to the lease and may consist of photographs and a CD of the premises as well as a written report. The lease provides that the tenant will not be liable to put the premises into any better state of repair than evidenced by the schedule of condition. Agreeing the terms of a schedule of condition may take considerable negotiation. A tenant may be able to persuade a landlord to bear some responsibility for repair beyond an agreed level.

10.3.3 Collateral warranties

In the case of new or nearly new premises, it cannot be assumed that there is no need for a survey; there may be faults and defects in design, materials and construction. These are collectively called 'inherent defects', sometimes 'latent defects'. The tenant is likely to be responsible for rectifying these under a typical repairing covenant. Furthermore, tenants should not rely on the law of contract and tort to seek remedies from the various professionals and contractors involved in designing and building the premises: *Murphy v Brentwood District Council* [1991] 1 AC 398. The developer will be expected to provide collateral warranties obtained from those involved in the design and construction of the building. Collateral warranties give a tenant the contractual right to a remedy in the event of negligence by any of those involved. Whether advising a tenant on the grant of a lease of newly-built premises or an assignee of a lease of nearly new premises, the collateral warranties must be examined with care. In particular, where appropriate, they should extend their benefit to a mortgagee. No tenant should take a lease or assignment of a new or nearly new building without adequate collateral warranties.

Where a developer pre-lets premises (that is, grants leases during the course of planning or construction), the tenant should negotiate for access to the site for its own professionals, such as its architect and surveyor. These can then protect the interests of the tenant during construction.

10.4 Meaning of repair

The many cases in this area involve specific covenants, buildings and repairs, and so a precise meaning is not easy to give. A number of principles, however, can be gleaned from the authorities.

- Repair means such repair as, having regard to the age, character, and locality of the premises, would make them reasonably fit for the occupation of a reasonably-minded tenant of the class who would be likely to take them. Repair should be such as would make the premises reasonably fit for occupation by a reasonably-minded tenant: *Proudfoot v Hart* [1890] 25 QB 42.

- Repair does not involve giving back to the landlord something different from that which the tenant took: *Lister v Lane and Nesham* [1893] 2 QB 212; *Elmcroft Developments Ltd v Tankersley-Sawyer* [1984] 270 EG 140.

- The true test is that what is repair is always a matter of degree, namely, whether that which the tenant is asked to do can properly be described as repair or whether it would involve giving back to the landlord a wholly different thing: *Ravenseft Properties Ltd v Davstone (Holdings) Ltd* [1979] 1 All ER 929; *McDougall v Easington District Council* [1989] 1 EGLR 93.

- Repair necessarily involves a degree of restoration by renewal or replacement of subsidiary parts. But renewal, as distinguished from repair, is the reconstruction of the whole or substantially the whole of the premises: *Lurcott v Wakely and Wheeler* [1911] 1 KB 905.

- Repair is only necessary where there is disrepair. If the premises are in the same condition as they were when they were constructed there is no want of repair: *Post Office v Aquarius Properties Ltd* [1987] 1 All ER 1055. It follows that repair does not include preventative works: *Fluor Daniel Properties Ltd v Shortlands Investments Ltd* [2001] 2 EGLR 103; Janet Reger International.

- Where work involves more than one component, the question is whether the total work to be done can properly be described as repair since it involves no more than renewal or replacement of defective parts, or whether it is renewal or replacement of substantially the whole: *Brew Bros Ltd v Snax (Ross) Ltd* [1970] 1 All ER 587.

- In the case of a very long lease, it may not be intended by the parties that the same building be kept in repair, but that other buildings may replace original buildings, so that demolition for the purpose of reconstruction is not a breach of a covenant to repair. Where a lease was granted in 1958 for a term of 1,000 years with no clauses restricting user, alteration and alienation, but with a repairing covenant in the usual form, the proposed demolition and redevelopment of the site of the premises was not a breach of the repairing covenant since the parties could not have intended that the building opened in 1959 should be the only building ever to be built on the site: *British Glass Manufacturers' Confederation v University of Sheffield* [2003] EWHC 3108.

10.5 Standard of repair

Once it has been established what repair is and that it is required, the question then to be asked is, how good does the repair have to be?

- The tenant can never say that the premises are so old that they need not be repaired: *Lurcot v Wakely and Wheeler*.

- The standard of repair may differ according to the age, character and location of the building. The standard for a mansion in Belgravia is different than for a house in Spitalfields. Repair does not have to be perfect: *Proudfoot v Hart*.

- Repair is an ongoing matter involving that which is necessary to keep the premises in such condition as might be expected to be found if they had been managed by a reasonably-minded owner having regard to the age of the premises, the locality, the class of tenant likely to take them at the date of the lease, not at some later date when the premises may have been allowed to deteriorate. There is not a fluctuating standard, so the standard may not go down if the area deteriorates or up if the area improves: *Anstruther-Gough-Calthorpe v McOscar* [1924] 1 KB 716.

- The standard of repair cannot be limited by reference to the commercial life of a building (such as 15 years). There can be no lesser expectation because the building was badly built and the lease had a long unexpired residue (such as 75 years): *Ladbroke Hotels Ltd v Sandhu* [1996] 72 P & CR 498.

- 'The test which I must apply is that of an intending occupier of an industrial warehouse building, with modern construction, who judges repair reasonably by reference to his intended use of the premises': *Commercial Union Life Assurance Co Ltd v Label Ink Ltd* [2001] L & TR 29, *per* HH Judge Rich QC at para 17.

- If there are two ways of effecting a repair, by substantial repairs or by replacement, the tenant is entitled to choose the less expensive option provided repair is effected: *Riverside Property Investments Ltd v Blackhawk Automotive* [2005] 1 EGLR 114. The position may be different, however, where the work is to be done to the satisfaction of the landlord's surveyor: see **10.6.4**.

10.6 Scope of repairing covenant

In *McDougall v Easington DC*, the Court of Appeal identified three criteria for determining the scope of a repairing covenant. These are: whether or not the work goes to the whole or substantially the whole of the structure or only to a subsidiary part and so amounts to renewal and not repair; whether the work involved would produce something wholly different from what had been let; the cost. The scope of the covenant (and indeed the standard or extent of repair) may be modified by a requirement to do work to the satisfaction of the covenantee's surveyor.

10.6.1 Repair or renewal

This criterion derives from a number of cases. In *Lurcott v Wakely & Wheeler*, all three Lords Justice made it clear that repair must involve a degree of renewal; a broken pipe or a rotten and decayed window needs repairing by replacing it, but repair cannot extend to the whole or substantially the whole. Since it is a matter of degree (*Ravenseft Properties Ltd v Davstone (Holdings) Ltd*), where is the cut-off point beyond which replacement goes beyond repair? In *Halliard Property Co Ltd v Nicholas Clarke Investments Ltd* (1983) 269 EG 1257, French J, acknowledging that the case was borderline, and confessing to some hesitation, thought that where the work involved restoring rather more than a third of the building, it could not properly be described as repair. There is obviously a connection here with cost.

10.6.2 Producing something different

This criterion has been described in many cases of which *Lister v Lane and Nesham* and *Ravenseft Properties Ltd v Davstone (Holdings) Ltd* are but examples. In *Lister v Lane and Nesham*, the defendants were not liable to rebuild a house which collapsed since the causes of collapse were natural over time, and rebuilding the house would necessarily involve making a house of a different kind. Improvements, modifications, inherent defects and replacements have all been considered judicially as to whether repair was involved.

In *Morcom v Campbell-Johnson* [1956] 1 QB 106, 115, Denning LJ (as he then was), whilst confessing to finding the distinction difficult, described the difference between repair and improvement in these terms:

> It seems to me that the test . . . is this: if the work which is done is the provision of something new for the benefit of the occupier, that is, properly speaking, an improvement; but if it is only the replacement of something already there, which has become dilapidated or worn out, then albeit that it is the replacement by its modern equivalent, it comes within the category of repairs and not improvements.

Modification to the premises may amount to producing something different from that which was let. Where the modification is very substantial, there can be little doubt that the work goes beyond repair: *McDougall v Easington DC*. But a less substantial modification may also produce something different from what was let. In *Eyre v McCracken* (2000) 80 P & CR 220, the tenant took a lease in 1976 for a term of seven and a half years of a house built in 1841 in St John's Wood, London. Houses built in the middle of the nineteenth century did not have damp-proof courses. Pill LJ held that to require a tenant to install a damp-proof course in such circumstances would mean giving back to the landlord a different thing – a house with a damp-proof course whereas what the tenant took was a house without one. (See Smith [2001] 65 Conv 102.)

This criterion does not mean, though, that a tenant may not have to attend to an inherent defect. In the *Ravenseft* case, stone cladding was falling from the elevation of the premises due to an inherent defect in design and construction. The tenant denied it was liable under its repairing covenant to attend to the cause of the problem, claiming there was a doctrine of inherent defect which excluded such liability. Forbes J held there was no such doctrine. The tenant argued, in effect, that to solve the problem would result in a different building – what it had rented was a building which had stone panels dropping from it and what it had to hand back to the landlord was a building with stone panels dropping from it. It does not follow that a tenant will always have to remedy an inherent defect, but it will if that is the only realistic and practical way of doing the repair.

In *Gibson Investments Ltd v Chesterton plc* [2002] EWHC 19, the tenant and the landlord contended for different methods of repairing cracked brickwork and stonework caused by rusting of the steelwork of the building (which rusting did not, however, threaten the structural integrity of the building). The difference in cost between what the parties each proposed was considerable. Neuberger J held that the covenantor must carry out such repair as would be prudent. Depending on the circumstances, that may mean eradicating the cause of the disrepair (as in *Ravenseft*), or only lesser, preventive work. His lordship said (see para 35) that the choice of work was that of the person paying but that the work must be appropriate and not futile, and so in some cases the covenant may not be performed if the cause is not eradicated. This would be so in the case of a simple covenant to repair, not only when there were further words imposing a further obligation. Where it is contended that the work should extend to eradicating the causative problem, the work will not be repair if it would involve giving back to the landlord something different.

In *Elite Investments Ltd v TI Bainbridge Silencers Ltd* [1986] 2 EGLR 43, the tenant had to repair a roof by replacing it. In any case, there was a specific covenant to replace the roof. The tenant argued that, even so, a new roof would be of better, modern materials and so make the building different from that which it had rented. The judge disagreed: what the tenant had rented was a building with a roof – what it would be giving back was a building with a roof. Use of current materials was unavoidable and any consequent improvement was incidental.

10.6.3 Cost

In the *Ravenseft* case, the cost of the repair was £55,000. The rebuilding cost was £3m, and so the repair was 1.83% of the rebuilding cost. In *Elite Investments Ltd v TI Bainbridge Silencers Ltd*, the cost of replacing a roof was £85,000. The value of the building was £150,000 which the tenant argued was the figure to take for comparison. The rebuilding cost was £1m. HH Judge Paul Baker QC held that, for comparison, the rebuilding cost is the figure to use, and that meant the cost of repair was 8.43% of the rebuilding cost.

Taking the *Halliard Property Co Ltd* case as a guide, it seems that if the cost is more than one-third of the rebuilding cost, then the work will be outside the scope of repair. Thus, in *Brew Bros v Snax (Ross) Ltd*, repairs to a wall and drains cost nearly the rebuilding cost, and in *McDougall v Easington DC*, renovation of a house cost more than its value, nearly doubled its value and greatly increased its lifespan. In both cases, the works were well beyond the meaning of repair.

10.6.4 To the satisfaction of the covenantor's surveyor

Clearly, there will be cases involving all these criteria. One such case is *Mason v TotalFinaElf* [2003] EWHC 1604 (which included, also, consideration of the standard of repair). The case was actually about liability of the tenant in a claim for damages for terminal dilapidations (the tenant's obligation to give the premises back to the landlord in a stated condition) but concerned consideration of the extent of the tenant's obligation where the works of repair were required to be done to the satisfaction of the landlord's surveyor. Can that requirement displace the general principle that it is for the covenantor to choose how to comply with the covenant? The surveyor is not entitled to require work beyond the operative words of the covenant nor to require the work to be done to an unreasonably high standard. But if the tenant chooses a way of doing the repair which is not to the surveyor's satisfaction, it fails to comply with the covenant. As Blackburne J said (at para 35), 'provided [the surveyor] reaches a decision which a reasonable surveyor could reach, it matters not that the tenant's surveyor favours another cheaper but no less reasonable decision as to what should be done'. It is up to the covenantor (the tenant in this case) to find out what the landlord's surveyor might require.

10.7 Construction of the repairing covenant

Not all the words in a covenant will add significance to the basic concept of repair. In *Anstruther-Gough-Calthorpe v McOscar*, both Bankes LJ and Scrutton LJ held that there was no significance in words such as 'well and sufficiently', 'good', 'tenantable' and 'substantial' when used adjectivally in relation to repair. In *Simmons v Dresden* [2004] EWHC 993 (TCC), the court confirmed that the words 'well and substantially' did not make the standard of repair different from that set in *Proudfoot v Hart*. However, in *Lurcot v Wakely and Wheeler*, Fletcher Moulton LJ thought that 'thorough repair' meant something more than repair and that this expression was similar to an obligation to keep in good condition. But words which may extend the obligation beyond the meaning of repair must be given their true significance.

Construction of the words of a repairing covenant has varied over the years. Words beyond those which were merely adjectival were originally given their full meaning in earlier cases. Later, the approach relaxed. More recently, there has been a return to the original approach.

A covenant to keep premises in repair includes an obligation to put the premises into repair if they are in disrepair when the lease begins: *Proudfoot v Hart*. Where, however, the covenant is to maintain the state and condition of the premises, there is no such obligation, but the meaning of such a covenant may not be clear.

In *Lurcot v Wakely and Wheeler*, Fletcher Moulton LJ said that the words of the covenant must be given their proper legal significance and that it was the duty of the court to give full effect to each word used. Similarly, in *Anstruther-Gough-Calthorpe v McOscar*, Atkin LJ said that effect should be given if possible to every word used.

Forbes J, in the *Ravenseft* case noted the typically verbose form of the covenant but took no point on the various words used. In *Post Office v Aquarius Properties Ltd*, Ralph Gibson LJ noted that no reliance had been placed on additional words, including 'amend', renew', and 'condition'. In *Norwich Union Life Insurance Society v British Railways Board* [1987] 2 EGLR 137, Hoffmann J commented on the 'torrential' style of drafting of the repairing covenant. His lordship accepted (at 138) 'that in the construction of covenants such as this one cannot . . . insist upon giving each word in a series a distinct meaning'.

However, there was a return to the approach of the early cases in *Credit Suisse v Beegas Nominees Ltd* [1994] 1 EGLR 76, an approach confirmed by the Court of Appeal in *Welsh v Greenwich London Borough Council* [2000] 3 EGLR 41. In the first case, Credit Suisse were the tenant and Beegas Nominees Ltd (the British Gas pension scheme) the landlord. The premises were the first four floors of a prominent and prestigious building in central London built in the early 1980s. Lindsay J noted, for the purposes of considering the 'class of tenant', that the first tenant had been J Rothschild & Co Ltd and that Credit Suisse (assignee from Rothchilds) was (and remains) a leading Swiss bank and one of the world's strongest banks. It is hard to imagine a higher class of tenant. The building proved defective and water came in through the windows and walls. Staff had to mop up and catch water in bins and buckets, and lights in client interview areas exploded. Credit Suisse said this was not a tolerable situation for an organisation in their position. The landlord had covenanted 'to maintain repair amend renew cleanse repaint and redecorate and otherwise keep in good and tenantable condition' the structure of the building. Solving the problem of the ingress of water meant replacing the cladding of the building and that went beyond the scope of repair. Reviewing the cases, Lindsay J agreed with the approach to construction of Fletcher Moulton LJ in *Anstruther* (amongst other cases) and held that the words in the covenant, 'renew and amend' and 'otherwise keep in good and tenantable condition' imposed a higher degree of liability than the covenant to repair so that the landlord was obliged to replace the cladding and to make the building watertight. The premises being, in effect, unassignable, Credit Suisse were awarded very substantial damages.

In *Welsh*, the repairing covenant of the landlord borough council obliged the council to 'maintain the dwelling in good condition and repair'. Mrs Welsh's flat suffered from severe mould caused by condensation, in turn caused by a lack of insulation. The problem was not caused by disrepair and so the council could not be liable under a simple obligation to repair: *Quick v Taff-Ely Borough Council* [1985] 3 All ER 321. Only if the covenant went beyond the obligation to repair would the council be liable to attend to the problem. The council argued that to maintain in good condition meant 'structural condition'. Mrs Welsh argued that the first words of the covenant were not circumscribed by the obligation to repair but added to the council's obligation. Robert Walker LJ agreed that the reference to 'good condition' marked a separate concept from repair and made a significant addition to the council's obligation.

Welsh constituted 'a stark warning to all that *Beegas* was not simply a one-off and that the insertion of an obligation can (perhaps inadvertently) extend what might have been intended as a mere obligation to repair': S Murdoch, (2000) Estates Gazette, 21 October, 172. It has been suggested that *Welsh* demonstrated 'a shift in judicial interpretation' such that 'well-established principles have been turned on their heads . . . in an attempt to do justice' and thereby departing 'from concepts of strict legal precedent': Hancock and Lloyd, (2001) Estates Gazette, 22 September, 182, 183. It is submitted that, given the clarity of the judgments in *Lurcot* and *Anstruther*, *Credit Suisse* and *Welsh* mark a welcome return to a precision in the interpretation of words which had sometimes been lacking.

The position now is as described by Blackburne J in *Mason v TotalFinaElf*. His lordship said (at para 13):

> . . . where, as here, the draftsman has employed a variety of closely related expressions . . . while I should not expect to give each word used a meaning distinct from the others, I should not assume that the draftsman was merely using different words to express the same concept. In short, I should endeavour, where the context allows, to give each word its proper meaning without striving to give each word a wholly distinct meaning.

A case from July 2006 illustrates a number of points of covenant construction. It also illustrates the difficulties that can arise where the premises are part of a building, and the landlord is responsible for repair of the building and the tenant for the premises. In *Janet Reger International Ltd v Tiree Ltd* [2006] EWHC 1743, the claimant tenant held the landlord liable for curing dampness in the basement of the building, the basement forming part of the premises occupied by the tenant. The tenant's covenant required the tenant to 'put and keep [the premises] in good and substantial repair and condition'. The premises included the surface finishes of the walls whilst the walls themselves were retained by the landlord. The landlord had covenanted to use reasonable endeavours to maintain repair and renew the retained structure. Dampness to the premises was caused by a defectively installed damp proof membrane. Though that membrane was part of the retained structure there was no damage to the retained stucture. Consequently, there was no obligation to repair; *Quick v Taff-Ely Borough Council* and *Post Office and Aquaris Properties Limited* [1987] 1 All ER 1055 applied. That principle applies to both bad design and bad workmanship. Unlike the tenant's covenant which did, the landlord's covenant had no obligation in it to put the structure into good condition. Tenants' advisors should check that, in such situations, there is parity between the respective obligations of tenant and landlord.

10.8 Decorating

A covenant to repair does not extend to decorating and painting. But if the state of decoration is so bad that a reasonably-minded tenant would not take the premises as they stood, then redecoration could be required under the repairing covenant: *Proudfoot v Hart*.

Leases normally include a separate covenant to decorate, usually to decorate the interior every three years and the outside every five years.

10.9 Drafting

Given the possible expense involved, it is obvious from the all the foregoing that drafting the repairing covenant is one of the most important jobs of the landlord's solicitor and that the most careful and critical scrutinising of the covenant is demanded of the tenant's solicitor. Unfortunately, drafting is often not of the standard required. In *Credit Suisse*, Lindsay J commented (at 85) on the poor quality of the draftsmanship; in *Holding & Barnes plc v Hill House Hammond Ltd* [2002] 2 P & CR 1334, the Court of Appeal judged that certain words in parentheses in a repairing covenant simply made no sense and should be ignored. On the other hand, even a well-drafted lease may not provide the answer to a problem of construction which later arises through no fault of the draftsman: see *Ibrahim v Dovecorn Reversions* [2001] 2 EGLR 46.

Drafting must consider the following matters:

- Avoidance of words which add nothing to the meaning, eg 'good', 'substantial' and 'tenantable'.

- Will the expressions 'to put into and keep in repair' or 'to keep in repair' be used so as to oblige a tenant to put premises into repair that are in disrepair at the start of the term?

- Is the covenant to be a simple obligation to repair, or will it go further and require an obligation to keep in good condition?

- Will there be further obligations, eg to renew, replace and rebuild?

- Will liability for inherent defects be excluded, and if so, will liability be accepted by the landlord?

- Is liability to be limited by reference to a schedule of condition?

- Will liability for repairing damage caused by insured risks be excluded? It usually is, save where the insurance money is irrecoverable due to the tenant's fault.

10.10 Enforcement and remedies

During the term of a lease under which the tenant is liable for repairs, the landlord will inspect the premises at intervals to view the state of repair pursuant to a covenant by the tenant to permit this. When disrepair is found, the landlord's surveyor will serve notice on the tenant specifying what should be done. Such notice is usually in the form of a 'schedule of dilapidations'. During the term, this will be called an 'interim schedule of dilapidations'; at the end of the term it will be called a 'terminal schedule of dilapidations'. Dilapidations are very much the preserve of the surveyor who must not only draw up the schedule but carry out valuations to assess any damages. Enforcement and the pursuit of remedies are clearly matters of property litigation; in most firms, commercial property and property litigation are separate areas of work.

10.10.1 Landlord's remedies

The landlord has a range of remedies against the tenant in breach of a repairing covenant.

10.10.1.1 Sue for damages

Damages are limited by s 18(1) of the Landlord and Tenant Act 1927 to the diminution in the landlord's reversion. This may be less than the cost of repair and, at the end of the lease, it may be to the tenant's advantage to pay damages rather than to do the repair. In *Mason v TotalFinaElf*, these figures were £73,500 and £135,000 respectively and so damages were the lower figure. If the lease is for seven years or more with more than three years left, the landlord must comply with the further procedure in the Leasehold Property (Repairs) Act 1938.

10.10.1.2 Forfeit the lease

See **Chapter 14**.

10.10.1.3 Self-help

The lease should give the landlord power, on default by the tenant, to enter the premises and carry out (or finish) the work. The cost to the landlord should be made to be recoverable from the tenant, not as damages, but as a debt. That is because s 18(1) of the LTA 1927 will not then apply since any action will be between the parties as creditor and debtor, not as landlord and tenant.

10.10.1.4 Specific performance

This is an equitable remedy and so in the discretion of the court which will consider all the circumstances, including, eg whether the term of the lease was near its end, so perhaps making spending on repairs oppressive to the tenant. Though rare in practice, specific performance of a repairing covenant may be granted in certain circumstances: see *Rainbow Estates Ltd v Tokenhold Ltd* [1988] 2 All ER 860. Specific performance was sought by the claimant in the *Janet Reger* case. The judge did not have to consider that remedy since he found no breach of obligation by the landlord, but he did not suggest it would not have been available as a remedy.

10.10.2 Tenant's remedies

Where the landlord is responsible for repairs, the tenant may have recourse to the following remedies.

10.10.2.1 Damages

The usual contractual principle applies, namely, that an award of damages is to 'place the [claimant] in the position which he would have occupied if he had not suffered the wrong complained of, be that wrong a tort or a breach of contract': *Calabar Properties Ltd* v *Stitcher* [1984] 1 WLR 287, 295 to 296, *per* Stephenson LJ at 295–6.

Many cases concern domestic property, but in the *Credit Suisse* case, substantial damages were awarded under a number of heads: general damages for inconvenience; loss of premium on assignment and abortive associated costs; rent, insurance and service charges after the date the underlease might have been assigned.

10.10.2.2 Specific performance

As already said, this is an equitable remedy which may or may not be granted according to the circumstances.

10.10.2.3 Do repairs and set off cost against rent

Where the landlord will not carry out repairs for which it is liable, the tenant may do the repairs and recover the cost by withholding rent. Alternatively, the tenant may simply withhold rent and counterclaim for damages when the landlord sues for rent arrears. In the *Janet Reger* case, the tenant did withhold rent but was not held to have done so wrong. Many leases, though, specifically exclude a right of set-off. Bean J considered the position in *Edlington Properties Ltd v JH Fenner and Co Ltd* [2005] EWHC 2158. His lordship said (at para 9) that it is well established that a tenant may claim set off since the decisions in *British Anzani (Felixstowe) Ltd v International Marine Management (UK) Ltd* [1980] QB 137 and *Muscat v Smith* [2003] 1 WLR 85.

10.10.2.4 Repudiatory breach

This is a claim imported from the law of contract. It can perhaps be called the tenant's counterpart to forfeiture. If the landlord persistently refuses to comply with its obligations, the tenant may regard the refusal as repudiation by the landlord of the contract and quit the premises: *Hussein v Mehlman* [1992] 2 EGLR 87. The court will be astute, however, to detect any use by a tenant of repudiatory breach to get out of a lease by which it no longer wishes to be bound: *Nynehead Developments Ltd v RH Fibreboard Containers Ltd* [1999] 1 EGLR 7.

10.10.3 Alternatives to litigation

It is important to consider ways of solving problems without recourse to litigation. Many disputes regarding repairs and dilapidations are solved by negotiation and agreement. Where agreement cannot be reached, alternative dispute resolution (ADR) may be tried. As in rent review disputes, arbitration is appropriate for high value or complex disputes. For lower value disputes, determination by an expert will be appropriate. The Royal Institution of Chartered Surveyors provides a dispute resolution service. The Property Litigation Association runs a mediation service.

It is possible that a lawyer would be negligent for failing to advise a client to consider some form of ADR. In *Halsey v Milton Keynes General NHS Trust* [2004] EWCA Civ 576, Dyson LJ said:

> All members of the legal profession who conduct litigation should now routinely consider with their clients whether their disputes are suitable for alternative dispute resolution.

11 Alienation

11.1 Introduction

This chapter concerns the covenant in the lease which restricts the tenant's right to alienate the premises. A lease can be alienated, ie dealt with, in a variety of ways: assignment, subletting, mortgaging and any parting with possession. Any form of alienation may be described as a disposition, and the person disposing of the interest (whether by way of assignment, subletting or otherwise) is called the disponor and that taking the interest is the disponee. Parting with possession means parting with the possession granted by the lease and so would not include a licence as a licence does not confer possession: see **4.3.1** and **4.3.2** and see **11.7**.

At common law, there is no restriction on a tenant's ability to alienate the premises. Landlords, though, naturally wish to keep control of who is actually in the premises or who may have an interest in them. By such control, they preserve security of rental income. The financial standing of any assignee is of prime importance for landlords. This will especially be so in the case of longer leases to which the Landlord and Tenant (Covenants) Act 1995 applies.

There will invariably be an express clause in a business lease restricting alienation. Alienation clauses:

(a) may be absolute, qualified or fully qualified;

(b) usually draw a distinction between alienation of the whole and of part of the premises, generally permitting the former and prohibiting the latter;

(c) relate closely with the user clause.

11.2 Absolute covenant

Here, the tenant simply covenants not to alienate the premises. It is always open to the landlord to relax the covenant but it does not have to do so and only would at a price. The landlord has to bear in mind that an absolute covenant has a severely depressing effect on rent and it would need a compelling reason to choose such a covenant. It may be more acceptable in the case of a very short lease of low-value premises.

11.3 Qualified covenant

Where the covenant provides that the landlord's consent must be obtained, the covenant is qualified. Statute intervenes to make a qualified alienation covenant fully qualified. Section 19(1)(a) of the Landlord and Tenant Act 1927 provides that where a lease contains a covenant, condition or agreement against assigning, underletting, charging or parting with possession of the demised premises or any part thereof without the landlord's licence or consent, the covenant is deemed to be subject to a proviso that such licence or consent is not to be unreasonably withheld, notwithstanding any express provision to the contrary. In short, a qualified alienation clause is converted into a fully-qualified clause. Section 19(1)(a) applies only to qualified alienation clauses and has no application to absolute alienation clauses.

Section 19(1)(a) allows a landlord to claim a reasonable sum for legal and other expenses incurred in the giving of consent. The other expense the landlord may incur is the surveyor's fee where his advice is needed in connection with the giving of consent. Section 144 of the LPA 1925 provides that no fine or sum of money in the nature of a fine shall be payable for a landlord's licence or consent to assign, underlet, part with possession or other disposition of the premises. But it is possible to contract out of this section and it is of limited effect.

It is important to note that an apparently fully qualified covenant may be rendered absolute by a proviso. In *Crestfort Ltd v Tesco Stores Ltd* [2005] EWHC 805, a fully qualified alienation clause was subject to a proviso that said (among other things), 'any permitted underlease shall be granted subject to like covenants and conditions as are herein contained except as to the rent thereby reserved and the length of the term thereby granted'. On the facts, the repairing clause in the intended underlease was not like that in the head lease. Lightman J judged that the effect of the proviso was to limit the circumstances in which the absolute prohibition on underletting was qualified and the tenant had a right to request consent (see para 43). In other words, the tenant only had the right to request consent if the underlease was on the same terms as the head lease. He noted that such provisions are common in commercial leases in order to control the terms of any underlease. This effect had been conceded by the tenant in *Allied Dunbar Assurance v Homebase Ltd* [2002] EWCA Civ 666. Accordingly, the landlord had no obligation to consider the application for consent and s 1 of the Landlord and Tenant Act 1988 had no application (see para 50). The effect of such provisos on rent must be considered by the landlord at review.

11.4 Alienation in breach of covenant

Where an assignment takes place in breach of the covenant to obtain the landlord's consent, then, at common law, the assignment is nevertheless effective to pass the legal estate: *Old Grovebury Farm Ltd v W Seymour Plant Sales & Hire* (No 2) Ltd [1979] 1 WLR 1397. This means that the landlord must take any enforcement action (such as forfeiture proceedings) against the assignee. The assignee may also be liable to the landlord for the tort of conspiracy in having induced the assignor to break the covenant: *Midland Bank Trust Co Ltd v*

Green [1981] AC 513. The effect of a subletting without consent is the same: in *Crestfort Ltd v Tesco Stores Ltd*, Lightman J held that the intended undertenant had committed against the landlord the tort of wrongful interference with contract by agreeing to accept and accepting the grant of an underlease without consent of the superior landlord, and was liable therefore in damages. In such a case, the underlease may be ordered to be surrendered, as it was in that case. (It is to be noted that the lease in this case was granted in 1981 for a term of 25 years and so was not registrable, and the intended underlease was proposed in 2004 when the residue of the term was only about 2 years.)

The position will be different where registration formalities are required. Since 19 June 2006, leases which require registration at the Land Registry (which means leases granted for a term of more than seven years: s 27(2)(b) of the LRA 2002) must comply with the Land Registration (Amendment) (No 2) Rules 2005. Any lease granted on or after 19 June 2006 must contain 'prescribed clauses' where the lease is a disposition of a registered estate in land. (There are very limited exceptions.) Full details are to be found in Land Registry Practice Guide 64, September 2005. See further at **1.4.6.1**. Alienation clauses are included as prescribed clause LR8. One of two statements must be given: 'This lease does not contain a provision that prohibits or restricts dispositions' or 'This lease contains a provision that prohibits or restricts dispositions'. If the second option is chosen – as it most commonly will be – the Land Registry will make an entry on the register. Then, if there is an attempt to assign the lease without consent, the assignment will not be registered by the Land Registry and so legal title will not pass.

The Land Registry will not examine the lease itself, and any error by way of including or omitting both statements will result in no entry of a restriction on the register. Where a lease contains a clause restricting alienation and because of the error there is no restriction on the register, an assignment without consent could end up being registered. Since it is clearly in the interests of the grantor of the lease to have the restriction entered on the register of the lease where there is an alienation clause, the landlord's solicitor should require the tenant's solicitor to produce copy title documentation after registration. Such a requirement is likely to be in the form of a covenant in the lease. It remains to be seen what will happen if a mistake is made by the landlord's solicitor in drafting the lease as to prescribed clause LR8, there is no restriction on the register, and there is then an assignment by way of transfer without consent. Clearly, if registration of an assignment in such circumstances is completed (which it will be instantly when e-conveyancing arrives), the legal title will pass to the assignee in breach of covenant and the common law position will apply, though perhaps with a claim by the landlord for rectification in respect of the restriction.

Assuming that the second option is chosen and the entry made on the register, no disposition of the lease, for example by assignment, will be registered unless the necessary consent is produced to the Land Registry. Since legal title will not pass until registration is effected (s 27(1) of the LRA 2002), it follows that the common law position will not apply to relevant leases.

The common law position will, of course, continue to apply to leases granted for seven years or less. Having regard to the trend, since 2004, towards shorter terms, eg the average term for leases granted in 2004–2005 was 6.4 years (see British Property Federation

Annual Lease Review, 11 November 2005), the common law position will apply to a great number of leases. If, however, the requirement of first registration is extended to leases for a term of more than three years (as has been mooted), then most leases will be affected by the prescribed clauses requirements.

11.5 Assignment

Assignment is the most common form of alienation. The outgoing tenant is called the assignor and the incoming tenant the assignee. The assignment may be of just the lease or it may be of the business carried on at the premises as well. For instance, a shop held on a lease may be sold as a business and the assignment will be of the lease, the goodwill of the shop (the 'reputation' of the shop, which can be valued), and the stock. This section is concerned only with the assignment of the lease.

Section 52 of the LPA 1925 provides that all conveyances of land or of any interest therein are void for the purpose of conveying or creating a legal estate unless made by deed. Even if the tenancy was created orally, as s 54(2) of the LPA 1925 provides, it must still be assigned by deed: *Crago v Julian* [1992] 1 WLR 372. For the formalities involved in the making of a deed, see **3.7**.

The assignment of an unregistered lease with more than seven years to run is subject to the requirement of compulsory first registration at the Land Registry: ss 4(1)(a) and 4(2)(b) of the LRA 2002. If the lease is registered land, there must be a transfer to effect the assignment and, as already mentioned, legal title will pass when registration takes place: s 27(1) of the LRA 2002. When a lease containing an alienation clause is submitted for registration at the Land Registry and the second LR8 prescribed clause is given, an entry will be made on the property register of the title in the following form:

> There are excepted from the effect of registration all estates, rights, interests, powers and remedies arising upon, or by reason of, any dealing made in breach of the prohibition or restriction against dealings therewith inter vivos contained in the Lease.

An assignment may proceed much like a transfer of freehold title, though sometimes the contract stage is omitted. Where the lease is registered title, the assignor simply needs sight of the official copies of the title by way of investigation of title. Care should be taken to have sight of any documents referred to in the register, and to check that the lease is registered with absolute leasehold title. Where the lease has more than seven years to run and the title out of which it was granted is unregistered then, since the assignment will trigger first registration, the assignee must call for the freehold title to be deduced.

The lease will usually provide that notice of assignment must be given to the landlord. A typical clause may say that, within 28 days, any assignment, subletting, charge, or transmission relating to the premises must be registered with the landlord's solicitors, the tenant producing a certified copy of the relevant instrument and paying the landlord's solicitor's reasonable costs of registration.

The position regarding enforcement of covenants as between successive tenants has been considered at **Chapter 6**.

11.6 Sublettings

An alienation clause will commonly permit a subletting of the whole of the premises. Tenants may want to sublet rather than assign so as to have the opportunity of recovering the premises near the end of the term. The landlord will want control of sublettings because, in some circumstances, the head lease may cease and the subtenant become the immediate tenant of the landlord, as, for example, on the surrender of the head lease. A sublease is created by granting a lesser term out of the term of the head lease. If the sublease is granted for the residue of the term of the head lease, this operates as an assignment: *Keydon Estates Ltd v Eversheds LLP* [2005] EWHC 972. The sublease must, therefore, be granted for a lesser term even if by a few days, so that the immediate landlord retains a reversion. This means that the immediate tenant may be in possession for the purposes of security of tenure. If the head lease has security of tenure excluded, then any sublease should also be contracted out of the security of tenure provisions. If the head lease is not contracted out, both landlord and tenant may well want the sublease to be contracted out.

The alienation clause will often have elaborate provisions relating to permitted sublettings. These provisions may include:

(a) no subletting permitted by the subtenant;

(b) no fine (a sort of fee, not a penalty) or premium to be paid;

(c) rent to be not less than the greater of the rent payable under the head lease and the current open market rent of the premises;

(d) any rent review clause to be upwards only;

(e) a covenant by the subtenant directly with the landlord to comply with the head lease covenants save as to rent;

(f) that the sublease contains tenant covenants consistent with and no less onerous than those in the head lease.

The requirement that the rent under the sublease be not less than the greater of the rent reserved under the head lease and the current open market rent of the premises, is clearly a problem for the tenant who has no need for the premises and wishes to reduce its losses at a time when the market means that the premises are overrented. An assignment is out of the question, and so is subletting unless a way can be found to structure the subletting in such a way that there is no breach of the alienation clause (see **11.8.3**).

Where a sublease requires registration at the Land Registry, the application for registration must be accompanied by a consent from the superior landlord, otherwise only 'good leasehold' title will be granted.

11.7 Construction of alienation clauses

The general rule is that alienation covenants are construed against the landlord. In *Yorkshire Metropolitan Properties Ltd v Co-operative Retail Services Ltd* [1997] EGCS 57,

Neuberger J said that the courts should construe such covenants in favour of the tenant where there is ambiguity. Where the court had to consider the meaning of the phrase 'sharing occupation', the link with the user clause had to be taken into account: *Mean Fidler Holdings Ltd v Islington London Borough Council* [2003] EWCA Civ 160. In that case Carnwath LJ held that, in a lease of a nightclub, there was no breach of the alienation clause in which the tenant covenanted (amongst other things) 'not to . . . share the occupation of the Property or any parts thereof whether as licensee or otherwise . . . ' when the tenant offered the premises to external promoters who staged club nights. His lordship was reluctant to lay down strict guidelines of construction, considering that the market would be more likely to handle such matters by negotiation than litigation. He acknowledged that alienation clauses are to be construed against the landlord, but said that in grey areas such as always exist at law between clear extremes, the Court Appeal is unlikely to interfere with the conclusion of the trial judge unless there is a clear error of law. Delivering the second judgment, Sir Christopher Staughton did offer some guidance when he said:

> [t]he test, in my opinion, is whether the promoter . . . is operating a separate business on the premises from that carried on by the tenant . . . If, on the other hand, the tenant is carrying on a business and the promoter participates in that business under the tenant's supervision and control, I would say not that the promoter is sharing occupation of the property'.

In construing an alienation clause, the difference between possession and occupation is important if the clause mentions possession but not occupation. This issue was discussed at some length by Neuberger LJ in *Akici v LR Butlin Ltd* [2005] EWCA Civ 1296. His lordship said (at para 23), '[t]he difference between possession and occupation is rather technical . . . Nonetheless, it is . . . particularly important . . . in relation to alienation covenants'. He went on (at para 25):

> although one cannot lay down any immutable rule as to how a particular word or expression is to be construed in every document or lease, I consider that any court must be very cautious before construing the word 'possession' as extending to occupation that does not amount to possession.

His lordship was guided by the clear wording in *Lam Kee Ying Sdn Bhd v Lam Shes Tong (t/a Liam Joo Co)* [1975] AC 247 at 256, PC:

> A covenant which forbids a parting with possession is not broken by a lessee who in law retains the possession even though he allows another to use and occupy the premises.

The effect of a proviso on the construction of an alienation clause has been noted: see *Crestfort Ltd v Tesco Stores Ltd* at **11.4**.

11.8 Landlord's consent

11.8.1 General

The landlord's consent, or licence, must be obtained by the disponor who cannot force completion of the disposition without it. Where there is a contract for the disposition, it will normally be an express term of the contract that the disponor obtains the landlord's consent before completion. The disponor will be required by the landlord to pay its solicitor's costs for the preparation of the consent whether the matter proceeds to completion or not, but the disponor may well contract to recover these from the disponee.

As already indicated, where the alienation covenant is absolute – that is, there is an outright prohibition on any disposition of the lease – the landlord can refuse any request by the tenant for consent, however unreasonably: *FW Woolworth & Co Ltd v Lambert* [1937] Ch 37. The landlord has complete freedom to refuse or give consent.

Where the covenant is fully qualified, whether by its wording (as is usual) or by operation of s 19(1) of the LTA 1927, the question will arise whether consent was reasonably or unreasonably withheld. This may also involve considering whether conditions attaching to a consent are reasonable or not.

11.8.2 Reasonableness of refusal of consent

The general approach is that a broad view is to be taken when considering whether a landlord has reasonably withheld consent, based on the test of reasonableness. In setting out the test of reasonableness Lord Denning MR, in *Bickel v Duke of Westminster* [1976] 3 All ER 801, said that the question of reasonableness is one of fact to be decided according to the circumstances of each case, not a proposition of law to be applied in all cases. In *International Drilling Fluids Ltd v Louiseville Investments (Uxbridge) Ltd* [1986] 1 All ER 321, Balcombe LJ distilled the case law in a number of propositions:

1. The purpose of a covenant against assignment without consent is to protect the landlord from having his premises used or occupied in an undesirable way or by an undesirable tenant.

2. Consent cannot be refused on grounds unrelated to the relationship of landlord and tenant, such as some collateral purpose unconnected with the lease.

3. The onus of proving that consent has been unreasonably withheld is on the tenant.

4. It is not necessary for the landlord to prove that the conclusions which led him to refuse consent were justified if they were conclusions which a reasonable man might reach in the circumstances.

5. It may be reasonable for the landlord to refuse consent on the grounds of the intended use of the premises by the proposed assignee even if that use is not forbidden in the lease.

6. Refusal of consent may be unreasonable where it causes disproportionate harm to the tenant compared with the benefit to the landlord.

7. Subject to the foregoing, whether consent is being unreasonably withheld is a question of fact depending on the circumstances.

11.8.3 Landlord and Tenant Act 1988

In any but an absolute covenant, the landlord must not unreasonably withhold consent to an application for some form of alienation permitted under the alienation covenant. The LTA 1988 was passed to ensure that landlords who had been asked for consent did not delay in dealing with the application. The landlord is under a statutory duty to:

(a) give consent unless it is unreasonable to do so;

(b) serve on the tenant a written notice of its decision within a reasonable time;

(c) specify any conditions where conditional consent is given.

Breach of its statutory duty exposes the landlord to a claim for damages in tort. The burden of proof is on the landlord to show the reasonableness of a refusal or of any conditions attached to the consent.

The 1988 Act does not say what is a 'reasonable time', but a few weeks may be reasonable. In *Midland Bank plc v Chart Enterprises* [1990] 2 EGLR 59, 10 weeks' delay was unreasonable. Twenty eight days was held to be reasonable in *Dong Bang Minerva (UK) Ltd v Davina Ltd* [1995] 1 EGLR 41. Factors affecting the timescale will include what information the landlord seeks, when it is asked for and when it is provided.

Trivial reasons for refusing consent combined with delay and an agenda for getting a tenant out may lead to a finding that the landlord unreasonably withheld consent. In *Mount Eden Land Ltd v Folia Ltd* [2003] All ER (D) 374, an unpaid solicitor's bill of less than £600 and breach of a signage covenant (a covenant restricting the putting up of signs) were among the reasons put forward by the landlord for refusing consent to assign to a tenant who was desperate to assign. It was suspected that the landlord wanted to get the tenant out and relet at a higher rent. The landlord's aggressive stance was an abuse of the 1988 Act and Peter Smith J said (at para 198), 'I raise the possibility that as the breach [of L's statutory duty under the 1988 Act] was a tortious breach of statutory duty it would be quite possible to claim exemplary or punitive damages'.

The landlord should aim to avoid prolonging the matter by seeking further information in case it is held to have unreasonably withheld consent. In *Design Progression Ltd v Thurloe Properties Ltd* [2004] EWHC 324, a case which attracted much attention after it was decided, the defendant landlord was found to have deliberately delayed progress of the proposed assignment by repeated requests for further information, causing the tenant and the proposed assignee to miss a deadline and also causing the withdrawal of the proposed assignee. The landlord's motive for its cynical conduct was to try to force a surrender. Peter Smith J, following what he had said about the awarding of exemplary damages in *Mount Eden Land Ltd v Folia Ltd*, awarded the claimant £25,000 exemplary damages.

Allowance may be made, however, for the consideration of complex and significant financial matters and for holiday periods. So, in *NCR Ltd v Riverland Portfolio Ltd* [2005] EWCA Civ 312, 23 days was held by the Court of Appeal to be a reasonable time in which the landlord could consider its decision to refuse consent.

The 1988 Act does not give any guidance on the reasonableness or otherwise of a land-lord's response to a tenant's request to alienate but only requires a response to be given as the Act provides; as Lord Bingham said in *Ashworth Frazer Ltd v Gloucester City Council* [2002] 1 All ER 377 at para [2], 'the landlord owes the tenant a duty within a reasonable time to give consent, or give consent subject to notified conditions, or refuse consent for notified reasons'. If challenged by the tenant, the onus is on the landlord to show that its withholding of consent or the condition attached to a consent is reasonable.

11.8.4 Particular cases

11.8.4.1 User

Where an assignment will necessarily result in breach of the user clause, the landlord may reasonably refuse consent to the assignment: *Wilson v Flynn* [1948] 2 All ER 40. In *Killick v Second Covent Garden Property Co Ltd* [1973] 2 All ER 337, however, a landlord refused consent to assign because the proposed assignee intended to use the premises for a dif-ferent use from that authorised. The Court of Appeal held that where the landlord reasonably believed that the assignment was likely to lead to a breach of the user clause, a refusal of consent was unreasonable since the landlord was able to enforce the user clause against the assignee, in the event of a breach, in the same way as it could against the assignor. This decision tended to a proposition of law.

Following the decision in *Bickel* and approving of Lord Denning's test of reasonableness, the House of Lords in *Ashworth Frazer* overruled the decision of the Court of Appeal in *Killick*. Though Lord Bingham and Lord Rodger dissented on the construction of the user clause, all five law lords agreed that the test in Killick was too narrow and rigid. Lord Rodger pointed out (see para [67]) that the test of reasonableness, used in so many areas of law, is useful because it prevents the law from becoming unduly rigid. It allows the law to respond to different situations as they arise. Lord Rodgers said (para 68):

> it cannot be said, as a matter of law, that the belief of the landlord, however reasonable, that the proposed assignee intends to use the demised premises for a purpose which would give rise to a breach of a user covenant cannot, of itself, be a reasonable ground for withholding consent to the assignment.

He went on, '[t]he rule of law derived from *Killick's* case introduces a rigidity which makes it impossible to apply that approach. It should, for that reason, be rejected' (para 69). For comment, see: P Luxton, 'Inevitable or merely likely? Anticipated user and consent to assign', (2002) JBL, Jul, 466–74.

Since *Ashworth Frazer*, it can be said that where the landlord reasonably believes that a proposed assignee's use of the premises will breach the user clause, it may be reasonable to refuse consent, thought that reason alone may not suffice; if there is no objection to the proposed use beyond that it would breach the user clause, withholding consent could still be unreasonable.

In the case of a subletting, since the landlord is then not in a direct relationship with the subtenant, refusal of consent under *Ashworth Frazer* may be reasonable. Where the user clause is clearly positive (and the construction of the relevant clause in *Ashworth Frazer* was arguable), or where there is a 'keep-open' covenant (see **8.11**), it is likely that refusal of consent may be reasonable if a breach is thought likely: *FW Woolworth v Charlwood Alliance Properties Ltd* [1987] 1 EGLR 53.

11.8.4.2 Financial standing of proposed disponee

Landlords are obviously concerned to know, so far as possible, that a prospective assignee will be able to pay the rent and other payments due under the lease. It is reasonable for the landlord to require:

(a) references to be taken from accountants, banks, solicitors, traders and current and previous landlords;

(b) audited trading accounts covering three years;

(c) a guarantor if the landlord is not completely satisfied with the financial standing of a proposed assignee. In the case of a limited company, it will usually require two directors to guarantee the company;

(d) a rent deposit agreement. This is where the tenant puts on deposit in an account in joint names with the landlord a sum of money to which the landlord has recourse in the event of failure by the tenant to pay the rent.

If the landlord has reasonable reasons for doubt as to the financial strength of the tenant and its guarantor, then it may reasonably refuse consent.

Where a landlord has the right to insist on guarantors and the further right to approve them, it does not have to act reasonably but is free to dispute the suitability of any guarantors offered: *Mount Eden Land Ltd v Towerstone Ltd* [2002] EWHC 2545. In that case, the alienation clause allowed the claimant landlord to require two or more guarantors in the case of a proposed assignment to an unlisted company. The landlord had the right to approve the guarantors, and when it disapproved of those offered, the defendant claimed that the landlord had unreasonably refused to accept its guarantors. It was held that the landlord did not have to act reasonably in the exercise of its own judgment. The decision was given notwithstanding that the motive of the landlord was that it really wanted the tenant out and, indeed, no relief from forfeiture was granted.

However, reasons for refusal must be given to the tenant in writing within a reasonable time of the tenant's request and in replying to the tenant, the landlord brings to an end the 'reasonable time': *Go West Ltd v Spigarolo* [2003] 2 WLR 986.

To insist on a guarantor at a later stage when no guarantor could reasonably be required may amount to an unreasonable condition on consent to assign: *London & Argyll Developments Ltd v Mount Cook Land Ltd* [2002] 50 EG 111.

When deciding whether to give consent, the landlord should look beyond the accounts of a proposed assignee. Where a tenant wanted to assign to the company of a celebrity chef who was one of the few chefs in England to have been awarded three Michelin stars and whose company had strong guarantees, it was not in accord with commercial reality to base a decision only on accounts which showed an overall deficiency on the balance sheet due only to directors' drawings: *Old English Inns plc v Brightside Ltd* (2004) *The Times*, 30 June.

Where the lease was granted before 1 January 1996 (and so an old lease for the purposes of the Landlord and Tenant (Covenants) Act 1995), the existence of an original tenant whom the landlord could sue does not necessarily lessen the landlord's right to refuse consent to assign to a doubtful assignee. In *Ponderosa International Development Inc v Pengap Securities (Bristol)* [1986] 1 EGLR 66, L granted a lease of restaurant premises to T, a substantial concern. L's intention was then to sell its reversion. T wished to assign to M, a new company and franchisee of M. L refused on the ground that a weak tenant like M would harm the value of its reversion, though it would have consented to a subletting by T to M. In the circumstances, notwithstanding the covenant strength of T, L's refusal was reasonable. However, in *Venetian Glass Gallery Ltd v Next Properties Ltd* [1989] 2 EGLR 42, Harman J noted not only the apparent soundness of the assignee but referred to the fact that the original tenant would remain liable.

A landlord may be found to refuse unreasonably if it requires a guarantor for a subsidiary of sufficient substance since it is commercially unlikely that a parent company will allow its subsidiary to default: *Re Greater London Properties' Leases* [1959] 1 WLR 503.

In *Footwear Corporation Ltd v Amplight Ltd* [1998] 2 EGLR 38, Neuberger J, in disagreeing with the landlord's view that the accounts of a proposed subtenant were unsatisfactory, thought that covenant strength was more important in the case of an assignment than a subletting. His lordship pointed out that there is no rule that for accounts to be satisfactory a proposed tenant should show profits after tax equal to three times the rent.

11.8.4.3 Terms of proposed disposition

A landlord is entitled reasonably to refuse consent if the terms of a proposed disposition are not in accord with the terms of the lease. In *Allied Dunbar Assurance plc v Homebase Ltd* [2002] 2 EGLR 23, Homebase wanted to sublet overrented premises. It agreed in a collateral agreement with the prospective subtenant that the rent would be the same as the rent reserved by the head lease, as required by the alienation clause, but that Homebase would pay a rebate so that the real rent was the lower rent agreed. The Court of Appeal upheld the landlord's objections to the terms of this arrangement. But where, in a similar situation, the tenant agreed to pay the subtenant a reverse premium, the court held that this was not a breach of the alienation clause: *NCR Ltd v Riverland Portfolio No 1 Ltd* [2004] EWHC 921.

11.8.4.4 Breach of repairing covenant

A landlord may only reasonably refuse consent on the grounds of a breach of covenant by the tenant if the breach is serious. In relation to a repairing covenant, the more serious and longstanding the breach, the more likely that the landlord's refusal of consent, or the granting of consent subject to conditions, will be reasonable. Since the House of Lords' decision in *Ashworth Frazer*, the tenant is unlikely to be successful in arguing that the landlord would have the same rights of enforcement against the assignee as it would have against the tenant. Rather, it will be reasonable for the landlord to want to be satisfied that an assignee will be able to remedy any serious disrepair.

In *Orlando Investments Ltd v Grosvenor Estate Belgravia* (1990) 59 P & CR 21, the defendant sublet a large house in Belgravia. The claimant became the subtenant and agreed with the defendant to a scheme of repair for the property which was (unaccountably for a house in Belgravia) in very bad condition, being not even windtight and watertight. This agreement explains why the defendant had not taken proceedings for breach of the repairing covenant, though as a result of delays in implementing the scheme, this was later contemplated. The subtenant then decided to assign and asked for consent under the fully qualified alienation clause. The defendant responded that it would only consent to the assignment if the proposed assignee covenanted directly with the defendant to carry out the repair works and to offer security of £500,000 against failure to do the repairs.

Nourse LJ referred to the *International Drilling Fluids* case as providing guiding principles and the general rule that consent may be reasonably withheld if there is reason to suppose that the proposed assignee may commit substantial breaches of covenant. His lordship distinguished *Killick* on the grounds that where, as in the present case, there are existing serious breaches of covenant, the landlord is entitled to refuse consent unless it is reasonably satisfied that the proposed assignee is able to remedy the breaches. In the circumstances, the landlord was not being unreasonable.

11.8.4.5 Landlord's interests and estate management

Where the landlord lets out two premises near each other, it will be concerned to ensure that business competition does not prejudice the profitability of each. In *Premier Confectionery (London) Co Ltd v London Commercial Sale Rooms Ltd* [1933] Ch 904, a tenant ran two similar businesses and wanted to assign one of the premises. The landlord was held reasonably to have refused consent to the assignment because of the danger that the resulting competition would harm trade and so the ability to pay rent.

Similarly, in *Whiteminster Estates v Hodges Menswear Ltd* [1974] 232 EG 715, when a tenant wanted to assign premises to an assignee who planned to use the premises for a use similar to the landlord's use of its own nearby premises, refusal of consent was held to be reasonable.

In *Bromley Park Garden Estates Ltd v Moss* [1982] 2 All ER 890, a statement in *Woodfall* (28th edn, 1978) Vol 1, para 1181 was challenged by counsel for the appellant defendant and that challenge was upheld by the Court of Appeal. The statement said 'that a landlord may reasonably be influenced in his decision [to refuse consent] by considerations of the proper management of the estate of which the demised property forms part'. Cumming-Bruce LJ said (at 899) that, on the authorities he cited, this statement was 'misleading, and its reference to good estate management as a valid reason for withholding consent is altogether too wide'. His lordship did not say in what way the statement was too wide, but he cannot have meant that estate management could not be a valid reason for refusing consent. It cannot be inferred from this decision that estate management considerations may not be a ground for making refusal reasonable. Clearly, where estate management is put forward as a reason for refusing consent (whether of an assignment or a subletting), there must be sufficient evidence to support the reason: see *Footwear Corporation Ltd v Amplight Ltd.* Two cases deal with the point directly and substantively, and another makes reference to it.

In *Crown Estate Commissioners v Signet Group plc* [1996] 2 EGLR 200, the defendant tenants assigned the lease of premises in London's Regent Street (accepted as a premier retail site of international significance) to TTT without the landlord's consent. Signet (formerly Ratners) and TTT must have assumed that, faced with a *fait accompli*, the landlord would accept TTT as tenant. It did not, but served a s 146 of the LPA 1925 notice on TTT to forfeit the lease. The landlord's solicitors set out very carefully the reasons for their refusal. Those reasons focused on the landlord's estate management strategy for Regent Street which essentially aimed to increase, not decrease, retail floor space at ground floor level. TTT's use would have been in the service sector: travel agency, bureau de change and ticket sales. The landlord's retail management strategy was not set out in the lease or related documentation, but Judge Bromley QC considered that the landlord's estate management strategy was well-enough known and should not have been any surprise to any tenant. He thought that the 'unity' of the Regent Street Crown estate was known to tenants and that, in relation to one small unit of the estate, the landlord was entitled to have regard to 'general estate management considerations' on the facts of the case. He said further that 'while the lack of knowledge of policies in a particular case may go to the reasonableness of the refusal, this is not such a case, where the essential estate unity was known'.

Moss Bros Group plc v CSC Properties Ltd [1999] EGCS 47 concerned a shop unit in the Metro Centre in Gateshead. The fully-qualified user clause was subject to the user being, in the reasonable opinion of the landlord, consistent with the principles of good estate management. The authorised use was retail clothing and the surrounding units were also engaged in retail clothing. The claimant, trading as Cecil Gee, sought consent for assignment to Game (Stores) Ltd and for change of use to the sale of computer games and related items. The landlord refused consent to both applications on the grounds that the proposed use would be inconsistent with the landlord's tenant mix policy in that part of the Centre. Neuberger J, in contrast to his decision a year earlier in the *Footwear Corporation* case, rejected the tenant's complaint of unreasonable refusal. There was an overall policy of attracting anchor tenants (leading retailers who attract the public to wherever they are) and within that policy was a more limited policy of retail management in the relevant part of the centre. It did not matter that the latter policy was not published in a formal policy document.

In *NCR Ltd v Riverland Portfolio No 1 Ltd* (No 2) [2005] EWCA Civ 312, Carnwarth LJ said that a landlord needed adequate time to consider serious legal and financial implications when deciding whether to give consent. His lordship referred (at para [20]) to the 'estate-management issues that merited serious consideration'.

The first two of these three last-mentioned cases have been given more attention by surveyors than by lawyers. In a Royal Institution of Chartered Surveyors' research paper on landlord's perceptions of retail tenant mix and the management of shopping centres (ISBN 1-84219-031-8), Downie, Williamson and Fisher stress the *Moss Bros* case as 'most significant'. The authors quote other research as indicating that landlords should make known their tenant mix policy to facilitate using it as grounds for refusal of consent to assignment. At least such a policy should be enforced consistently. However, such a policy, when put in writing, needs to be drafted in such a way (that is, loosely) as to minimise depression of rental value. Moreover, as retail trends change ever more rapidly, the tenant mix policy needs constantly to be reviewed and changes implemented. The chief tools of implementation are suitably drafted user and alienation clauses combined with a clear and constantly updated tenant mix policy. Other tools are buying out tenants, moving tenants around, and landlords' break clauses. Whilst *Signet* and *Moss Bros* were decided the way they were, the boundary line between estate management being a means of defeating unwanted assignments and its being held to be unreasonable or unconnected to the terms of the lease or the policy being 'entirely outside the intention to be imputed to the parties at the time of the granting of the lease . . . or the assignment' (*Bromley Park Garden Estates Ltd v Moss per* Cumming-Bruce LJ at 899) is not easily drawn. Best practice, especially for shopping centres, is for landlords to:

(a) have a tenant mix policy;

(b) keep the policy under review;

(c) have a carefully drafted policy document;

(d) provide the policy document to all tenants and assignees;

(e) add a suitable proviso to the alienation clause to the effect that consent to an assignment may be refused if the proposed use is contrary to the published estate management strategy of the landlord as revised from time to time;

(f) respond early in writing to the tenant's request for consent.

11.8.4.6 Break clause

The landlord may refuse consent to an assignment where the tenant merely seeks to use the assignment as a way of avoiding overrenting by operation of a break clause. In *Olympia & York Canary Wharf Ltd v Oil Property Investments Ltd* [1994] 2 EGLR 48, L let office premises to T1 in 1985, a boom time in the market. In 1990, the reviewed rent was over £1m. In 1994, as a result of the recession of the early 1990s, the open market rent was put at £450,000. T1 had the benefit of a break clause. In 1987, T1 had assigned to T2 which later became insolvent. The premises were unassignable because of the rent and, because of T2's insolvency, T1 was obliged to pay the rent. Both T1 and T2 wanted to get out of the lease, so they had the idea of assigning the lease back to T1 who would then operate the break clause. Not surprisingly, L refused consent and the Court of Appeal upheld L's refusal. Furthermore, such a scheme would be objectionable on the grounds that it would diminish the value of the landlord's reversion.

11.8.4.7 Security of tenure

Where a tenant without security of tenure wanted to grant a sublease, it was reasonable for the landlord to require that the sublease be contracted out of security of tenure: Re *Cooper's Lease* [1968] 19 P & CR 541.

12 Service charges

12.1 Introduction

Service charges arise when there is multiple occupation of the landlord's premises. Throughout this chapter, the landlord's property is referred to as 'premises', whilst the parts let to tenants are called 'units'. Shopping centres, office blocks, some industrial and mixed use buildings are the types of premises designed for multiple occupation. When leases of units are granted in such premises, they are called 'leases of part'. The physical definition of each of the units in the parcels clause of the lease of the unit is of the highest importance. When all the units in the premises are let, their total and the parts of the premises retained by the owner should add up to the whole of the premises. There must be no gaps left for which responsibility is then uncertain: see **10.2**.

In multi-let premises, it is often the case that tenants will be responsible for very little in the way of repair and maintenance because what is let is really just space bounded by surface finishes. The landlord will retain the structure of the building and of what are called 'common parts': entrance areas, corridors, stairs, lift shafts, service areas and all other parts of the premises not to be let. There may be also external areas such as driveways, car parks and gardens; the landlord will retain these. The landlord will also retain plant and machinery servicing the premises: lifts, escalators, air conditioning and heating, plant associated with services (water, gas and electricity) and so forth. In some cases, management and security personnel are provided. Shopping centres must promote themselves and so marketing will then be undertaken. The more complex the premises, the greater the range of provision to be made.

Landlords aim to maintain the value and quality of their premises whilst receiving rental income without deduction. Tenants aim to have their businesses benefit from the services provided at reasonable cost to keep down overheads. These respective concerns clearly offer scope for conflict and, given the often high cost of service charges and their complexity, there is as much scope for disagreement as there is with payment of rent, and perhaps even more scope for ill feeling.

There is no statutory regulation of commercial service charges. They are entirely matters of contract and so depend on the relevant clauses in the lease. In order to promote good practice and good relations between landlords and tenants, the property industry (in the form of the Royal Institution of Chartered Surveyors, the British Council of Shopping

Centres, the British Property Federation, the British Retail Consortium, the Property Managers Association, and the Shopping Centre Management Group) published *Service Charges in Commercial Property: A Guide to Good Practice* (2nd edn, August 2000) (available at www.servicechargeguide.co.uk) (referred to here as 'the Guide'). Landlords and tenants were encouraged to use the Guide in the interpretation of service charge clauses and in resolving differences. Much of the Guide is taken up with Appendices which illustrate the various mechanisms for managing service charge matters.

A new Code has been published: the *Service Charges in Commercial Property RICS Code of Practice*, published on 26 June 2006 ('the Code'). The Code replaces the Guide for service charges from 1 April 2007. It is available at www.servicechargecode.co.uk. The Code is an official RICS publication and it is clear that practitioners are expected to use it even though it is not binding.

It remains, however, that landlords expect none of their rental income to suffer deduction but that all expenditure on services should be recoverable from the tenants. Landlords want what are called 'clear leases' which are 'leases in which the tenants bear all the costs and risks of repairing, maintaining and running the building of which their demised premises form part, so that the rent payable reaches the landlord clear of all expenses and overheads': *O'May v City of London Real Property Co Ltd* [1982] All ER 660, 671 *per* Lord Wilberforce. This is especially the concern of institutional landlords – insurance companies and pension funds – which have liabilities of their own to meet.

On the other hand, service charges should not be a way of generating profit for landlords. It is suggested in *Woodfall* (Part 1, 7.175) that service charge provisions would be construed so as not to allow a landlord to make a profit but there is no clear authority on this.

The construction of service charge clauses was considered by HH Michael Rich QC in *Earl of Cadogan v 27/29 Sloane Gardens Ltd* [2006] 24 EG 178. Though concerned with the service charge for a caretaker's flat, the judge made the following remarks on the construction of service charges (at para 20):

(i) It is for the landlord to show that a reasonable tenant would perceive that the underlease [as it happened to be in the case] obliged it to make the payment sought.

(ii) Such conclusion must emerge clearly and plainly from the words used.

(iii) Thus, if words used could reasonably be read as providing for some other circumstance, the landlord will fail to discharge the onus upon it.

(iv) This does not, however, permit the rejection of the natural meaning of the words in their context on the basis of some other fanciful meaning or purpose, and the context may justify a 'liberal' meaning.

(v) If consideration of the clause leaves an ambiguity, the ambiguity will be resolved against the landlord as 'profferor'.

(The reference to 'profferor' is a reference to the *contra proferentum* rule, one of the rules of construction, which is that, when ambiguity arises in a matter of construction, that ambiguity is to be resolved by construing wording against the party 'proffering' (from the verb to 'proffer', Latin *pro* and *offerre*, to offer forward). A lease is 'proffered' by a landlord.)

Thus, a service charge clause should be construed in the usual way by construing words according to their natural meaning in their context, but against the landlord if ambiguity prevents such construction. See comment by S Murdoch, (2006) Estates Gazette, 17 June, 175.

12.2 **Provision in the lease**

A typical lease will provide for the service charge in the following ways:

- the definition section at the beginning of the lease will define 'service charge' and 'services';

- there will be a specific tenant's covenant to pay the service charge;

- there will be a landlord's covenant to provide services;

- details of the service charge, often in a schedule, setting out definitions of terms, eg 'accounting' or 'financial' year; 'plant'; accounting procedures; actual services provided. These details are important because the tenant can only be charged for services specifically set out in the lease.

The services provided will include (depending on the nature of the premises):

- repairing, decorating and maintaining retained parts – the wording of this provision must be read carefully by the tenant's solicitor who should try to avoid tenant's liability for reimbursing the cost to the landlord of inherent defects;

- plant and machinery;

- heating, air conditioning and lighting of retained parts;

- fire precautions and equipment;

- refuse collection;

- cleaning;

- garden and landscape maintenance;

- services to retained parts (water, gas, electricity, toilets);

- maintaining the structural parts of the premises and boundary features;

- signage;

- payment of outgoings for retained parts;

- legal and other professional fees;

- employment of staff to provide security, reception, management and administration;

- CCTV systems;

- promotional activities – shopping centres must advertise, maintain a website, and provide seasonal decorations and activities since the weeks before Christmas are the busiest time of the year (so retailers hope) and income during November and December accounts for a large proportion of income for the year.

The costs of these items vary a great deal, but cleaning and security may account for about half the total expenditure.

Tenants need to have regard to a number of concerns. As premises get older, they need more repair and maintenance, and costs may well increase over previous years. If high-cost remedial work is needed, this may inflate the service charge significantly for one or two years which would be burdensome for a tenant who did not plan to stay so long as to gain a proportionate benefit. A tenant may feel aggrieved if it has to pay a share of the cost of some work in, say, a distant part of a centre, from which it thinks it gains no benefit. Since the wording in the lease is determinative, close reading of the service charge provisions is necessary.

12.3 Apportionment of service charges

In paras 58–65, the Guide (see **12.1**) sets out its recommendations for apportionment:

58   Apportionment of costs to each occupier should be on a fair and reasonable basis, in accordance with the principles of good estate management and applied fairly and consistently throughout the property having regard to the physical size, nature of use and the benefit to the occupier or occupiers.

59   An apportionment schedule should be available showing the total apportionment for each unit within the property/complex.

60   The occupiers should not be charged through the service charge or otherwise collectively toward the costs attributable to unlet premises. Also, the owner should meet the costs of any special concession given by an owner to any one occupier. A properly constituted weighting formula is not regarded as a special concession.

61   The owner should bear a fair proportion of costs attributable to his use of the property e.g. where a centre management suite is used in part as the owner's regional office.

62   Where there is a separate cost/profit centre within a property complex that generates income for the owner, which is not credited to the service charge account, the costs associated with maintaining and running the costs centre should not be allocated to the service charge account (e.g. car parks).

63   Where services are provided for the benefit of specific occupiers only, these costs should be allocated to the specific occupiers that benefit from or need them.

64   If the property is fully let the owner should normally be able to recover all expenditure on services through the service charge.

65   The estimated budget of service charge expenditure and certified accounts should set out the method and calculation used to determine each occupier's share of the costs and how costs are apportioned.

As with the rest of the Guide, these recommendations cannot take precedence over the terms of the lease, but the Guide does aim to provide parties with a basis for interpretation and application of lease terms.

The Code (see **12.1**) sets out apportionment methods at section D4.

There are a number of ways of calculating the amount of service charge each tenant has to pay. None of them is entirely satisfactory but it is clear that some methods are more appropriate to certain kinds of premises than others, and that some methods are fairer than others. Solicitors acting for prospective tenants and assignees must examine the service charge provisions very carefully; of course, leases for units must be in standard form and landlords are unlikely to agree variations – leases of units in large complex premises such as a major shopping centre are offered on a 'take it or leave it' basis. The solicitor, however, must advise his client so that the client understands the likely measure of its liability.

12.3.1 Fixed proportion

This method fixes the amount payable according to the number of units in the premises, eg if there are 10 units, the charge is 10%. This has the advantage of being certain and simple, but it is inflexible, can lead to under- or over- recovery, and may be unfair since it takes no account of varying usage by tenants of services. It is only likely to be used in small premises with a few similar units let for short terms.

12.3.2 Rateable value

The Government calculates that there are 1.75 million business properties in England for the purposes of valuation for rates (Scotland and Wales have their own systems). The Valuation Office Agency is responsible for administering the system. Business properties do not pay council tax as owners of domestic properties do; they pay business rates. All non-domestic properties have a rateable value which is based on an assessment of the annual rent of a property if it was available to rent on the open market at a certain date, the 'fixed valuation date'. New rating lists for all these properties came into effect on 1 April 2005 and will endure for five years. Rateable value is not the amount paid in business rates. It is a calculation arrived at by multiplying the rateable value of the property by a fixed multiplier which is set by the Government each year. This multiplier is called the 'uniform business rate'. For further details, see www.mybusinessrates.gov.uk.

This method is calculated as the percentage that the rateable value of the unit bears to the rateable value of the total number of units (and so excludes the retained parts). It can be unfair since it takes no account of changes in rateable values and may be unrelated to the services provided. However, a formula can be built in to allow for recalculation as rateable values change. There may be problems associated with this system if a tenant successfully appeals against assessment by the valuation officer since this would trigger a claim for reimbursement of a portion of the service charge. Such a scenario creates undue administrative and accounting difficulties.

12.3.3 Floor area

The Guide notes (Appendix 5) that this is the most common method of apportioning charges and is the fairest in most cases. The standard floor area is the ratio of the unit to the total lettable parts of the premises. In calculating floor area, two means of measurement are used: for industrial units, the gross internal area; for offices and shops, the net internal area. Floor areas are calculated using the RICS *Code of Measuring Practice*, and the lease ought to provide for this if this is the method of apportionment used. The *Code of Measuring Practice* is published by the RICS (5th edn, 2001). For the importance of correct measurement, see: *Kilmartin SCI (Hulton House) v Safeway Stores* [2006] EWHC 60. This method may be suitable where all tenants make proportionate use of services but could cause unfairness in some situations where they do not.

12.3.4 Weighted floor area

In large shopping centres, there is no simple relation between the size of a unit and the costs involved. As the Guide notes (Appendix 5), 'a 5.000sq. m. unit will not cost 5 times that of a 1,000 sq. m. unit, but a 500 sq. m. unit may cost twice that of a 250 sq. m. unit.' The Guide has illustrations of tables for weighting of floor areas. Most lawyers will be happy to leave such matters to the surveyors! The Code similarly has tables for calculating weighted floor area.

12.3.5 Payment of service charge

The amount of service charge for an accounting year cannot be known until the accounts have been prepared. During the year, the landlord incurs expenditure on a regular basis. To meet this, there will be provision for tenants to pay advance or interim payments either quarterly or half-yearly. These sums may be such as the landlord's surveyor certifies to be fair and reasonable and based on the anticipated amount of the service charge, subject to revision to cover some known or expected increase in expenditure.

The lease may provide that the landlord must prepare final accounts as soon as possible after the financial year end and give the service charge account to the tenant. The service charge must be paid within a set time, say seven days, after the delivery of the landlord's account. Credit will be given for the sums paid on account.

Payments of service charges are often reserved as additional rent. This means that the landlord has the same remedies for non-payment as for non-payment of rent, that is, it can distrain as for rent, and service of a s 146 notice (see **14.2.3.2**) is not required. On the other hand, the procedure for non-payment of rent gives the tenant statutory and equitable rights of relief. The landlord must consider whether payments of service charges are to be treated as rent or not.

12.3.6 Sinking funds

A sinking fund involves tenants paying a fixed amount regularly into a fund which builds up over time and can be used to pay for items which will incur expenditure at intervals, such as redecoration every 5 years, or replacement of, say, air conditioning every, say, 20 years. It is much like the case of a householder who puts so much aside each month into a separate bank account as a contingency fund. A sinking fund avoids one-off heavy items of expenditure which can be planned for, and is fairer to tenants who come and go in the meantime.

Tenants, however, have to check what happens to the money in a sinking fund if it is not used. In *Secretary of State for the Environment v Possfund (North West) Ltd* [1997] 2 EGLR 56, £1 million of sinking fund money had not been used to replace air conditioning equipment by the time the lease ended, and the court held that the money belonged to the landlord since it had been by way of indemnity and not on account. Clearly, tenants should press for a provision that unused sums in the sinking fund should be returned to them.

12.3.7 Taxation

The tax position in relation to service charges is complex and specialist advice should be sought.

12.3.8 Disputes

As in other areas of practice, parties are nowadays encouraged to use dispute resolution procedures rather than litigation. The courts encourage this and at trial a judge will want to know why any available form of alternative dispute resolution (ADR) was not used. The Code, at section D8, sets out details of the RICS dispute resolution scheme, use of which is part of best practice.

13 Ending a business tenancy

13.1 Introduction

There are many ways a tenancy can be ended, some of which are remedies by the landlord or the tenant. Some of these methods are not often encountered in the practice of commercial property law, and general books such as Gray and Gray and *Megarry & Wade* deal with all the possible methods.

There are two distinct areas of law: termination at common law and termination under the Landlord and Tenant Act 1954. Most business tenancies will be terminated, if not continued, in accordance with the 1954 Act: see **Chapter 15**. A distinct and very controversial method of termination is forfeiture which may well be abolished in the near future. Forfeiture is dealt with in **Chapter 14**. In this chapter we look at other common law methods of termination. These are:

- effluxion of time;
- notice to quit;
- break clause;
- surrender;
- repudiatory breach;
- disclaimer.

13.2 Effluxion of time

'A lease or tenancy for a fixed term comes to an end by effluxion of time on the date fixed for its determination': *Barrett v Morgan* [2000] 1 All ER 481 at 484 *per* Lord Millett. Such is the position at common law. Where statutory regulation intervenes, the common law position does not apply. In the case of business tenancies, Pt II of the Landlord and Tenant Act 1954 may operate: see **Chapter 15**. Where, however, that statutory protection applied but has then been lost, the common law applies: *Esselte AB v Pearl Assurance plc* [1997] 2 All ER 41 (see **15.2.2**).

13.3 Notice to quit

Notice to quit is the common law method of ending a periodic tenancy. 'A periodic tenancy comes to an end on the expiry of a notice to quit served by the landlord on the tenant or by the tenant on the landlord': *Barrett v Morgan* at 484 *per* Lord Millett. It is of the essence of a periodic tenancy that either party be able to give notice since it is an inherently consensual arrangement. The length of notice may be express in which case, of course, the notice must comply with the express terms to be effective. If there is no express provision as to notice (perhaps because the tenancy itself arose by implication), then the length of notice must end the tenancy at the end of the rental period. For a yearly tenancy, there must be six months' notice expiring on the anniversary of the start of the tenancy. For a monthly tenancy, the notice must be one month, and for a weekly tenancy, one week.

13.4 Break clauses

These are sometimes called 'options to determine'. Commercially, break clauses can be very valuable and there is a considerable body of case law about them. A break clause is an agreement that a fixed-term lease can be ended early on notice by either or both the landlord or the tenant. The most common provision is that the break clause can be operated by one party at an agreed time during the lease. For example, in a lease for 12 years, the break clause may be operated in the sixth year of that term. It is usual in the property industry to speak of a 'landlord's break clause' and of 'a tenant's break clause'.

13.4.1 Who may break?

A break clause which is not expressed to be personal to the party with the benefit of it but is for the benefit of the party for the time being, runs with the term of the lease or the freehold reversion (according to whether it is for the tenant or the landlord respectively). That means that if, for instance, an original tenant has the benefit of a break clause but then assigns the lease to an assignee, the benefit passes to the assignee. Similarly with a landlord's break clause and any assignment of the reversion. Such will only be the case where the assignment is legal and not merely equitable and, in many cases, the assignment will only become legal on completion of registration at the Land Registry.

Often, however, a break clause is expressed to be personal to the party who has the benefit of it and then will not run with the term. If it is personal to, say, the tenant, the benefit will be lost on any assignment by that tenant. In *3M United Kingdom plc v Linklaters & Paines* [2006] EWCA Civ 530, leases were granted by Provident Mutual Life Assurance Association to 3M United Kingdom plc and included break clauses which were an important part of 3M's corporate restructuring. On assignment from one company to another within the 3M group, the benefit of the break clauses was lost because the break clauses had been personal to the original tenant in the following terms:

> If the Tenant (here meaning only 3M United Kingdom plc) shall desire to determine the term hereby granted at the expiration of the tenth year thereof and shall give to the

Landlord not less than twelve months' notice in writing of such desire (in this Clause referred to as 'the Option Notice') then on the expiration of the Option Notice this lease shall absolutely cease and be void but without prejudice to the rights of the Landlord in respect of any antecedent breach of covenant.

Such is the rigour of this rule that even if there is an assignment which causes the tenant to lose the break clause and there is then a reassignment to that same tenant, the break clause will still be lost. This issue arose in *3M* and Chadwick LJ said (at para 25):

The suggestion . . . that the problem could be solved by a reassignment of the leases to the original tenant was based on a misunderstanding of the law – as Mr Justice Lightman had pointed out in *Max Factor Limited v Wesleyan Assurance Society* [1996] 74 P & CR 8, decided some three and a half months earlier.

Furthermore, as we saw at **11.8.4.6**, a landlord in such circumstances cannot be required to consent to a reassignment for that purpose: *Olympia & York Canary Wharf Ltd v Oil Property Investments Ltd* [1994] 2 EGLR 48.

In short, once a party with the benefit of a break clause which is expressed to be personal to it and it alone parts with its interest (the tenant assigns the lease or the landlord assigns its reversion), the benefit is lost for good and cannot be revived for that or any other person.

Where a tenant has the benefit of a break clause which is personal to it and the landlord then assigns the reversion, the tenant may exercise the break clause against the new landlord: *System Floors Ltd v Ruralpride Ltd* [1995] 1 EGLR 48. This case involved a lease granted in 1987 and a side letter of the same date containing terms for the determination of the lease on three months' notice after any rent review date. The Court of Appeal, comprising Leggatt, Millett and Morritt LJJ, held that the obligation to accept notice under the terms of the side letter was binding on the assignee of the reversion. The commercial reality for such a finding was 'compelling' in that it cannot have been the intention that the benefit and burden of the terms for determination could have been so easily circumvented by the original landlord.

13.4.2 Break clauses and security of tenure

Where a lease containing a landlord's break clause is one to which Pt II of the Landlord and Tenant Act 1954 applies, the landlord's notice according to the terms of the break clause is only effective at common law to end the tenancy which will continue to have statutory protection until determined in accordance with the 1954 Act (see **Chapter 15**). The landlord must therefore also serve notice under s 25 of the 1954 Act.

If a lease with security of tenure has a tenant's break clause, then the tenant may activate it according to its terms. What a tenant may not do is to use a break clause to end a lease when the premises are over-rented and then apply for a new tenancy under the 1954 Act with a view to getting a new tenancy at a market rent which, because of the state of the market, would be lower than that currently payable: *Garston v Scottish Widows Fund* [1998] 3 All ER 596, CA.

13.4.3 Break clause notices

There is a lot of case law about the construction and validity of break clause notices. Break clause notices must comply strictly with the terms of the break clause and failure to do so will usually cause loss of the benefit of the break clause.

13.4.4 Time is of the essence

Because a break clause is a privilege, there is a presumption that time is of the essence in the service of notices: *United Scientific Holdings v Burnley Borough Council* [1977] 2 All ER 62, 72 *per* Lord Diplock. Where there is no mistake as to the computation of time, this rule will stand: see **1.3.4**.

13.4.5 Mistakes in notices

Failure properly to serve a break clause notice in time when there is no mistake as to the computation of the relevant time is one thing. A separate issue is where there is a mistake in a break clause notice due to miscalculation of the date by which the notice must be served. This is one of those instances in which there can be confusion as to what is meant by terms which set deadlines.

The leading case is *Mannai Investment Co Ltd v Eagle Star Life Assurance Co Ltd* [1997] 3 All ER 352. It is worth mentioning that the judge at first instance came to his decision on the basis of an authority which the House of Lords thought was not authority for his decision, that the Court of Appeal unanimously found in favour of the landlord, and that the House of Lords found in favour of the tenant only by a majority of three to two. Thus, of the nine judges who considered the case, five favoured the landlord's position, but the majority decision of the House of Lords meant that the tenant won the case.

The facts were as follows. The tenant, Mannai, held a lease of premises in Jermyn Street, London for term of 10 years from 13 January 1992. The tenant's break clause allowed the tenant to end the lease by serving not less than six months' notice in writing, such notice to expire on the third anniversary of the term. The tenant served a notice purporting to end the lease on 12 January 1995. This was a mistake. The anniversary of a date is not the day before: after all, if someone was born on 13 January, he celebrates the anniversary of his birthday on 13 January, not the day before on 12 January. Had the break clause said, 'the end of the third year of the term', then 12 January would have been correct. Was the mistake fatal to the exercise of the break clause?

Lords Goff and Jauncey said it was. A notice must comply with the specification in the lease. The settled practice was clear and certain and to depart from it would create uncertainty even if a strict test were devised under which such errors might not make a notice void. The majority favoured such a test which has become known as the 'reasonable recipient test'. This is an objective test which asks how a reasonable recipient of the notice with knowledge of the terms of the lease would have understood it. In the case itself, the reasonable recipient would have had no doubt of the intended purpose of the notice and would not have been perplexed by the error.

The decision of the House of Lords in *Mannai* has spread to other areas of the law where notices have to be construed, and not only to common law notices but in some cases to statutory ones also: see *York v Casey* [1998] 2 EGLR 25 and *Speedwell Estates Ltd v Dalziel* [2002] 02 EG 104. *Mannai* has also been used to defeat an argument that the timescale in a break clause was ambiguous: *Trafford MBC v Total Fitness (UK) Ltd* [2003] 2 P & CR 8 (and see Precedent Editor's Case Notes [2003] 67 Conv 270). It should not be assumed, however, that *Mannai* will always come to the rescue.

In *Procter & Gamble Technical Centres Ltd v Brixton plc* [2002] EWHC 2835, Ch, Procter & Gamble was the claimant tenant and Brixton was the defendant landlord. The lease contained a tenant's break clause which was not personal to the original tenant and allowed the tenant to end the lease on either 24 December 1999 or 24 December 2002 (the end of the fifth and eighth years of the term – note the difference from the wording in *Mannai*). There was a restructuring of Procter & Gamble which involved two assignments of the lease. When it was decided to operate the break clause in 1999, notice was served on the landlord. However, the name of the tenant given in the notice was wrong. The landlord argued (i) that the tenant did not have the necessary desire to end the lease; (ii) that the notice was not served by the tenant; and (iii) that the notice was not valid on its face. The tenant got over the first two hurdles but fell at the third. Neuberger J, following the Court of Appeal decision in *Lemmerbell Ltd v Britannia LAS Direct Ltd* [1998] 3 EGLR 67, reluctantly agreed that the solicitor's serving the notice on behalf of a company which was not the tenant made the notice invalid. The fact that a mistake had been made could not make it obvious to a reasonable recipient that the real tenant intended to break (even though it did), since how could the landlord know this? The notice could not tell the landlord what the tenant's solicitor knows about the tenant. The authority that the tenant's solicitor certainly had to act for the real tenant could not somehow correct the mistake because, again, how could the landlord know that the necessary desire should be imputed to the real tenant just because the company which purported to operate the break clause was in the same group? As Neuberger J pointed out (at para 23), 'those who live by the sword of choosing to set corporate structures, often to take advantage of company and revenue law, sometimes die by the sword'.

More generally, his lordship made clear that there are two aspects of validity of notices to be considered. The first is the formal requirements for the notice. Time limits and other conditions must be complied with strictly. Secondly, there are the contents of the notice, and, following *Mannai*, these are not to be so strictly assessed. If the notice clearly and unambiguously communicates the required message, some error will not invalidate the notice. But even so, said his lordship (at para 20), that does not mean 'that the proper approach to the validity of the contents of a notice enables any error to be overlooked'. He added (at para 35) that the House of Lords in *Mannai*, 'did not give a green light to inaccurate and sloppily drafted notices'. (See article by S Murdoch (2003) Estates Gazette, 7 June, 133.)

13.4.6 Material compliance

Break clauses may be unconditional and only correct service of notice at the right time is needed to make the break. It is common for the operation of a tenant's break clause to be conditional on the tenant having complied with conditions. The most usual of these conditions are that the rent has been paid; there are no breaches of covenant outstanding; and the tenant gives vacant possession on the date of the break. Since, as Neuberger J mentioned in the *3M* case (see **13.4.1**), compliance with conditions in the break clause is strict, it may be very difficult or even impossible for the tenant to comply. For example, the landlord may claim that there is a breach of the repairing covenant: any property, as every householder knows, is always in need of some attention. The *Mannai* case did not relax the rule that there must be strict compliance with conditions in a break clause. As Lord Hoffmann, in his speech in *Mannai* put it, '[i]f the clause had said that the notice had to be on blue paper, it would have been no good serving a notice on pink paper, however clear it might have been that the tenant wanted to terminate the lease': [1997] 3 All ER at 377. Given that it could be impossible to comply absolutely with them, conditions are sometimes qualified so that the tenant must comply 'materially', 'reasonably' or 'substantially' with the conditions. These matters were reviewed by Jacob J in *Reed Personnel Services plc v American Express Ltd* [1997] 1 EGLR 229 where his lordship cited *Bass Holdings Ltd v Morton Music Ltd* [1987] 1 EGLR 214 as an example of a requirement of absolute compliance. In *Reed*, there was a condition of reasonable performance and observance of the covenants in the lease. On the facts, there had been a failure to comply, so there was no break and the tenancy continued.

The issue has been more recently considered by the Court of Appeal in *Fitzroy House Epworth Street (No 1) Ltd v The Financial Times Ltd* [2005] EWCA Civ 329; [2006] 19 EG 174. The case concerned a building worth some £12m with a rental value of £750,000 a year. The break clause required material compliance by the tenant with its obligations in the lease. The tenant operated the break clause and carried out substantial repairs in order to effect compliance. The landlord did not take the opportunity offered by the tenant to inspect the works but, after the tenant quit the building, claimed non-compliance. The effect of the outstanding works on reletting was valued at £15,000. The Chancellor, Sir Andrew Morritt (with whose speech Jacob and Moore-Brick LJJ agreed), said that 'material' and 'substantial' meant the same thing but 'reasonable' meant a different test. Materiality did not modify the strict test so as to create fairness between the landlord and the tenant, but neither did it mean that only trivial and trifling breaches could be overlooked. The correct test is an objective one, applying 'material' as an ordinary English word. The test is that in a commercial context '[m]ateriality must be assessed by reference to the ability of the landlord to relet or sell the property without delay or additional expenditure' (at para 35). On the facts as found by the judge at first instance, the defects complained of were insubstantial and had no effect on the landlord's ability to relet, and the damage to the landlord's reversion was negligible or nil. Accordingly, there had been compliance and the operation of the break clause was effective.

Landlords should be aware that if, following proper operation of a break clause, they then enter into a settlement with the tenant, releasing it from its liabilities in return for payment, they cannot then resile from the settlement but will be taken to have waived their rights under the break clause even though the tenant is in breach. A full and final settlement will mean that the lease had been validly ended: *Legal & General Assurance Society Ltd v Expeditors International (UK) Ltd* [2006] 18 EG 151.

13.5 Surrender

In the context of business tenancies, surrender will normally mean express surrender. Implied surrender is more likely to be encountered in the area of residential tenancies. Surrender is the giving up of the lease to the landlord so that the lease merges with the superior estate. Since it is a dealing with a legal estate, the surrender must be by deed, unless the lease is for three years or less. If the lease is registered at the Land Registry, an application must be made to close the register for that title.

If the lease to be surrendered is protected by the provisions of Pt II of the Landlord and Tenant Act 1954, a surrender may still be effected because s 24(2) says that s 24(1), which confers security of tenure, shall not prevent the coming to an end of a tenancy by surrender.

Where, before a lease which will be protected by the 1954 Act is entered into, the parties wish to agree that it may be surrendered, then the procedure in the 1954 Act must be followed. Section 38A(2) provides that the parties may agree that the tenancy shall be surrendered on such date or in such circumstances as may be specified in the agreement and on such terms as may be specified. To be a valid agreement, the landlord must have served notice on the tenant using a form as prescribed in Sch 3 to the Regulatory Reform (Business Tenancies) (England and Wales) Order 2003 (SI 2003/3096) and have complied with the requirements in Sch 4 to that Order. The form has a 'health warning' telling the tenant that it will be giving up its rights under the 1954 Act. The requirements are that the landlord should serve the notice on the tenant not less than 14 days before the lease is entered into or the tennant becomes contractually bound to do so. The tenant must then make a simple declaration acknowledging the notice. If the parties cannot wait 14 days, the landlord must serve notice on the tenant before the lease is entered into or before the tenant is contractually bound to do so. In this case, the tenant must make a statutory declaration which is in similar terms to the simple declaration.

13.6 Acceptance of repudiatory breach

This relatively recent aspect of business tenancies is an example of the import of contract law into landlord and tenant law. Under the general law of contract, a breach by one party which indicates an intention not to be bound by the contract can be accepted by the other party as repudiating the contract. One party repudiates the contract – the other accepts that, and the contract is ended.

The first case which applied this principle was *Hussein v Mehlman* [1992] 2 EGLR 87. At the Wood Green (London) Trial Centre, Stephen Sedley QC, sitting as an Assistant Recorder, had to deal with the following facts. The landlord, Mr Mehlman, had let a house to Mr Hussein. The landlord became in breach of his repairing obligations. Such was the extent of the breach that Mr Hussein left the house and handed in the keys to the agent. The Assistant Recorder noted how much contract law had been imported into landlord and tenant law, and he held that the landlord's breach amounted to repudiation of the tenancy agreement and the tenant's action in leaving was acceptance of that repudiation. This decision meant that a tenancy, though an estate in land, could be ended according to contract law.

This decision was echoed by the Court of Appeal in *Chartered Trust plc v Davies* [1997] 2 EGLR 83. When the landlord (actually, the mortgagee in possession) of a shopping centre consistently failed, over some 18 months, to prevent a nuisance caused by a neighbouring shop to the tenant's shop, the tenant, driven out of business by the nuisance, left the shop. The landlord sued for arrears of rent but the court held that the landlord's failure to abate the nuisance was repudiatory breach which the tenant had accepted by quitting the shop.

The courts will be alert to attempts by tenants to use acceptance of repudiatory breach to get out of a lease it no longer wants. In *Nynehead Developments Ltd v RH Fibreboard Containers Ltd* [1999] 1 EGLR 7, the landlord, Nynehead, owned part of an industrial estate. The defendant was tenant of a unit on that part of the estate. On the forecourt of the units of which that of the defendant was part, tenants could park vehicles. The defendant complained to the landlord about inconsiderate parking by other tenants which was claimed to be damaging to its business. The landlord did nothing about this. The defendant found it needed larger premises but had not been able to assign its current premises. When the tenant handed in the keys and left, claiming acceptance of the landlord's alleged repudiation, the judge was not inclined to allow the tenant an easy escape route from a lease it did not want. For comment, see: P. Luxton, 'Repudiatory Breach of Leases: Furore on the Forecourt, *Nynehead Developments Ltd v RH Fibreboard Containers Ltd* [1999] 1 EGLR 7, [1999] JBL 471.

13.7 Disclaimer

It has already been said in various parts of this book that a number of areas of legal practice within the field of commercial property are best dealt with by specialists. Insolvency is one of them. In firms of any size, property lawyers, property litigation lawyers, banking and finance lawyers, and insolvency lawyers all bring to the client's property matters their respective skills. Disclaimer is an aspect of insolvency law and so what is said here serves only to highlight some basic points; insolvency lawyers will deal with matters of any complexity.

A trustee in bankruptcy (in respect of an individual) or a liquidator (in respect of a company) may disclaim onerous property. A lease may be disclaimed because it involves liability to pay money and to perform onerous obligations. Commercial leases have little or no capital value and so disclaimer is likely to follow on from any insolvency of the tenant.

Proceedings to disclaim are governed by the Insolvency Act 1986. There are, however, separate provisions according to whether the insolvency is the bankruptcy of an individual or the liquidation of a company.

The effect of disclaimer is to end all rights and liabilities of the tenant under the lease. If rent or other sums are outstanding, the landlord must stand in line with other creditors.

14 Forfeiture

14.1 Introduction

Forfeiture is the early termination of the lease by the landlord when the tenant is in breach of covenant either to pay the rent or some other obligation. This is so provided a lease contains a clause allowing forfeiture, called a proviso for re-entry, which commercial leases invariably do. Periodic tenancies can be terminated by notice to quit, so forfeiture relates to fixed-term tenancies. The remedy is drastic. The lease is brought to an end and the tenant loses – forfeits – its right to the lease. So draconian is this action that it is sometimes called the landlord's 'nuclear option'. Forfeiture is part of the general law of landlord and tenant and so does not apply only to business tenancies. So far as business tenancies are concerned, forfeiture is not affected by the security of tenure provisions in Pt II of the Landlord and Tenant Act 1954. Section 24(2) expressly says that security of tenure shall not prevent the coming to an end of a tenancy by forfeiture.

Given the extreme nature of forfeiture as a remedy, it is unfortunate that the law of forfeiture 'is notoriously complicated, out-dated, and difficult to use': S Bridge, Why forfeiture should go, NLJ Vol 154, No 7113. Elsewhere, Stuart Bridge, the Law Commissioner urging reform, has said that the law of forfeiture is 'complex, confused and defective'. It is universally acknowledged that the law of forfeiture needs reform. That reform may be in sight. Since 1985, the Law Commission has advocated and made suggestions for reform. Earlier suggestions have been revised, and a consultation paper, Law Com No 174, was published in 2004. In 2006, it is expected that there will be a final report and draft Bill. For more on the proposals for reform, see **14.3** below.

14.2 The current law of forfeiture

14.2.1 The right to forfeit

The landlord's right to forfeit the lease is not automatic. Without a forfeiture clause, the landlord's remedy for breach of covenant by the tenant lies in damages. To be able to forfeit the lease, there must first be a clause in the lease which allows forfeiture. An example of such a clause is as follows:

If and whenever:

1. the rent or any sum reserved as rent is in unpaid for 14 days after the same shall have become due (whether formally demanded or not), or

2. there shall be a breach by the Tenant of any of the provisions of this lease, or

3. the Tenant has any distress levied on its goods, or

4. the Tenant is insolvent or enters into any arrangement or composition with its creditors, or

5. the Tenant (being a body corporate) has a winding up order made in respect of it (other than a members' voluntary winding up of a solvent company for the purposes of amalgamation or reconstruction approved by the landlord (such approval not to be unreasonably withheld)) or has a receiver administrator or an administrative receiver appointed of it or any of its assets or is dissolved or struck off the Register of Companies

then the Landlord may re-enter the Premises or any part thereof at any time and thereupon this Lease shall end but without prejudice to any right of the Landlord in respect of any breach of the Tenant's obligations contained in this Lease.

Secondly, of course, there must have been a forfeiting event of the kind described in the clause. From the example given, it can be seen that just failing to pay the rent or being in breach of covenant are not the only forfeiting events. If the tenant becomes in some form insolvent, that is enough to trigger the landlord's right to forfeit.

14.2.2 The decision to forfeit

Just because a tenant is in breach of a covenant and a forfeiting event has occurred, neither the landlord nor its advisors should think that forfeiture ought always then to follow. Commercial awareness of the circumstances is most important. Forfeiture, if completed, brings the lease to an end and the premises are empty. Empty premises generate no rental income. The landlord must ask itself – or its advisors must so advise – what is the state of the market for those premises? How easy, or difficult, will it be to relet them? Unless the tenant is so insolvent that the question answers itself, it has to be asked, is it better to have somebody in the premises, perhaps paying something, rather than have empty premises which may be difficult to relet? The remedy must be proportionate to the problem.

In the case of a lease granted before the coming into force of the Landlord and Tenant (Covenants) Act 1995, there should be considered any earlier tenant which may be liable in the event of a breach, particularly to pay rent. In *Scottish & Newcastle plc v Raguz* [2006] EWHC 821, Ch, National Car Parks Ltd (NCP) was landlord under two underleases granted in 1967 and 1969 respectively and expiring in 2062. The current tenant defaulted on the rent (which was substantial). The claimant, Scottish & Newcastle (S&N), was the original tenant under the underleases which it had then assigned to Raguz (from whom it had taken an indemnity covenant under which it was claiming, which claim Raguz was defending). Clearly, there was no incentive for NCP to forfeit the underleases for non-payment of rent whilst it had S&N on the hook for decades to come; as Hart J put it (at para 8):

[a]n additional feature of this situation [liability as earlier tenants], horrid for both claimant and defendant, was that it was in the highest degree unlikely that NCP would resolve matters for both of them by forfeiting the lease [his lordship meaning the underleases]. The claimant is a major quoted public company and, from the point of view of any landlord, a 'blue chip' covenant.

14.2.3 Action to forfeit

There may be a forfeiture clause in the lease and there may have been a forfeiting event but forfeiture does not take place until the landlord takes action to bring about forfeiture of the lease. The landlord may take one of two forms of action according to whether the breach is non-payment of rent, or breach of any other covenant. The service of the writ for forfeiture and possession does not give the landlord physical possession. Only once the appropriate proceedings have taken place, may the landlord then re-enter, that is, physically retake the premises. Actual re-entry may be effected under a court order gained in the proceedings, or it may be effected without a court order by what is called 'peaceable re-entry'.

The courts do not like peaceable re-entry: see *Billson v Residential Apartments Ltd* [1992] 1 All ER 141. There, Lord Templeman called re-entry 'dubious and dangerous' and the re-entry in that case a 'farce', and referred to the alternative of court proceedings as 'civilised' (146). He also pointed out that re-entry is unlawful where the premises are occupied by the tenant but not unlawful where the premises are occupied by the tenant's goods. Re-entry is dangerous because if any violence is threatened or used against either persons or property, the landlord is liable to prosecution under s 6 of the Criminal Law Act 1977. Peaceable re-entry can only safely be contemplated if there is no one in the premises.

We turn now to consider the two forms of proceedings to bring about forfeiture of the lease.

14.2.3.1 Forfeiture for breach of a covenant other than to pay rent

This procedure is governed by s 146 of the Law of Property Act 1925. The section requires the service of a notice on the tenant, commonly called a s 146 notice. Section 146(1) is as follows:

(1) A right of re-entry or forfeiture under any proviso or stipulation in a lease for a breach of any covenant or condition in the lease shall not be enforceable, by action or otherwise, unless and until the lessor serves on the lessee a notice—

  (a) specifying the particular breach complained of; and

  (b) if the breach is capable of remedy, requiring the lessee to remedy the breach; and

  (c) in any case, requiring the lessee to make compensation in money for the breach;

and the lessee fails, within a reasonable time thereafter, to remedy the breach, if it is capable of remedy, and to make reasonable compensation in money, to the satisfaction of the lessor, for the breach.

(Note that the words, 'by action or otherwise' refer to peaceable re-entry which cannot be effected unless this notice has first been served.)

Service of s 146 notice

The notice must be served on the tenant. If there has been an unauthorised assignment, the assignee may be the tenant: see *Old Grovebury Manor Farm Ltd v W Seymour Plant Sales & Hire Ltd* (No 2) [1979] 1 WLR 1397 and what is said at **6.3.2**.

The purpose of the notice is twofold: to give the tenant the opportunity to remedy the breach, and to apply for relief (see below): *Expert Clothing Service and Sales Ltd v Hillgate House Ltd* [1986] Ch 340. Of course the breach must be capable of remedy, and some breaches may be irremediable.

Remediable and irremediable breaches

It used to be said that a breach of a positive covenant will normally be remediable but a breach of a negative covenant is likely to be irremediable: see Law Commission Consultation Paper 174, para. 2.46 n. 79. In *Savva v Houssein* (1977) 73 P & CR 150, the Court of Appeal said that the test was more practical: if the breach could be remedied it was remediable, whether the covenant was positive or negative. For comment, see R Duddridge and J Brown, 'A step in the right direction' 1(4), L & TR 70–2. In *Expert Clothing*, Slade LJ thought that the test of whether a breach was remediable or not was whether the breach had caused irreparable harm to the landlord. More recently, the Court of Appeal has visited this point and done much to clarify and improve perceptions about remediable and irremediable breaches. In *Akici v L R Butlin Ltd* [2005] EWCA Civ 1296, Neuberger LJ said (paras 65 and 66):

> In principle, I would have thought that the great majority of breaches of covenant should be capable of remedy, in the same way as repairing or most user covenant breaches . . . I consider that it would follow, as a matter of both principle and practicality, that breaches of covenants involving parting with possession should be capable of remedy.

His lordship went on to say that he thought the argument that breach of a covenant against assigning or subletting is incapable of remedy was 'somewhat technical' and, were the matter free of authority, he would be attracted by the view that a surrender or assignment back would remedy such a breach. As the authorities stand, however, breaches against subletting and breach involving illegal or immoral use are, in principle, incapable of remedy. An example of the former is *Scala House & District Property Co Ltd v Forbes* [1974] QB 575. An example of the latter is *Egerton v Esplanade Hotels London Ltd* [1947] 2 All ER 88 (hotel in Paddington, London, used for prostitution in breach of the user clause): although the activity can be made to cease, it is said to cast a stigma on the premises. However, in *Ropemaker Properties Ltd v Noonhaven Ltd* [1989] 2 EGLR 50, the court did not grant forfeiture. The premises had been used for prostitution in breach of the user clause but the judge felt that since the immoral use had ended and the tenant was otherwise excellent, the stigma would be short-lived.

Breach of a covenant to repair would normally be remediable simply by doing the repair. As Slade LJ put it, 'in the ordinary case, the breach of a promise to do something by a certain time can for practical purposes be remedied by the thing being done, even out of time': *Expert Clothing* [1986] Ch at 355.

If the breach is remediable, the notice must give the tenant a reasonable time to effect the remedy. If the breach is irremediable, there is need only for enough time for the tenant to consider its position. In *Scala House*, 14 days was held to be enough.

Excusable breach

The tenant may have a lawful excuse for the breach of covenant. In *John Lewis Properties plc v Viscount Chelsea* [1993] 2 EGLR 77, leases had been granted in 1934 in which the tenant covenanted to develop certain premises by specified dates. The development would have involved demolition of existing buildings. In 1969, those buildings were listed which meant they could not be demolished.

Breach of repairing covenant

There is further statutory regulation of the landlord's ability to take action for breach of a repairing covenant.

Section 18(2) of the Landlord and Tenant Act 1927 provides that the s 146 notice is actually received by the tenant. The general law on the service of notices applies so that registered and recorded delivery methods suffice to provide prima facie knowledge of the addressee. The tenant must be given a reasonable time from the date the tenant knew of the s 146 notice to do the repairs.

The Leasehold Properties (Repairs) Act 1938 provides further protection for tenants. The aim of this provision was to stop unscrupulous developers buying up premises that needed repair, forfeit the lease when the tenant did not do the repair and so get the premises with vacant possession. To be able to forfeit the lease, the lease must be a qualifying lease. That means it must be for a term of not less than seven years with at least three years to run. The s 146 notice must tell the tenant it has 28 days to serve a counternotice. If it does, the landlord cannot enforce forfeiture without leave of the court. The court is not to grant leave unless the landlord proves one or more of the criteria set out in s 1(4) of the 1938 Act.

14.2.3.2 Forfeiture for breach of covenant to pay rent

A formal demand is necessary at common law but this can be and invariably is exempted by a clause in the lease. Section 146 of the LPA 1925 does not apply. Instead, there are two ways of proceeding. The most common is by action in the county court under s 138 of the County Courts Act 1984. Once a summons is served, the tenant has five days to pay. If it does not, and the court thinks the landlord is entitled to forfeiture, the court will order possession at the end of a stated period not less than four weeks. If the tenant does pay, then forfeiture is avoided. The other way is by action in the High Court if more than six months' rent is due.

14.2.4 Waiver of forfeiture

The landlord's entitlement to forfeiture may be lost if the landlord does something which affirms that the lease is continuing. Landlords must be careful because waiver can occur unintentionally and by accident. The following are cases where there was held to be a waiver:

(a) making a demand for rent: *Segal Securities Ltd v Thoseby* [1963] 1 QB 887;

(b) L's agents instructed their staff to refuse all rent from T but a clerk did not receive this instruction and sent out a routine rent demand: *Central Estates (Belgravia) Ltd v Woolgar (No 2)* [1972] 1 WLR 1048;

(c) Accepting rent after knowledge of the breach in respect of which forfeiture was claimed: *Iperion Investments Corporation v Broadwalk House Residents* [1992] 2 EGLR 235.

In *Expert Clothing Service and Sales Ltd* v *Hillgate House Ltd* [1986] Ch 340, Slade LJ thought the rule should be less strict than it had been in earlier cases. The court should look at all the circumstances to see whether there really was an unequivocal act of waiver. In *John Lewis Properties plc* v *Viscount Chelsea* [1993] 2 EGLR 77, the landlord told the tenant it would not accept rent but the tenant still paid rent by cheque to the landlord's bank. The landlord returned the money to the tenant. Mummery J said that the clearing of a cheque was banking procedure should not be taken as waiver. In *Yorkshire Metropolitan Properties Ltd* v *Co-operative Retail Services Ltd* [1997] EGCS 57, Neuberger J held that a demand for insurance money not reserved as rent was not an act of waiver.

Waiver, if it happens, does not release the tenant from its obligations under the lease. Furthermore, if the landlord does an act of waiver and the breach then continues, it can start another action: *Penton* v *Barnett* [1898] 1 QB 276; *Greenwich LBC* v *Discreet Selling Estates Ltd* [1990] 2 EGLR 65. But if the breach is irremediable (sometimes called 'once and for all'), an act of waiver will be final. 'It is not the breach itself which is waived, but merely the right to forfeit in respect of the breach: P Luxton and M Wilkie, *Commercial Leases* (1998), 339.

14.2.5 Relief from forfeiture

When the landlord takes steps to forfeit the lease, the tenant may defend itself by applying for relief from forfeiture. How the tenant does this depends on whether the breach is of a covenant other than to pay rent or of one to pay rent. The granting of relief is equitable and therefore discretionary.

14.2.5.1 Relief from forfeiture for breach of a covenant other than to pay rent

The court's discretion is contained in s 24(2) of the Landlord and Tenant Act 1954 which reads as follows:

> (2) Where a lessor is proceeding, by action or otherwise, to enforce such a right of re-entry or forfeiture, the lessee may, in the lessor's action, if any, or in any action brought by himself, apply to the court for relief; and the court may grant or refuse relief, as the court, having regard to the proceedings and conduct of the parties under the foregoing provisions of this section, and to all the other circumstances, thinks fit; and in case of relief may grant it on such terms, if any, as to costs, expenses, damages, compensation, penalty, or otherwise, including the granting of an injunction to restrain any like breach in the future, as the court, in the circumstances of each case, thinks fit.

The tenant does not need to wait until proceedings have started but can apply as soon as the landlord has served its s 146 notice (see **14.2.3.1**): *Pakwood Transport Ltd* v *15 Beauchamp Place Ltd* [1977] 36 P & CR 112. This case concerned peaceable re-entry without a court order and it was thought that the wording of s 146(2) of the Law of Property Act 1925 meant that the tenant could not apply for relief after the landlord had re-entered. The House of Lords in *Billson* v *Residential Apartments Ltd* [1992] 1 All ER 141 firmly rejected this idea. But where the landlord re-enters with a court order, it is too late for the tenant to apply for relief because the landlord relied not on its own action but on the sanction of the court.

The court will usually grant relief where the breach is remediable and the tenant will perform its obligations. Relief may be granted on terms so that the landlord is put into the position it would have been but for the breach. The terms may involve payment of compensation or an injunction to restrain further breach. In framing any terms, the court will have regard to all the circumstances including the conduct of the tenant, the nature and gravity of the breach and the value of the property. For example, in *Ropemaker Properties Ltd v Noonhaven Ltd* [1989] 2 EGLR 50 the judge was influenced by the high value of the lease – about £1m.

The extent of the terms on which relief may be granted is illustrated in the case of *Fuller v Judy Properties Ltd* [1992] 1 EGLR 75. There, the tenant assigned the lease to the defendants in breach of the alienation clause, the defendants paying £30,000. The claimant peaceably re-entered and then granted a lease to H Ltd which knew nothing of the action regarding the defendant. It seemed to the court unfair that the defendant should have paid £30,000 for nothing despite the lack of landlord's consent. The solution was to restore the defendant's lease and for H Ltd to stay in occupation, paying rent to the defendant who in turn paid rent to the (now) head landlord.

14.2.5.2 Relief from forfeiture for breach of a covenant to pay rent

It must be remembered that rent includes any sum reserved as rent such as a service charge or insurance premium payment. The equitable jurisdiction of the court is now in statute, namely s 38 of the Supreme Court Act 1981 and ss 138 and 139 of the County Court Act 1984. If the tenant pays what is owed, relief is automatic. Most actions are in the county court and the situation there has been described at **14.2.3.2**. The tenant may apply for relief in the High Court which has an inherent equitable jurisdiction to grant relief or in the county court whose equitable jurisdiction flows from the High Court.

14.2.6 Derivative interests

These are those of subtenants and mortgagees. Forfeiture of a head lease automatically results in the extinguishing of any sublease. A subtenant – called an 'under-lessee' in the section – may apply for relief under s 146(4) of the Law of Property Act 1925 which reads as follows:

(4) Where a lessor is proceeding by action or otherwise to enforce a right of re-entry or forfeiture under any covenant, proviso, or stipulation in a lease, or for non-payment of rent, the court may, on application by any person claiming as under-lessee any estate or interest in the property comprised in the lease or any part thereof, either in the lessor's action (if any) or in any action brought by such person for that purpose, make an order vesting, for the whole term of the lease or any less term, the property comprised in the lease or any part thereof in any person entitled as under-lessee to any estate or interest in such property upon such conditions as to execution of any deed or other document, payment of rent, costs, expenses, damages, compensation, giving security, or otherwise, as the court in the circumstances of each case may think fit, but in no case shall any such under-lessee be entitled to require a lease to be granted to him for any longer term than he had under his original sub-lease.

The terms of relief are similar to those for forfeiture of the head lease save that s 146(4) applies also to non-payment of rent. The landlord must endorse the writ with the name and address of any derivative interest holder of whom it is aware and serve them a copy of the writ. It is therefore important that derivative title holders make sure the head landlord is aware of their existence.

In *Abbey National Building Society v Maybeech Ltd* [1985] Ch 190, the court invoked its equitable jurisdiction to grant relief to the mortgagee even after the landlord had re-entered pursuant to a court order. Luxton and Wilkie (at 328) consider that the authority of this case is uncertain.

14.3 Proposals for reform

The proposals in Law Comm 174 do not seek to abolish the right of the landlord to end a tenancy when the tenant is in default but to cure a number of defects and obsolete requirements. The law on re-entry is anachronistic and full of anomalies; the rules for relief from forfeiture are complex and irrational; the difference in proceedings for breach of covenant to pay rent and for other covenants has no logic behind it; and the position of holders of derivative interest is unsatisfactory. It is considered that the best way to reform the law is to abolish the existing law and make new law. It is to be hoped that there is now a very real prospect that a new law of forfeiture will be in place in the near future. Briefly, the proposals, subject to the final report, are as set out below.

- To abolish the current law of forfeiture and the related doctrine of waiver.

- To create a new statutory scheme for fixed term commercial tenancies (and certain long-term residential tenancies).

- To make any breach of covenant a tenant default entitling landlords to start an action to terminate the tenancy (so there is no need to construe forfeiture clauses in leases).

- To require landlords to give to tenants a pre-action notice in prescribed form of their intention to terminate the tenancy for default, giving particulars of the breach complained of and requiring remedial action.

- To enable landlords to apply to the court for a termination order which will be available on proof of specific grounds.

- That in exceptional circumstances landlords may be permitted to exercise self-help and recover possession without a court order but only where there has been prior service of a pre-action notice stating the intention to use this procedure. The tenancy will then terminate within three months unless the tenant applies to the court. (This will be a modified form of what is currently called peaceable re-entry which landlords value highly, though landlords must wonder why they cannot relet until three months have passed.)

- Otherwise, a tenancy will only terminate when a court order takes effect.

15 Security of tenure

15.1 Introduction

It is worth remembering that, during the business tenancy, there is little statutory interference with the contract made by the original parties: the law that applies to business tenancies applies to all tenancies (though it must be conceded that the Landlord and Tenant (Covenants) Act 1995 is most likely to apply to business tenancies). The security of tenure legislation has to do only with what happens at the end of the contractual term. In many jurisdictions, business tenants have no security of tenure. In England and Wales, most business tenants may enjoy the protection of their tenancy under Part II of the Landlord and Tenant Act 1954 (the 1954 Act).

The aim of the 1954 Act was to give business tenants protection from eviction at the end of the contractual term, provided the tenant was not a 'bad' tenant and the landlord did not establish grounds for recovery of the premises. The reason was that it was thought unfair that a good tenant with a flourishing business should suffer the expense and upheaval of having to leave its premises and find others if the landlord simply refused to grant a new lease. Apart from the property complications for the tenant, there could be a serious threat to the tenant's goodwill which has much to do with the location of premises, especially retail premises. Furthermore, it would be unfair if the landlord were able to demand a higher rent on the grant of a new lease simply because the existing tenant would be especially anxious to stay on in the same premises. These considerations were thought to justify interfering with the common law position that the tenancy would end when the agreement said it would. Additionally, where the business tenant does in fact leave, it may be entitled to compensation for disturbance. These two rights – security of tenure and compensation – are clearly most important for many business tenants.

Despite the aims of the 1954 Act, there came a time when it was felt that the parties to a lease ought to be able to decide for themselves whether it should apply. The Law Commission in 1969 recommended that the 1954 Act could be made less restrictive and so the 1954 Act was amended to allow parties to contract out of the security of tenure provisions of the 1954 Act provided certain procedures were followed. There are no qualifications as to which business tenancies may be contracted out, and perhaps between a quarter and a half of tenancies are contracted out. Whether the landlord can negotiate contracting out depends upon the state of the market, but a landlord may have a specific need to contract out. However, the difference contracting out makes to the level of rent is probably small. For contracting out, see **15.3**.

The 1954 Act is said to have worked well in its first half century of existence, but then reform was thought to be necessary. In March 2001, the Government published a Consultation Paper. The result was the Regulatory Reform (Business Tenancies) (England and Wales) Order 2003 (SI 2003/3096) (referred to in this chapter as the 2003 Order) which came into force prospectively from 1 June 2004. The reforms were considerable and wide-ranging and practitioners had to get used to a new regime. Some had hoped for a more radical reform, in particular that the dangers of date-sensitive procedures would be abandoned, but it remains the case that tenants wanting the protection of the 1954 Act do still have to make an application to the court and the date by which that must be done, though now more flexible, can still be a trap.

The current procedures under the 1954 Act are set out, with appendices setting out all necessary forms, in *Business tenancies: new procedures under the Landlord and Tenant Act 1954, Part 2*, published April 2004 by the Office of the Deputy Prime Minister and available online from the DCLG website.

15.2 **Protected tenancies**

The 1954 Act protects those tenancies which qualify under s 23. This section is as follows:

23 Tenancies to which Part II applies

(1) Subject to the provisions of this Act, this Part of this Act applies to any tenancy where the property comprised in the tenancy is or includes premises which are occupied by the tenant and are so occupied for the purposes of a business carried on by him or for those and other purposes.

[(1A) Occupation or the carrying on of a business—

(a) by a company in which the tenant has a controlling interest; or

(b) where the tenant is a company, by a person with a controlling interest in the company,

shall be treated for the purposes of this section as equivalent to occupation or, as the case may be, the carrying on of a business by the tenant.

(1B) Accordingly references (however expressed) in this Part of this Act to the business of, or to use, occupation or enjoyment by, the tenant shall be construed as including references to the business of, or to use, occupation or enjoyment by, a company falling within subsection (1A)(a) above or a person falling within subsection (1A)(b) above.]

(2) In this Part of this Act the expression 'business' includes a trade, profession or employment and includes any activity carried on by a body of persons, whether corporate or unincorporate.

(3) In the following provisions of this Part of this Act the expression 'the holding', in relation to a tenancy to which this Part of this Act applies, means the property

comprised in the tenancy, there being excluded any part thereof which is occupied neither by the tenant nor by a person employed by the tenant and so employed for the purposes of a business by reason of which the tenancy is one to which this Part of this Act applies.

(4) Where the tenant is carrying on a business, in all or any part of the property comprised in a tenancy, in breach of a prohibition (however expressed) of use for business purposes which subsists under the terms of the tenancy and extends to the whole of that property, this Part of this Act shall not apply to the tenancy unless the immediate landlord or his predecessor in title has consented to the breach or the immediate landlord has acquiesced therein.

In this subsection the reference to a prohibition of use for business purposes does not include a prohibition of use for the purposes of a specified business, or of use for purposes of any but a specified business, but save as aforesaid includes a prohibition of use for the purposes of some one or more only of the classes of business specified in the definition of that expression in subsection (2) of this section.

There are several key terms here: *tenancy, occupation, business and holding*. These terms are now examined.

15.2.1 Tenancy

'Tenancy' is defined in s 69(1) of the 1954 Act and includes:

(a) fixed term and periodic tenancies;

(b) subtenancies;

(c) an agreement for a lease.

The 1954 Act specifically excludes those tenancies mentioned in s 43:

43 Tenancies excluded from Part II

(1) This Part of this Act does not apply—

(a) to a tenancy of an agricultural holding [[[which is a tenancy in relation to which the Agricultural Holdings Act 1986 applies or a tenancy which would be a tenancy of an agricultural holding in relation to which that Act applied if subsection (3) of section 2 of that Act] did not have effect or, in a case where approval was given under subsection (1) of that section], if that approval had not been given];

[(aa) to a farm business tenancy;]

(b) to a tenancy created by a mining lease;

(c), (d) . . .

(2) This Part of this Act does not apply to a tenancy granted by reason that the tenant was the holder of an office, appointment or employment from the grantor thereof and continuing only so long as the tenant holds the office, appointment or employment, or terminable by the grantor on the tenant's ceasing to hold it, or

coming to an end at a time fixed by reference to the time at which the tenant ceases to hold it:

Provided that this subsection shall not have effect in relation to a tenancy granted after the commencement of this Act unless the tenancy was granted by an instrument in writing which expressed the purpose for which the tenancy was granted.

(3) This Part of this Act does not apply to a tenancy granted for a term certain not exceeding [six months] unless--

(a) the tenancy contains provision for renewing the term or for extending it beyond [six months] from its beginning; or

(b) the tenant has been in occupation for a period which, together with any period during which any predecessor in the carrying on of the business carried on by the tenant was in occupation, exceeds [twelve months].

Put shortly, this excludes:

(a) agricultural holdings;

(b) mining leases;

(c) service tenancies;

(d) fixed-term tenancies not exceeding six months (though note the provisos that such a lease must not provide for renewal beyond that period, and that there should not have been prior occupation).

Also excluded, but by operation of the general law, are:

(a) licences (see **Chapter 4**);

(b) tenancies at will (see **3.6.4**).

Of course, there are excluded tenancies which are contracted out of the 1954 Act by an agreement under s 38A: see **15.3**.

Tenancies of premises licensed to sell alcohol are generally included. Not included are those (not including tenancies of hotels, restaurants and other premises where the sale of alcohol is not the main use) granted before 11 July 1989.

15.2.2 Occupation

15.2.2.1 Requirement of occupation

To qualify, the premises must be occupied by the tenant or for the tenant in some representative capacity. In most cases, this will be a clear fact. The occupation must, however, be for the purposes of a business carried on by the tenant (see **15.2.3**). The 1954 Act will not apply to a tenancy in respect of which the tenant is not in occupation for the purposes of its business. Section 23 works, in this respect, with s 24 and s 27. In *Esselte AB v Pearl Assurance plc* [1997] 2 All ER 41, it was held that the 1954 Act cannot apply where the tenant has ceased occupation before the end of the contractual term. This decision is now reflected in s 27(1A).

15.2.2.2 Degree of occupation

Occupation need not be actual and completely unbroken: in *Bacchiocchi v Academic Agency Ltd* [1998] 2 All ER 241, an absence of 12 days did not break what is called the 'thread of continuity' which, Ward LJ said (at 253), 'has a degree of elasticity to it'. In considering the application of s 23, Simon Brown LJ said (at 249) that some periods of closure for repairs and the like would 'not destroy the continuity of business occupation' since such events are 'recognisable as an incident in the ordinary course or conduct of business life'; his lordship said further:

> Indeed, whenever business premises are empty for only a short period, whether mid-term or before or after trading at either end of the lease, I would be disinclined to find that the business occupancy has ceased (or not started) for that period provided always that during it there exists no rival for the role of business occupant and that the premises are not being used for some other, non-business purpose. That to my mind is how Pt II of the 1954 Act should operate in logic and in justice . . . If, of course, premises are left vacant for a matter of months, the court would be readier to conclude that the thread of continuity has been broken.

Occupation being a question of fact, the court will consider each case before it on its merits. Premises were held to be sufficiently occupied for the purposes of the 1954 Act in the following instances:

(a) a café and restaurant business were occupied seasonally, being open in the holiday season and closed outside it: *Artemiou v Procopiou* [1966] 1 QB 878, CA;

(b) the tenant had to leave when a fire badly damaged the premises, though the tenant kept the keys and stated its intention to resume business when possible: *Morrison Holdings Ltd v Manders Property (Wolverhampton) Ltd* [1976] 2 All ER 205;

(c) a piece of land was maintained weekly in the summer and fortnightly in the winter by the parks staff of the local authority tenant: *Wandsworth London Borough v Singh* [1991] 2 EGLR 75;

(d) the tenant ceased trading for seven months but intended to resume business if granted a new tenancy: *I & H Caplan Ltd v Caplan* [1963] 2 All ER 930.

The thread of continuity was held to have been broken in the following instances:

(a) a commercial choice was made by the tenant, which operated casinos, between premises where it had ceased its activity and surrendered its gaming licence as it wished to run a gaming club at other premises, even though it had the intention of reopening the first premises if a new lease and licence were available: *Aspinall Finance Ltd v Viscount Chelsea* [1989] 1 EGLR 103;

(b) the tenant found other premises and cleared most of his stock out of the first premises, going back there from time to time: *Webb v Sandown Sports Club Ltd* [2000] EGCS 13.

15.2.2.3 Occupation for the tenant

Occupation may be representative as where employees carry on the tenant's business. Personal occupation is clearly not possible in the case of certain tenants such as companies and charities. Such tenants occupy through their employees or agents. Sections 41(1), 41A and 42(2) make specific provision for occupation on behalf of trusts, partnerships and companies within a group. Furthermore, s 23(1A) provides that occupation or the carrying on of a business may exist where:

(a) the tenant is not in occupation but a company controlled by the tenant is

and; conversely

(b) a tenant company is not in occupation but a person with a controlling interest in that company is.

This in effect means that protection applies to tenancies where the tenant and the occupier are not the same but one has control of the other. For all purposes under the 1954 Act, however, the tenant remains the tenant – it is just that the other's occupation feeds the right of the tenant to protection.

15.2.2.4 Occupation by a third party

It remains the case that there cannot be shared rights under the 1954 Act: there can be only one tenant who qualifies for protection. Where a tenant T allows some other person S into occupation, for example by way of subletting, of part or whole of the premises, and such part or whole is occupied by S at the time that T seeks renewal of its tenancy under the 1954 Act, then T is not in occupation of the part or whole occupied by that other person for the purposes of s 23(1). Indeed, it may be S who qualifies for the protection. It should be noted that the premises can be split for these purposes: see **15.2.4**.

The leading case on this point is *Graysim Holdings Ltd v P & O Property Holdings Ltd* [1995] 4 All ER 831. Graysim operated a market hall in which traders had lock-up stalls. A superintendent managed the hall, opening and closing it each day. Facilities and services were provided for the traders but Graysim had no access to the stalls. Graysim tried to renew its tenancy from P & O but failed at first instance because it was not in occupation for the purposes of s 23 (1). The Court of Appeal allowed Graysim's appeal against the first instance decision, but the House of Lords reversed the Court of Appeal, Lord Nicholls of Birkenhead giving the only reasoned judgment with which the other law lords agreed. Lord Nicholls described 'occupation' as a central feature to the statutory structure of the 1954 Act but pointed out that the concept of occupation is not a legal term of art. Occupation, he said, is an ordinary English word with shades of meaning. His lordship considered a scale of occupation from the occasional use of a field for a car boot sale to a subletting of the whole of office accommodation. Occupation is thus a matter of degree. Lord Nicholls mentioned that the degree of control retained by a landlord could make a difference to whether the landlord was in occupation or not, a point which was in issue in some lease/licence cases: see **4.3.2**.

Lord Nicholls mentioned that it was common ground between the parties that the traders' tenancies were business tenancies and so protected under the 1954 Act. It could not be the case that Graysim was in occupation and also entitled to protection. True, Graysim had retained some part of the hall and the common parts, but no business was being carried on in these parts and so Graysim did not qualify for protection. The only business being carried on was by the traders who had exclusive possession of their stalls.

It is worth commenting that it is strange that the concession was made by Graysim that the traders had tenancies; there was surely a strong argument that they had licences.

Graysim was considered and followed in *Smith v Titanite* [2005] 20 EG 262. There, a tenant of a house sought to acquire the freehold under the Leasehold Reform Act 1967 but to succeed had to show that it did not have a business tenancy to which Part II of the 1954 Act applied. The house was divided into flats, the tenant providing certain services, including the presence of a manager who used an office in the house. The occupiers of the flats had tenancies and the tenant had not retained sufficient control so as to be in occupation itself and so qualify under the 1954 Act. See comment by M Pawlowski, (2005) 9(4) L & T Review 103–107.

An open question is whether dual occupation could ever be possible. In *Graysim*, Lord Nicholls said there were no hard and fast rules about dual occupation though he doubted it was possible for the purposes of the 1954 Act. *Lee-Verhulst (Investments) Ltd v Harwood Trust* [1972] 3 All ER 619 was a case in which a tenant company of a house let furnished rooms with services and exercised a great degree of control over the whole premises such that the Court of Appeal was able to find that the tenant was in occupation for the purposes of the 1954 Act but this did not add up to dual occupation.

Where a tenant is in the business of letting out premises, it needs to consider carefully how to protect its rights under the 1954 Act. In many cases, it will be too risky to assume that a licence will be upheld as such, and even where an agreement is a licence, there is nothing to stop a licensee claiming a tenancy, a claim that will have to be challenged and resisted, however unmeritorious the claim might be. The obvious and safest course is to grant subtenancies with security of tenure excluded. This is easy to do.

15.2.3 Business

The premises must be occupied for the purposes of a business carried on by the tenant. The business need not actually be carried on at the premises; they may be occupied for some purpose ancillary to the business so long as such occupation is necessary. Thus, in *Sandhu Menswear Co Ltd v Woolworths plc* [2006] EWHC 1299, TCC, the claimant tenant occupied a small industrial unit for the purposes of keeping stock for its retail business which was carried elsewhere. See also *Methodist Secondary Schools Trust Deed Trustees v O'Leary* [1993] 1 EGLR 105.

'Business' is widely defined in s 23(2). A close reading of the provision shows that an individual should be carrying on some trade, profession or employment, but that a body of persons, corporate or unincorporated, simply has to carry on 'any activity'; thus, for example, a charity carrying on its work would qualify. Even in the narrower sense of trade, profession or employment, it is not necessary that such business should be profitable, nor should it follow that if a body of persons carries on a trade, profession or employment, that cannot be also an activity: see *Hawkesbrook Leisure Ltd v Reece-Jones Partnership* [2003] EWHC 3333 and comment thereon by S Murdoch (2004) Estates Gazette, 10 April, 103.

The following are examples of cases where the activity carried on was a business for the purposes of the 1954 Act:

(a) a not-for-profit hospital: *Hills (Patents) Ltd v University College Hospital Board of Governors* [1956] 1 QB 90;

(b) a members' tennis club: *Addiscombe Garden Estates Ltd v Crabbe* [1958] 1 QB 513;

(c) provision of residential accommodation: *Lee-Velhulst (Investments) Ltd v Harwood Trust* [1973] QB 204;

(d) a local authority's maintenance of a park: *Wandsworth London Borough v Singh* [1991] 2 EGLR 75.

In the following cases, there was no or insufficient business or activity:

(a) dumping waste (being merely casual user): *Hillil Property and Investment Co Ltd v Naraine Pharmacy Ltd* (1979) 39 P & CR 67;

(b) taking in of lodgers by an individual: *Lewis v Weldcrest Ltd* [1978] 3 All ER 1226.

Where there is partial use of premises for business, then whether the premises qualify for protection depends on whether the business activity is significant or only incidental. A caretaker's flat in an office block would not detract from the office block being business premises but one room in a house used for professional purposes would not make the house business premises.

15.2.4 Holding

Section 23(1) refers to 'the property comprised in the tenancy'. Section 23(3) equates this expression with the term 'holding' and says that there is excluded from the qualifying property or holding any part thereof which is not occupied for the purposes of the 1954 Act. As mentioned in **15.2.2.4**, the premises comprised in a tenancy may be split with the tenant parting with possession of part and retaining part. The problems that arise from this were discussed in relation to *Graysim Holdings Ltd v P & O Property Holdings Ltd* at **15.2.2.4**. The effect of s 23(3) is that the tenant's right to a new lease applies only to the tenant's holding which could be less than the premises originally comprised in the lease if the tenant has allowed another to occupy part of the premises. Thus, if a tenant takes a lease of a five-storey office block and sublets one floor, then the tenant's holding is the remaining four floors (assuming the subtenant is in occupation at the relevant time).

The importance of the test of occupancy is that a tenant only has renewal rights for premises it occupies; unoccupied parts will be excluded as well as any parts sublet. Any subtenant gains the benefit of renewal rights for the part it occupies (unless contracted out under the 1954 Act).

The tenant's holding may include incorporeal hereditaments which go with the tenancy. In *Pointon York Group plc v Poulton* [2006] EWCA Civ 1001, designated car parking spaces were held to be part of the holding, and occupation of them was sufficient for the purposes of the Act.

The date at which the extent of the holding is determined is when the order for the grant of a new tenancy is made under s 29. Section 32(1) provides that an order under s 29 shall be an order for the grant of a new tenancy of the holding.

15.3 Contracting out

Contracting out refers to the exclusion of the tenancy from the provisions for security of tenure in the 1954 Act. Whether a landlord will be able to have a tenancy contracted out will depend on the state of the market but most tenants will be keen to have the benefit of security of tenure. There are no statistics available from the Royal Institution of Chartered Surveyors as to what is the proportion of tenancies contracted out but some legal practitioners estimate that up to half of tenancies granted are contracted out. Security of occupation is especially important to retail businesses, and retail tenants will normally not expect to be asked to accept an agreement to contract out.

The provisions for contracting out are set out in ss 38 and 38A of the 1954 Act. Section 38A refers to the forms to be used and the requirements to be met set out in Schs 1 and 2 to the 2003 Order.

15.3.1 Agreement to contract out

Section 38(1) provides as follows:

38 Restriction on agreements excluding provisions of Part II

(1) Any agreement relating to a tenancy to which this Part of this Act applies (whether contained in the instrument creating the tenancy or not) shall be void [(except as provided by [section 38A of this Act])] in so far as it purports to preclude the tenant from making an application or request under this Part of this Act.

Section 38A then provides:

38A Agreements to exclude provisions of Part 2

(1) The persons who will be the landlord and the tenant in relation to a tenancy to be granted for a term of years certain which will be a tenancy to which this Part of this Act applies may agree that the provisions of sections 24 to 28 of this Act shall be excluded in relation to that tenancy.

(3) An agreement under subsection (1) above shall be void unless—

(a) the landlord has served on the tenant a notice in the form, or substantially in the form, set out in Schedule 1 to the Regulatory Reform (Business Tenancies) (England and Wales) Order 2003 ('the 2003 Order'); and

(b) the requirements specified in Schedule 2 to that Order are met.

Schedule 2 to the 2003 Order is as follows:

SCHEDULE 2

Article 22(2)

REQUIREMENTS FOR A VALID AGREEMENT THAT SECTIONS 24 TO 28 OF THE LANDLORD AND TENANT ACT 1954 ARE NOT TO APPLY TO A BUSINESS TENANCY

1. The following are the requirements referred to in section 38A(3)(b) of the Act.

2. Subject to paragraph 4, the notice referred to in section 38A(3)(a) of the Act must be served on the tenant not less than 14 days before the tenant enters into the tenancy to which it applies, or (if earlier) becomes contractually bound to do so.

3. If the requirement in paragraph 2 is met, the tenant, or a person duly authorised by him to do so, must, before the tenant enters into the tenancy to which the notice applies, or (if earlier) becomes contractually bound to do so, make a declaration in the form, or substantially in the form, set out in paragraph 7.

4. If the requirement in paragraph 2 is not met, the notice referred to in section 38A(3)(a) of the Act must be served on the tenant before the tenant enters into the tenancy to which it applies, or (if earlier) becomes contractually bound to do so, and the tenant, or a person duly authorised by him to do so, must before that time make a statutory declaration in the form, or substantially in the form, set out in paragraph 8.

5. A reference to the notice and, where paragraph 3 applies, the declaration or, where paragraph 4 applies, the statutory declaration must be contained in or endorsed on the instrument creating the tenancy.

6. The agreement under section 38A(1) of the Act, or a reference to the agreement, must be contained in or endorsed upon the instrument creating the tenancy.

7. The form of declaration referred to in paragraph 3 is as follows: –

I
_____

(*name of declarant*) of
_____

(*address*) declare that –

1. I/
_____

(*name of tenant*) propose(s) to enter into a tenancy of premises at
_____

(*address of premises*) for a term commencing on
_____

2. I/The tenant propose(s) to enter into an agreement with
_____

(name of landlord) that the provisions of sections 24 to 28 of the Landlord and Tenant Act 1954 (security of tenure) shall be excluded in relation to the tenancy.

3. The landlord has, not less than 14 days before I/the tenant enter(s) into the tenancy, or (if earlier) become(s) contractually bound to do so served on me/the tenant a notice in the form, or substantially in the form, set out in Schedule 1 to the Regulatory Reform (Business Tenancies) (England and Wales) Order 2003. The form of notice set out in that Schedule is reproduced below.

4. I have/The tenant has read the notice referred to in paragraph 3 above and accept(s) the consequences of entering into the agreement referred to in paragraph 2 above.

5. (*as appropriate*) I am duly authorised by the tenant to make this declaration.

DECLARED this

_____

_____

day of .

_____

To:

_____

_____

_____

[*Name and address of tenant*]

From:

_____

_____

_____

[*name and address of landlord*]

8. The form of statutory declaration referred to in paragraph 4 is as follows: –

I

_____

(*name of declarant*) of

_____

(*address*) do solemnly and sincerely declare that –

     1. I

_____

(*name of tenant*) propose(s) to enter into a tenancy of premises at

_____

(*address of premises*) for a term commencing on

_____

2. I/The tenant propose(s) to enter into an agreement with (name of landlord) that the provisions of sections 24 to 28 of the Landlord and Tenant Act 1954 (security of tenure) shall be excluded in relation to the tenancy.

3. The landlord has served on me/the tenant a notice in the form, or substantially in the form, set out in Schedule 1 to the Regulatory Reform (Business Tenancies) (England and Wales) Order 2003. The form of notice set out in that Schedule is reproduced below.

4. I have/The tenant has read the notice referred to in paragraph 3 above and accept(s) the consequences of entering into the agreement referred to in paragraph 2 above.

5. (*as appropriate*) I am duly authorised by the tenant to make this declaration.

To:

_____

_____

_____

[*Name and address of tenant*]

From:

_____

_____

_____

[*name and address of landlord*]

AND I make this solemn declaration conscientiously believing the same to be true and by virtue of the Statutory Declaration Act 1835.

DECLARED at _____

this _____

day of . _____

Before me

(*signature of person before whom declaration is made*)

A commissioner for oaths or A solicitor empowered to administer oaths or (as appropriate)

The agreement thus requires three elements:

(a) landlord's 'health warning' in the form or substantially the form prescribed in Sch 1 to the 2003 Order (s 38A(3)(a)). The warning tells the prospective business tenant that it will have no rights of renewal, and stresses the importance of getting legal advice. This warning must be served on the tenant not less than 14 days before the tenant enters the tenancy or contracts so to do (Sch 2, para 2 of the 2003 Order);

(b) tenant's declaration in the form or substantially the form set out in para 7 of Sch 2 (see above) to be signed by the tenant (or authorised person, usually the tenant's solicitor). This is called a simple declaration, and is used if the tenant received the landlord's health warning at least 14 days being contractually bound (Sch 2 para 3). 'Contractually bound' presumably means that any conditional contract has become unconditional. This is called (by the ODPM) the 'advance notice procedure'.

If the parties do not want to wait 14 days, the tenant must give a statutory declaration in the form or substantially the form set out in para 8 of Sch 2 (see above) (Sch 2, para 4). This is called the 'statutory declaration procedure';

(c) reference to the landlord's health warning and the relevant declaration and to the agreement to contract out must be contained in or endorsed on the lease.

Care must be taken in the service of notices because the 14-day period runs from when the landlord's health warning was served. Section 66(4) of the 1954 Act provides that the rules for service of notices in s 23 of the Landlord and Tenant Act 1927, s 23 apply. Section 23(1) provides for service to be:

(a) personal;

(b) by leaving the notice at the last known place of abode in England and Wales of the person to be served;

(c) by registered post,

Registered post and recorded delivery are treated in the same way: Recorded Delivery Services Act 1962. Service is deemed to have taken place on the date of posting and non-receipt is irrelevant: *C A Webber (Transport) Ltd v Network Rail Infrastructure Ltd* [2003] EWCA Civ 1167. Actual receipt of the landlord's health warning notice is, however, necessary otherwise the tenant cannot make its declaration.

Many deals are done in a hurry and often the 14-day option will be impracticable. Also, landlords will wish to avoid any doubt about whether all the terms of the lease had been agreed before the contracting out machinery is activated. For both reasons, it is likely that the alternative statutory declaration procedure will be followed in many cases.

15.4 Continuation of tenancies

The core of the security of tenure provisions of the 1954 Act are in s 24 which reads as follows:

24 Continuation of tenancies to which Part II applies and grant of new tenancies

(1) A tenancy to which this Part of this Act applies shall not come to an end unless terminated in accordance with the provisions of this Part of this Act; and, subject to the [following provisions of this Act either the tenant or the landlord under such a tenancy may apply to the court for an order for the grant of] a new tenancy—

(a) if the landlord has given notice under [section 25 of this Act] to terminate the tenancy, or

(b) if the tenant has made a request for a new tenancy in accordance with section 26 of this Act.

(2) The last foregoing subsection shall not prevent the coming to an end of a tenancy by notice to quit given by the tenant, by surrender or forfeiture, or by the forfeiture of a superior tenancy [unless—

(a) in the case of a notice to quit, the notice was given before the tenant had been in occupation in right of the tenancy for one month; . . .

(b) . . .]

[(2A) Neither the tenant nor the landlord may make an application under subsection (1) above if the other has made such an application and the application has been served.

(2B) Neither the tenant nor the landlord may make such an application if the landlord has made an application under section 29(2) of this Act and the application has been served.

(2C) The landlord may not withdraw an application under subsection (1) above unless the tenant consents to its withdrawal.]

(3) Notwithstanding anything in subsection (1) of this section,—

(a) where a tenancy to which this Part of this Act applies ceases to be such a tenancy, it shall not come to an end by reason only of the cesser, but if it was granted for a term of years certain and has been continued by subsection (1) of this section then (without prejudice to the termination thereof in accordance with any terms of the tenancy) it may be terminated by not less than three nor more than six months' notice in writing given by the landlord to the tenant;

(b) where, at a time when a tenancy is not one to which this Part of this Act applies, the landlord gives notice to quit, the operation of the notice shall not be affected by reason that the tenancy becomes one to which this Part of this Act applies after the giving of the notice.

By s 24(1), the contractual term of the tenancy does not come to an end when it said it would but carries on, and does so indefinitely (which would be void at common law: see 3.4.2) until it is terminated in accordance with the provisions of the 1954 Act because the tenant wishes it, because the landlord successfully opposes the tenant's application for renewal, or because it is replaced by a new tenancy. During this interim period, the tenant is said to be 'holding over'.

Landlords as well as tenants can apply for a renewal of the tenancy, so putting them on an even footing and allowing either to avoid delay: s 24(1). Once either has made an application, the other cannot do so as well (s 24(2A)), and (by s 24(2B)) neither can make an application if the landlord has already made and served an application to terminate the tenancy under s 29(2). The landlord cannot withdraw its application for a new tenancy unless the tenant agrees but the tenant can withdraw at any time.

The timescale for applications to be made is set in s 29A:

29A Time limits for applications to court

(1) Subject to section 29B of this Act, the court shall not entertain an application—

(a) by the tenant or the landlord under section 24(1) of this Act; or

(b) by the landlord under section 29(2) of this Act,

if it is made after the end of the statutory period.

(2) In this section and section 29B of this Act 'the statutory period' means a period ending—

(a) where the landlord gave a notice under section 25 of this Act, on the date specified in his notice; and

(b) where the tenant made a request for a new tenancy under section 26 of this Act, immediately before the date specified in his request.

(3) Where the tenant has made a request for a new tenancy under section 26 of this Act, the court shall not entertain an application under section 24(1) of this Act which is made before the end of the period of two months beginning with the date of the making of the request, unless the application is made after the landlord has given a notice under section 26(6) of this Act.

Essentially, applications can be made at any time up to the termination or renewal date given in the landlord's s 25 notice or the tenant's s 26 notice, but the tenant cannot apply within two months of the date of its s 26 notice.

Under the terms of s 29B, the parties can agree to extend the time limits and can, from time to time, further extend the time limits.

15.5   Termination of tenancies under the 1954 Act

Section 24(1), as we have seen, provides for the continuation of a tenancy until it is terminated in accordance with the provisions of the 1954 Act. Section 24(2) refers to common law methods of termination which have already been discussed (see **Chapter 13**). Landlords must follow the procedures in the 1954 Act according to what they want to do. Although the 1954 Act is for the benefit of tenants, they cannot just vacate the premises at the end of the term; they too must follow the procedures of the 1954 Act both for leaving and for applying to stay on, save that a periodic tenancy can be terminated by common law notice to quit. Thus, a fixed term tenancy must be ended by notice even though the tenant wishes to leave: see **15.5.3**. There are four statutory methods of termination:

(a) landlord's notice under s 25;

(b) tenant's notice under s 26;

(c) tenant's notice under s 27;

(d) agreement under s 28.

15.5.1 Landlord's s 25 notice

Section 25 reads as follows:

25 Termination of tenancy by the landlord

(1) The landlord may terminate a tenancy to which this Part of this Act applies by a notice given to the tenant in the prescribed form specifying the date at which the tenancy is to come to an end (hereinafter referred to as 'the date of termination'):

Provided that this subsection has effect subject to [the provisions of section 29B(4) of this Act and] the provisions of Part IV of this Act as to the interim continuation of tenancies pending the disposal of applications to the court.

(2) Subject to the provisions of the next following subsection, a notice under this section shall not have effect unless it is given not more than twelve nor less than six months before the date of termination specified therein.

(3) In the case of a tenancy which apart from this Act could have been brought to an end by notice to quit given by the landlord–

(a) the date of termination specified in a notice under this section shall not be earlier than the earliest date on which apart from this Part of this Act the tenancy could have been brought to an end by notice to quit given by the landlord on the date of the giving of the notice under this section; and

(b) where apart from this Part of this Act more than six months' notice to quit would have been required to bring the tenancy to an end, the last foregoing subsection shall have effect with the substitution for twelve months of a period six months longer than the length of notice to quit which would have been required as aforesaid.

(4) In the case of any other tenancy, a notice under this section shall not specify a date of termination earlier than the date on which apart from this Part of this Act the tenancy would have come to an end by effluxion of time.

(5) . . .

[(6) A notice under this section shall not have effect unless it states whether the landlord is opposed to the grant of a new tenancy to the tenant.

(7) A notice under this section which states that the landlord is opposed to the grant of a new tenancy to the tenant shall not have effect unless it also specifies one or more of the grounds specified in section 30(1) of this Act as the ground or grounds for his opposition.

(8) A notice under this section which states that the landlord is not opposed to the grant of a new tenancy to the tenant shall not have effect unless it sets out the landlord's proposals as to—

(a) the property to be comprised in the new tenancy (being either the whole or part of the property comprised in the current tenancy);

(b) the rent to be payable under the new tenancy; and

(c) the other terms of the new tenancy.]

Thus, the landlord:

(a) serves notice in the prescribed form saying on what date the tenancy will end ('the date of termination');

(b) the notice must be given no more than twelve and no less than six months before the date of termination;

(c) the landlord must state whether it opposes the grant of a new tenancy;

(d) if the landlord opposes a new tenancy, it has to specify one or more of the grounds in s 30(1);

(e) if the landlord does not oppose a new tenancy, it must state:

    (i) what property will be comprised in the new tenancy (whole or part of the current tenancy);

    (ii) what the rent for the new tenancy will be;

    (III) the other terms.

Two terms need further explanation:

15.5.1.1 'Prescribed form'

The Landlord and Tenant Act 1954, Part 2 (Notices) Regulations 2004 (SI 2004/1005) (the Notices Regulations) provide for a Form 1 to be used where the landlord does not oppose a new tenancy and a Form 2 where it does. Both forms contain important 'health warnings' for tenants.

15.5.1.2 'The date of termination'

This cannot be earlier than the date on which the landlord could have ended the tenancy at common law. Three different situations need to be considered:

(a) fixed term tenancy without a break clause – this will simply be the contractual termination date;

(b) fixed term tenancy with a landlord's break clause – the landlord must satisfy the break clause terms as well as the s 25 procedure. One notice can do both jobs: *Scholl Manufacturing Co Ltd v Clifton (Slim-Line) Ltd* [1966] 3 All ER 16. It may be safer to serve two separate notices.

(c) periodic tenancies – common law notice to quit must be for a period the same as the intervals of the tenancy (eg one month for a monthly tenancy), but under s 25 still cannot be more than 12 months or less than 6.

So, in all cases, the termination date has to be calculated according to the relevant common law requirement and the 12- and 6-month periods worked out back from that date.

15.5.2 Tenant's s 26 notice

Section 26 reads as follows:

26 Tenant's request for a new tenancy

(1) A tenant's request for a new tenancy may be made where the [current tenancy] is a tenancy granted for a term of years certain exceeding one year, whether or not continued by section 24 of this Act, or granted for a term of years certain and thereafter from year to year.

(2) A tenant's request for a new tenancy shall be for a tenancy beginning with such date, not more than twelve nor less than six months after the making of the request, as may be specified therein:

Provided that the said date shall not be earlier than the date on which apart from this Act the current tenancy would come to an end by effluxion of time or could be brought to an end by notice to quit given by the tenant.

(3) A tenant's request for a new tenancy shall not have effect unless it is made by notice in the prescribed form given to the landlord and sets out the tenant's proposals as to the property to be comprised in the new tenancy (being either the whole or part of the property comprised in the current tenancy), as to the rent to be payable under the new tenancy and as to the other terms of the new tenancy.

(4) A tenant's request for a new tenancy shall not be made if the landlord has already given notice under the last foregoing section to terminate the current tenancy, or if the tenant has already given notice to quit or notice under the next following section; and no such notice shall be given by the landlord or the tenant after the making by the tenant of a request for a new tenancy.

(5) Where the tenant makes a request for a new tenancy in accordance with the foregoing provisions of this section, the current tenancy shall, subject to the provisions of [sections 29B(4) and 36(2)] of this Act and the provisions of Part IV of this Act as to the interim continuation of tenancies, terminate immediately before the date specified in the request for the beginning of the new tenancy.

(6) Within two months of the making of a tenant's request for a new tenancy the landlord may give notice to the tenant that he will oppose an application to the court for the grant of a new tenancy, and any such notice shall state on which of the grounds mentioned in section 30 of this Act the landlord will oppose the application.

Not every tenancy entitles the tenant to use this provision – only a fixed term exceeding a year, or one for a term of years certain and then from year to year: s 26 (1). Thus, periodic tenancies are excluded.

The request must:

(a) specify the commencement date of the new tenancy according to the requirements in (2). This cannot be before the current tenancy would end at common law;

(b) be in the prescribed form. This is Form 3 of the Notices Regulations;

(c) set out proposals for the new tenancy including:

    (i) what property will be comprised in the new tenancy (whole or part of the current tenancy);

    (ii) what the rent for the new tenancy will be;

    (iii) the other terms.

Whereas a tenant does not have to serve a counternotice to a landlord's s 25 notice, the landlord does have to respond to a s 26 notice. The landlord has two months to serve notice on the tenant opposing the tenant's application. There is no prescribed form but the landlord must state on which of the s 30 grounds it will oppose the application.

Tenants will consider the state of the market in deciding how to act. In a rising market, the sooner the new rent is fixed, the better. In a falling market, it may pay the tenant to delay if by so doing evidence of ever-lower rental levels is available. The tactics involved in these matters need to be considered with great care by someone with the necessary expertise. Solicitors should not play at being valuers but ought, unless they are very experienced, to advise the client to consult a chartered surveyor with specialist knowledge. Indeed, the area of lease renewals may be said to be more the preserve of the valuer than the solicitor.

15.5.3 Tenant's s 27 notice

This method of termination is used by the tenant under a fixed term tenancy who does not wish to stay on after the end of the contractual term. Notice must be given to the immediate landlord not later than three months before the date of expiry of the term. If the term has already expired but continues under the 1954 Act, the tenant still needs to give three months' notice.

15.5.4 Section 28 agreement

The current tenancy will be terminated on the date a new tenancy starts pursuant to an agreement between the landlord and the tenant for a new tenancy.

15.5.5 Competent landlord

Notices under ss 25 and 26 must be served by and on, respectively, the competent landlord, who is defined in s 44. Where the landlord is the freeholder and the tenant holds its tenancy from that person, there is no difficulty in identifying the competent landlord.

A subtenant, however, cannot assume that the immediate landlord is the competent landlord for the purposes of the 1954 Act. Section 44(1)(b) provides that the competent landlord is one who has a tenancy which will not come to an end within 14 months by effluxion of time. If the immediate landlord does not qualify, then the first up the chain with such a lease will be the competent landlord. The point here is that if the immediate landlord's own tenancy has little time left to run, it should be disregarded and the person with a more substantial interest be the one to grant a new tenancy.

15.5.6 Interim rent

The tenant holds over on the same terms as the current lease, including rent. Either party may wish that rent to be revised, and so either may apply to the court for an interim rent to be set. However, to avoid duplication of proceedings, one party may not apply if the other has already done so. An application cannot be made after six months from the end of the contractual term. Interim rent is payable from the earliest date for termination of the tenancy or start of the new tenancy which could have been specified in the s 25 or s 26 notice, not from the date which has been put in. The rent will be 'reasonable' unless either party can show a substantial change in the market or in the terms of the tenancy. Therefore, the interim rent is likely to be in line with the open market rent.

15.5.7 Landlord's grounds of opposition

The court must grant the tenant a new tenancy unless the landlord can establish one or more of the grounds for opposition set out in s 30. If the landlord decides to oppose the tenant's wish for a new tenancy, it must do so in its s 25 notice or in its response to the tenant's s 26 notice.

15.5.7.1 Landlord's application under s 29

By s 29(2), the landlord has the right to apply directly for an order terminating the tenancy without the grant of a new one. The landlord may do this provided (a) it has given notice under s 25 opposing a new tenancy, or (b) the tenant has served a s 26 notice and the landlord has responded to that within two months. Thus the landlord who opposes a new tenancy on one or more of the grounds set out in s 30 may do so either in defence of the tenant's application or by making its own direct application for termination.

By s 29(3), the landlord cannot make an application under s 29(2) if the tenant has made an application for an order for a new tenancy. Section 29(3) does not say, 'and served', and the question may arise as to how the landlord is to know that such an application has been made if it has not been served on the landlord.

If the landlord has made and served an application under s 29(2), the tenant cannot then apply for a new tenancy. If, however, the landlord's s 29(2) application fails, s 29(4)(b) provides that the court shall make an order for the grant of a new tenancy.

Section 29(6) says that the landlord may not withdraw its application under s 29(2) without the tenant's consent. This raises the question as to the tenant's position if it does so consent: this must mean that the court has no opportunity to make an order under s 29(4)(b). It is not clear what action the tenant can take to make an application for a new tenancy in such circumstances.

15.5.7.2 The seven statutory grounds under s 30(1)

These grounds, once put forward, cannot be withdrawn or amended. In some, the court has discretion whether to accept the ground; in others, it has no discretion. The exercise of discretion was considered in *Hazel v Akhtar* [2001] EWCA Civ 1883, a case concerning grounds (a) and (b). For comment, see: M Haley [2002] JBL 316. The grounds are:

(a) Tenant's breach of repairing covenant – *discretionary*

The landlord must give evidence of the extent of the covenant, of an existing breach and, by a surveyor's report, show that the breach is so serious that a new tenancy should be refused.

(b) Delay in paying rent – *discretionary*

The court will consider the payment history including the period of delay and the reasons for it. Any sums reserved as rent will be covered.

(c) Other breaches by tenant – *discretionary*

The court will want to see the covenants in respect of which breaches are alleged or anticipated.

(d) Landlord offering alternative accommodation – *obligatory*

Details of the alternative accommodation must be provided to the court and an important factor will be whether the offered accommodation enables the tenant to preserve its goodwill.

(e) Where sub-lease of part, landlord seeks to dispose of whole – *discretionary*

This is a rarely-used provision and concerns a superior landlord wishing to let the whole premises when that returns a higher rent than reletting in parts.

(f) Landlord intends to demolish or reconstruct – *obligatory*

Ground (f) has generated a large body of case law. It is:

> that on the termination of the current tenancy the landlord intends to demolish or reconstruct the premises comprised in the holding or a substantial part of those premises or carry out substantial work of construction on the holding or part thereof and that he could not reasonably do so without obtaining possession of the building.

The landlord needs to show a sufficient intention and the need for possession. There are two aspects to intention: it must be a fixed and settled desire, and there must be a reasonable prospect of bringing about that desire. As to the first aspect, in the oft-quoted words of Asquith LJ in *Cunliffe v Goodman* [1950] 2 KB 237, 254, the landlord's intention 'must have moved out of the zone of contemplation . . . into the valley of decision'. A resolution of the board of a corporate landlord will be good evidence of intention: *BP International Ltd v Newcastle International Airport Ltd*, Newcastle County Court, 18 January 2005, reported by Lawtel, LTL 25/1/2005, Document No AC0107710; *Dogan v Semali Investments Ltd* [2005] EWCA Civ 1036.

As to the second aspect – a reasonable prospect of bringing about the intention – the usual need is for planning permission. The threshold is not high: the landlord does not have to show that it will be granted on a balance of probabilities or that it is likely to be granted, merely that it has a real and not fanciful chance of getting it: *Dogan v Semali Investments Ltd*. Clearly, the more preparation is done, the better the prospect of success. The test is objective: would a reasonable person believe that the landlord has a reasonable prospect of being able to carry out its intention?

The time for establishing the landlord's intention is the date of the hearing: *Betty's Cafes Ltd v Phillips Furnishing Stores Ltd* [1959] AC 20.

The landlord's motive for its scheme is irrelevant: in *Turner v Wandsworth Borough Council* [1994] 1 EGLR 134, the motive was to demolish the premises and sell the site when the market was most favourable and the Court of Appeal held that this was not a reason for refusing possession.

The landlord's plans do not have to show a strong likelihood of commercial success: *Dolgellau Golf Club v Hett* [1998] 2 EGLR 75, CA.

The need for possession depends on whether the proposed work is sufficiently substantial which is a matter of fact and of degree. There are six possibilities: (i) demolition of whole of the premises; (ii) reconstruction of whole of the premises; (iii) demolition of a substantial part of the premises; (iv) reconstruction of a substantial part of the premises; (v) substantial construction on the whole holding; (vi) substantial construction on part of the whole. Thus, the first four relate to the premises and the last two relate to the holding. The obtaining of possession means ending the tenancy. Case law shows how extensive the proposed works must be for the landlord to succeed:

(a) landscaping of a field was insufficient: *Botterill v Bedforshire CC* [1985] 1 EGLR 82;

(b) resiting a staircase, rewiring the whole building, resiting toilets and providing new ones, reproofing, installing central heating, rebuilding some walls, and decorating were refurbishment and did not qualify under the paragraph: *Barth v Pritchard* [1990] 1 EGLR 109;

(c) the landlord of hotel premises had got planning permission and funding for £2m worth of work which was to include installing a lift, a basement kitchen, new bathrooms, realignment of partition walls and restoring a staircase. The landlord failed to establish the ground: *Marazzi v Global Grange Ltd* [2003] 34 EG 59; [2002] EWHC 3010 (Ch);

(d) the same landlord in respect of a another, nearby hotel, proposed to carry out similar works and did establish the ground: *Ivory Grove Ltd v Global Grange Ltd* [2003] 26 EG 179, CS; [2003] EWHC 1409, Ch;

These two last decisions show how finely-balanced the issue can be – too much so in the actual cases. It is lamentable that two cases involving the same landlord doing similar work to properties in the same location and heard only six months apart should lead to opposite results. This is not our jurisprudence at its most impressive. See articles by S Murdoch (2003) Estates Gazette, 21 June, 140 and (2003) Estates Gazette, 6 September, 109. Where the premises were an 'eggshell tenancy' of ground floor shop premises and the landlord intended to carry out substantial works to the building containing the premises, the tenant's argument that the premises had no structure failed, and the ground was made out: *Pumperninks of Piccadilly Ltd v Land Securities plc* [2003] 1 P & CR 14. See M Haley, *Business Tenancies: Renewal or Redevelopment?* [2003] JBL 76;

(f) where there are no premises on the site of the holding because those that were there (huts) were tenant's fixtures and would be removed, the ground could not be made out: *Wessex Reserve Forces & Cadets Association v White* [2005] EWHC 983.

Where the landlord fails under ground (f) (landlord intends to demolish or reconstruct) at the date of the hearing but the court is satisfied that the ground could have been made out if the termination date had been up to one year later, a new tenancy may not be ordered, though the tenant can apply to have the current tenancy continue to the later date. How much benefit this confers on the landlord depends on how long it takes to get a hearing.

One attempted tactic of a landlord has failed. In *Felber Jucker & Co Ltd v Sabreleague* (no report known but see (2005) Estates Gazette 19 November), the landlord served a s 25 notice citing opposition under ground (f) but, when the tenant had arranged to quit, the landlord applied for a new lease. This attempt was struck out as an abuse of process.

(g) Landlord intends to occupy – *obligatory*

Ground (g) is the next best generator of litigation. It provides that:

> on termination of the current tenancy the landlord intends to occupy the premises for the purposes or partly for the purposes of a business carried on by him or as his residence.

To qualify, the landlord must have owned its interest in the property for five years: s 30(2).

The test for the landlord's intention is similar to that in ground (f). Intention was considered in *Zarvos v Pradhan* [2003] 26 EG 180. Mr Zarvos had run a taverna (the Bitter Lemons) for many years and then decided to retire to Cyprus. He granted what was found to be a tenancy of the former taverna premises to Mr Pradhan who opened up his own restaurant (the Tandoori Garden). Later, Mr Zarvos changed his mind and sought possession under ground (g). Giving the only reasoned judgment, Ward LJ noted the two limbs to a landlord's opposition: the genuineness of the intention and the prospects of carrying it out. These two limbs may be considered separately. The landlord may have a genuine intention but have no realistic prospect of carrying it out; or, the lack of a realistic prospect of carrying out the intention may mean that the intention is not genuine. In *Zarvos*, it was found that the financial background caused failure of the landlord's case on the second limb. (This was harsh because there was inadmissible evidence that Mr Zarvos could, in fact, have raised the necessary cash.) There was no clear finding on the first limb, nor was it necessary that there should have been. Making a finding on the first limb would, as Ward LJ said, be harsh. The second limb is there to cater for the case where the landlord does believe in what he says he intends to do. Given the apparent inadequacy with which the landlord's opposition was initially handled, the case shows the importance of proper preparation and that landlords cannot take a relaxed approach to opposition on this ground. For comment, see M Haley [2003] JBL 504.

The landlord does not have to intend to occupy personally but can do so through an agent: *Parkes v Westminster Roman Catholic Diocese Trustee* [1978] 36 P & CR 22 (trustees would occupy through parish priest). The landlord may also occupy in accordance with the provisions of s 23(1A): see **15.2.2**. But the landlord cannot establish this ground if it intends to occupy with another for the purposes of that other's business. In *Zafiris v Liu* [2005] All ER (D) 261, the landlord, Mr Liu, contended that he and his wife were to run a business at the premises in partnership. In itself, that was not objectionable, but the business to be carried on was really Mrs Liu's business (in which Mr Liu had no part) which was being transferred from other premises of which Mr Liu was landlord. Accordingly, the landlord's claim failed.

15.6 Compensation

Where a tenant does not get a new tenancy because the landlord successfully opposes under grounds (e), (f) and (g), this is through no fault of the tenant (as it would be under grounds (a), (b), and (c)). Therefore, the tenant may be able to claim compensation, which is calculated by multiplying the rateable value by a multiplier which is notified from time to time by the Government.

There is usually a clause excluding the tenant's right to compensation but this is of no effect if the premises have been occupied for the purposes of a business carried on by the tenant or its predecessor for five years before the tenant has to leave.

If the tenant has been at the premises for 14 years or more, then it gets double compensation. To qualify for double compensation, the tenant must have been in occupation of the holding 'during the whole of the 14 years immediately preceding the termination of the current tenancy': s 37(3). The meaning of this provision was considered in *Bacchiocchi v Academic Agency Ltd* [1998] 2 All ER 241. Mr Bacchiocci ran a restaurant called La Pentola in Bath. He had a 20-year lease from 1974 so, by the time of the events, he qualified for double compensation. He applied to the court to discontinue his application for a new tenancy on 29 April 1994; formal discontinuance occurred on 11 May 1994. Because a tenant has three months to appeal, the real termination date became 11 August 1994. Mr Bacchiocci's solicitors mistakenly thought the three months ran from 29 April, they advised him accordingly, and Mr Bacchiocci vacated the premises on 29 July – actually 12 days early. The landlord claimed this disqualified Mr Bacchiocci from getting compensation (which worked out at £15,030). The Court of Appeal decided that such a literal reading of s 37 flew in the face of business reality and common sense dictated some reasonable leeway. However, Simon Brown LJ said (at 250) that if 'premises are left vacant for a matter of months, the court would be readier to conclude that the thread of continuity had been broken'.

15.7 The new tenancy

If the landlord does not oppose the grant of a new tenancy or where it is unsuccessful in its s 30 application, a new tenancy is ordered and if the parties cannot agree on any of the terms, the court will determine them. The terms to be determined are: *the premises, the term, the rent and other terms.*

15.7.1 Premises

These will normally be the whole of the holding comprised in the existing tenancy together with any rights enjoyed. Where the landlord is successful under s 30(f), the tenant may take a tenancy of a viable part of the remainder. If part is sublet, the holding excludes that part, save that the landlord can insist that the new tenancy nevertheless includes the whole of the premises comprised in the existing tenancy.

15.7.2 The term

The court can impose a term in default of agreement up to a maximum of 14 years. The court has wide discretion and will take account of all relevant factors. If the landlord failed in its s 30(f) application but it was clear that it still intends to carry out such works in the near future, the court may impose a short term or a term with a break clause to fit those circumstances: *National Car Parks v The Paternoster Consortium Ltd* [1990] 2 EGLR 99.

15.7.3 The rent

The court has to assess an open market value rent disregarding matters in a similar way as on rent review – occupation by the tenant, goodwill and improvements. Evidence from expert witnesses may be heard, and there may be a rent review clause included.

15.7.4 Other terms

The court will have regard to the terms of the existing lease when determining the terms of the new lease. If either party seeks to vary those terms, it must offer justification for this. Landlords may wish to update the lease especially if this will lead to a higher value on their reversion. Tenants will seek to oppose such attempts by landlords as a higher rental is sure to result. The leading case is *O'May v City of London Real Property Co Ltd* [1983] 2 AC 726. This concerned a five-year lease of an office block in the City of London. On renewal, the landlord wanted to introduce a variable service charge so as to shift the cost of structural repairs and maintenance onto the tenant. This would have increased the value of the landlord's reversion by well over £1m. The House of Lords upheld the tenant's objection, saying that any change must be fair and reasonable, the burden of establishing this being on the party proposing it.

Glossary of commercial property terms

Abandonment
The voluntary relinquishment of a property or an interest in a property, where there is no intention of resuming possession of the property or of maintaining rights in it.

AGA
See Authorised Guarantee Agreement.

Agreement for lease
Tenant contracting to take a lease in a development before the development is completed. Often called a pre-let.

Alienation
The transfer of an interest in property to another, usually by sale of a freehold or the grant or assignment of a lease, but can mean any parting with possession. Also called 'disposition'.

Arbitration
A method of settling disputes by reference to an independent and impartial third party, usually an arbitrator appointed by the President of the RICS. Arbitration is essentially an adjudication of the arguments of the parties, and as such differs from independent expert determination.

Arbitrator
Person appointed to carry out arbitration.

Assignee
A party to whom a lease has been assigned (see entry on assignment below).

Assignment
The transfer of a lease from one party to the other. Once a lease has been assigned, the assignee becomes responsible to the landlord for paying the rent and fulfilling the other obligations of the lease; however, in the event of default, the landlord can require the assignor to pay the rent (a) under the doctrine of privity of contract, where the latter still applies, or (b) under an Authorised Guarantee Agreement.

Assignor
One who assigns or transfers a lease.

Authorised Guarantee Agreement
Agreement under s 16 of the L&T (C) A 1995 that the assignor of a lease guarantees the performance of the tenant covenants by the assignee.

Bank finance
Funding of a development by a bank in return for a charge over the developer's property. Basically, a commercial mortgage.

Break clause
A clause in a lease giving either or both parties the right to terminate a lease in specified circumstances.

Building lease
A long-term lease, imposing an obligation on the lessee to erect one or more buildings on the leased land, which will become the property of the landlord after the lease expires.

Capital value
The value of an asset, freehold or leasehold, as distinct from its annual or periodic (rental) value.

Capitalisation
The value of an asset assessed in relation to the expected future income (rental) stream.

Certificate of practical completion
A certificate by the developer's architect or agent that a development has been practically completed.

Collateral warranties
Contractual promises for the benefit of third parties to whom they would otherwise owe no duty (eg tenants) given by contractors, architects, engineers and surveyors warranting that their obligations under their contracts or retainers have been and will be fulfilled.

Comparables
In determining the initial rent, or the market rent during the course of a rent review, parties and those acting on their behalf will have regard to evidence of rents for similar properties. Comparables may also be used to analyse properties' sale values.

Condition precedent
A term making a contract conditional until the condition has been fulfilled, until which time the contract will not come into effect.

Condition subsequent
The contract comes into effect immediately it is entered into but may cease to have effect if the condition is not fulfilled.

Confidentiality clause
An agreement between the parties to a lease or sale that some or all of the terms will remain confidential. Third parties can however compel the revelation of such terms (for example, where they are required to establish comparables) by means of a subpoena.

Contracting out
Agreement between parties who are to be landlord and tenant that the security of tenure provisions of ss 38 and 38A of the Landlord and Tenant Act 1954, shall not apply to the lease into which they propose to enter.

Covenant
The word is used in two senses. First, in the strict legal sense, it refers to a clause in the lease requiring the tenant (or landlord) to do something or not to do doing something (see also entry on restrictive covenant below). Secondly, it is used in the wider sense to denote the worth of a tenant (or, bearing in mind the doctrine of privity of contract, that of previous assignors) and hence the risk of default, which will have a bearing on the value of the lease. In this second sense, often called 'covenant strength'.

Demised premises
Premises which are the subject of a lease. Better described as just 'premises'.

Derogation from grant
An obligation on the landlord not to take away with one hand that which he has given with another (eg storing explosives next to the tenant's premises!).

Determination
The bringing or coming to an end of a lease, or an estate or interest in property, especially by notice as expressly provided for in the lease or as a consequence of a fundamental breach of a lease condition. See also entry on termination below.

Development lease
A lease in which the tenant agrees with the grantor to develop the site comprising the premises demised by the lease.

Disposition
See entry on alienation above.

Distraint
The enforcement of distress for rent.

Distress for rent
A common law remedy enabling landlords to recover rent arrears by the seizure and sale of goods within the defaulting tenant's property.

Estimated Rental Values (ERV)
An estimate of the rental which a property is likely to command in the open market at a given time.

Estoppel
A principle in English law that a person cannot go back on something he has previously affirmed. For example, a tenant serving a counternotice to a section 25 notice cannot subsequently argue that the latter was invalid, unless he expressly reserved his position.

Expert
Third party appointed to determine a dispute or resolve a failure to agree, as in a rent review.

Expert witness
One who is qualified to give technical or professional evidence, such as when a specialist surveyor gives evidence in support of one party.

'Flip flop' arbitration
A form of arbitration under which the arbitrator bases his award on the submission he considers most reasonable. It is claimed that this encourages parties to be more reasonable in their submissions and reduces polarisation.

Forfeiture
Forfeiture of a lease occurs when the landlord exercises his right to regain possession against the wishes of the tenant, where there is a breach in a condition of the lease, or a breach of a covenant. The tenant can apply for relief. The landlord may lose the right to forfeit by waiver.

Freeholder
Person holding an estate in 'fee simple absolute in possession', ie the freehold. Sometimes called the 'reversioner'.

Full repairing and insuring (FRI) lease
An FRI lease requires the tenant to pay all running costs, namely repairs and maintenance, rates and insurance.

Head tenant
Where a subtenancy (or series of subtenancies) exists, the highest leaseholder in the chain (who pays head rent to the freeholder).

Headline rent
The rent apparently being paid, which may not take account of concessions such as rent-free periods.

Independent expert determination
An independent determination of the rent to be paid on review. Independent expert determination differs from arbitration in that the independent expert is not confined to the evidence presented by the parties.

Indexation
The regular adjustment of a rent in accordance with a specified index, eg the Retail Price Index.

Institutional lease
A lease developed since the 1960s to meet the requirements of pension funds and insurance companies investing in property. The term is typically 25 years without options to break (see entry on break clause above) and with five-yearly upwards-only rent reviews. The aim of such leases is long-term investment as part of a portfolio which aims to enable financial institutions to succeed in the financial services market by meeting their commitments to investors in a competitive and attractive way.

Interim rent
A landlord may apply to the court to fix an interim rent when he has given notice of termination of a tenancy or where the tenant has served notice of a request for a new tenancy on the landlord.

Intermediate landlord
The landlord of a subtenant, and in turn being the tenant of the head landlord.

Investment yield
Annual passing rent as a percentage of the capital value.

Landlord
The party letting the property.

Lessee
See entry on tenant below.

Lessor
See entry on landlord above.

Market rent
See entry on Open Market Rental Value below.

Mesne landlord
See entry on Intermediate landlord above.

Off-balance sheet finance
Financial techniques which allow companies to incur debt, usually via associated companies or joint ventures, without the debt appearing in the group's consolidated accounts and affecting its gearing ratio.

O'May rules
The principle that the terms of a new lease will generally follow the terms of the existing one; the onus is on the party proposing a change to show that it is fair and reasonable (*O'May v City of London Real Property Co Ltd* [1983] 2 AC 726).

Open market rent review
Where the rent review clause provides that the rent on review should be based on the open market prevailing for new lettings.

Open Market Rent – OMR
The best rent at which a property might reasonably be expected to be let with vacant possession in the open market, with a willing landlord and tenant, taking full account of all terms of the tenancy offered. The term tends now not to be favoured by surveyors.

Overage
A sum of money over and above the purchase price which the buyer pays to the seller following compliance with agreed conditions as when, for example, the buyer applies for and gets planning permission and so increases the value of the property. The seller thus benefits from the increase. Overage may be secured by a restriction on the register or a charge on the property. Often used in development deals.

Over-renting
This occurs when the passing rent exceeds the current open market rent.

Overriding lease
An intermediate lease which the landlord grants to another party for a term longer than that of an existing lease, thereby creating a landlord and tenant, but not a contractual, relationship between the new and old lessee.

Passing rent
The actual current rent being paid.

Pre-let
See entry on agreement for lease above.

Premium
The price an actual or prospective tenant pays to a landlord, usually in return for the rent being reduced to below what would otherwise be payable. Or a sum paid at the outset for the purchase of a lease. (See also entry on reverse premium below.)

Prime covenant
The best quality of investment, represented by prime property.

Prime location
The most desirable or sought after location.

Prime property
A term used to define property of particular interest to investors. Broadly, prime property is likely to be a modern or recently refurbished building, finished to a high specification, well situated in a commercially strong geographical location and let to a good tenant.

Privity of contract
The principle in English common law that landlord and tenant continue to have obligations under the lease despite subsequent assignment. Privity of contract was abolished for new leases coming into force from 1 January 1996. Leases entered into before then are still subject to privity, but landlords wishing to sue previous tenants still bound by privity have to serve notice within six months of rent or service charges becoming due. The current legislation (L&T(C)A 1995) enables landlords in certain circumstances to require the outgoing tenant to guarantee the performance of the incoming tenant, until there is a further assignment. See entry on Authorised Guarantee Agreement above.

Quarter days
The four dates in the year when rent is normally due: 25 March, 24 June, 29 September, 25 December. Often termed, 'the usual quarter days'.

Quiet enjoyment
Most leases contain a covenant for quiet enjoyment, entitling the tenant to enjoy his lease without lawful entry, eviction or interruption, but not freedom from ordinary noise.

Rack rent
The best market rent obtainable.

Real estate
American term for real property now increasingly used in the UK, especially by large firms of solicitors.

Re-entry
A landlord may exercise his right to regain possession of premises by peaceable re-entry where there has been a breach of a condition by the tenant, or a breach of a covenant of a lease with a forfeiture clause. (See also entry on forfeiture above.)

Rent free period
Short period of, say, three months at the start of a lease when the tenant does not pay rent because it is preparing the premises for business.

Rent review
Lease clauses providing for a periodic review of the rent, usually at five-yearly intervals. The lease will generally specify what the basis of the review is to be: eg the open market rent prevailing at the time of the review or, as is frequently the case, upwards only (see entry on upward only rent reviews below).

Rental value
The rent that a property might reasonably be expected to command in the open market at a given time, subject to the terms of the lease.

Restrictive covenant
A covenant in a lease restricting the tenant in some respect, eg a covenant in a shop lease providing that only a particular type of trade may be carried out at the premises. More generally, an obligation in a deed whereby the covenantor undertakes to refrain from some act affecting the land of the covenantee.

Reverse premium
On assignment, the payment of a sum of money by the assignor to the assignee as an inducement to take the assignment and so reflecting unfavourable lease terms, or adverse market conditions, eg where there is over-renting.

Reversion
The right of the landlord to the return of premises on the expiry of a lease. As an interest, the reversion has value and may be transferred.

Reversioner
See entry on freeholder above. Also means the estate of any superior title holder, such as that of an intermediate landlord (see also entry above).

Sale and leaseback
An arrangement whereby a property is sold, with the vendor simultaneously being granted a lease on the property by the purchaser, generally either at a rack rent or at some lesser rent related to the price paid.

Schedule of dilapidations
List of repairing works which the landlord requires the tenant to do under its repairing covenant.

SDLT
See entry on stamp duty land tax below.

Securitisation
The conversion of assets into tradeable securities.

Security of tenure
The statutory right of a tenant to renew the lease at the end of a term. Part II of the Landlord and Tenant Act 1954 gives business tenants security of tenure, but parties may exclude it.

Service charge
The amount a tenant pays for services which his landlord provides.

Side agreement/side letter
Terms agreed separately by landlord and tenant, or by buyer and seller, which do not form part of the lease or contract of sale.

Stamp duty land tax
Replaced stamp duty from 1 December 2003. SDLT is payable on the consideration paid by the purchaser in a 'land transaction' as defined by s 43(1), of the Finance Act 2003, meaning any transfer of land, grant or assignment of a lease. Charities and transactions within a group of companies are exempt. The tax is self-assessed and then a certificate of payment is issued, without which a transaction registrable at the Land Registry will not be registered. SDLT is said to raise about £7bn a year.

Subletting
Where the tenant lets part or all of the premises to a subtenant, as permitted by the terms of the lease. It differs from assignment in that the head lessee remains responsible to the landlord for the payment of rent and fulfilment of other obligations.

Tenant
The party to whom a lease is granted or who is a successor to that party and so currently the holder of the lease.

Termination
The coming or bringing to an end of a lease, by mutual agreement, by the effluxion of time, or by the exercise of a right of one of the parties. Sometimes called 'determination'.

Turnover
Total sales or other business receipts, less VAT, in a given period, usually a year, thus 'annual turnover'.

Turnover rent
Where part or all of a rent, especially of retail premises, is based on a specified proportion of the tenant's turnover.

Upwards/downwards review clauses
See entry on open market rent review above.

Upwards only rent reviews – UORRs
Clauses in leases providing for regular reviews, at which the rent will be fixed at either the current passing rent or the open market level, whichever is the higher.

Waiver
The act of voluntarily giving up, or intentionally relinquishing, a claim, benefit or interest.

A landlord waives his right of forfeiture when a tenant is in breach of covenant, if he knows of the breach and accepts or demands rent or unequivocally recognises the continued existence of the lease.

Yield
See entry on investment yield above.

Bibliography

Abbey, R and Richards, M, *A Practical Approach to Commercial Conveyancing and Property*, (2nd edn. Oxford: Oxford University Press, 2003).

Encyclopaedia of Forms and Precedents, vol 22 (Butterworths).

Evans, D and Smith, P, *The Law of Landlord and Tenant*, (6th edn, London: LexisNexis, 2002).

Garner, S and Frith, A, *A Practical Approach to Landlord and Tenant Law*, (4th edn, Oxford: Oxford University Press, 2004).

Gray, K and Gray, S, *Elements of Land Law* (4th edn, Oxford: Oxford University Press, 2005).

Hill and Redman's Law of Landlord and Tenant (Butterworths, loose-leaf, 1988).

Luxton, P and Wilkie, M, *Commercial Leases* (Birmingham: CLT Professional Publishing, 1998).

Megarry, RE and Wade, W, *The Law of Real Property,* ed C Harpum (6th edn, London: Sweet & Maxwell, 2000).

Ross, *Commercial Leases* (Butterworths, loose-leaf).

Woodfall's Law of Landlord and Tenant (Sweet & Maxwell, loose-leaf, 1978).

Index

Lightning Source UK Ltd.
Milton Keynes UK
UKOW05f1227160816

280753UK00001B/25/P

9 781846 41024